Mary Baker Eddy

—— MBE ——

Mary Baker Eddy

Mary Baker Eddy

·M·B·E·

A Life Size Portrait

Lyman P. Powell

The Christian Science Publishing Society
Boston, Massachusetts, U.S.A.

© 1930, 1950, 1991, renewed 1958, 1978
The Christian Science Publishing Society
All rights reserved

ISBN: 0–87510–260–3
Library of Congress Catalog Card Number 91–72519

Printed in United States of America

Designed by Joyce C. Weston

To My Mother

MARY ANN POWELL

1829–1906

Ye shall know the truth, and the truth
shall make you free.   *John 8:32*

And we solemnly promise to watch, and
pray for that Mind to be in us which was
also in Christ Jesus; to do unto others as
we would have them do unto us; and to
be merciful, just, and pure.

Mary Baker Eddy

I love the prosperity of Zion, be it promoted by Catholic, by Protestant, or by
Christian Science. . . . I would no more
quarrel with a man because of his religion
than I would because of his art.

Mary Baker Eddy

If this . . . work be of men, it will come to
nought: But if it be of God, ye cannot
overthrow it.   *Acts 5:38, 39*

Contents

Illustrations

Introduction:
Twentieth-Century
Biographers Series

*O*N THE CLOSING YEARS OF THE TWENTIETH century, there is a growing awareness that the hundred years since 1900 will have registered a magnitude and pace of change, in every aspect of human affairs, which probably exceeds any historic precedent. In political, social and religious institutions and attitudes, in the sciences and industry, in the arts, in how we communicate with each other, humanity has traveled light years in this century.

"Earth's actors," said the Founder of Christian Science, Mary Baker Eddy, "change earth's scenes . . . ." As we look back over the landscape of this century, some towering figures emerge into view: political leaders, scientists and inventors, authors, artists and musicians, social and religious pioneers, industrialists, and many others who helped "change earth's scenes."

Typically, when someone comes along who changes human perceptions and ways of acting he or she attracts biographers. If an individual career is perceived, with growing distance, to have been especially significant in its impact on human affairs and changing ideas, the shelf of biography steadily expands; and each new published work, even though it may cover some of the ground already treated in earlier works, is expected to bring further insight into the meaning of a life, a mind, and a career.

Even among those who are not her followers, Mary Baker Eddy is customarily regarded as a major religious figure of the twentieth century and as a notable example of the emergence of women in significant leadership roles. Her works are visible today in virtually every country of the world: in church buildings, in Christian Science Reading Rooms, in the distribution of the newspaper and religious periodicals she established and their derivative broadcast forms, in the wide circulation of her own writings, and most important, in the way hundreds of thousands of people conduct their everyday lives.

Public interest in Mrs. Eddy, and curiosity about her, are as strong today as they were in 1910, the year of her decease. And yet, compared with other major figures of the century, the shelf of biography has increased little in the intervening years. A handful of early biographies, by those who knew her or stood close to her in time, were augmented in the late 1960s by Robert Peel's monumental three-volume work. Most of those early works, in spite of their great value as part of the historical record, have lapsed from print; and in fact some first-hand reminiscences by individuals who worked directly with her have only been privately published or circulated.

As we near the close of a century which directly witnessed some of Mary Baker Eddy's major contributions, The Christian Science Publishing Society, the publishing arm of the church she established, has been asked to reexamine the church's obligations to future generations and centuries, in providing an appreciation and understanding of her remarkable career.

Mrs. Eddy wrote only briefly about herself, in a short volume titled *Retrospection and Introspection*. She discouraged personal adulation or attention, clearly hoping that people would find her character and purpose in her own writings rather than in the biographic record. Yet, she came to see the need for an accurate account of her life and gave specific if possibly reluctant acquiescence in the year 1910 to the publishing of the first of the biographies — Sybil Wilbur's *Mary Baker Eddy*.

In addition to Robert Peel's trilogy, which is still in print, a number of significant biographic resources must remain, or become, permanently and readily available to future generations. These include: first-hand recollections of early workers who served directly under her leadership, not all of which have yet been published; and the various biographies which have already won their place in the history of Christian Science and in public use.

For these reasons, the Publishing Society welcomes the opportunity of publishing, and keeping in print, a major shelf of works on Mary Baker Eddy under the general series title: "Twentieth-Century Biographers Series."

Although a consistent set of editorial standards has been applied to such elements as indexing and footnoting, where required, with regard to dates, events, and statements of fact, the original texts of the authors have been preserved intact.

If the reader finds, through these volumes, occasional differing interpretations of events or concepts, this should serve as a strength rather than a weakness in a record which is so clearly synoptical in nature. Especially in the case of those who worked directly with Mrs. Eddy and shared many of her experiences, a special measure of respect and textual integrity is demanded. These are the workers she chose — individuals who served as her lieutenants, often for many years. To describe them as sturdy, strong-minded workers, patriarchal in their devotion and self-sacrifice, scarcely does them justice.

Mrs. Eddy's career and works have stirred humanity in the twentieth century and will continue to do so. Perhaps an appropriate introduction for this series is captured in her statement, in the Preface to *Science and Health:* "The time for thinkers has come." In that spirit, this series of biographies by many different twentieth-century writers is offered to all those who, now and in the future, want to know more about this remarkable woman, her life, and her work.

Preface

*T*HIS VOLUME, LYMAN POWELL'S *MARY BAKER Eddy: A Life Size Portrait*, first appeared in 1930. Although it was independently published by the Macmillan Company, it was written by Dr. Powell with the knowledge and cooperation of The Christian Science Board of Directors.

Dr. Powell appeared on the scene at an opportune moment. The previous year a scurrilous biography of Mrs. Eddy had been published. Containing relatively little that was new information, it was based largely on material already published during Mrs. Eddy's lifetime at the height of the muckraking craze. The Directors were naturally more than slightly interested in making available something that would set out the true course of Mrs. Eddy's unselfed life for others. Yet, during the then brief history of the Christian Science movement, they had already followed Mrs. Eddy's example of reticence when under attack. If divine Love was governing the progress of the Christian Science movement, there was clearly a better way. Thus one can understand their interest when a well-known Episcopalian clergyman knocked at their door, as it were, with the suggestion that he be allowed to write a new biography of Mrs. Eddy — and to tell the story as if it had never been told before.

Sixty years after the fact, most readers of this edition need to be reminded who Dr. Lyman P. Powell was and to gain some appreciation of the stature of this man who came forward at such an opportune moment. Dr. Powell's own story is related by his biographer, Charles S. Macfarland, in a book called *Lyman Pierson Powell: Pathfinder in Education and Religion*. Born in a small farming community in Delaware in 1866, Powell was some ten years junior to Woodrow Wilson, who was doing graduate work at the new Johns Hopkins University when Powell transferred there as an undergraduate. From his university days onward, Powell formed permanent friendships with many of the men who became intellectual forces in early twentieth century America. Among these were Albert Shaw, who for years edited the influential *Review of Reviews* and in 1930 encouraged him to tell the story of Mary Baker Eddy.

Lyman Powell devoted his life to the public good. While he should be remembered first for his work as an Episcopalian minister, the ministry of his church was not his only contact with the public. Following his graduation from Johns Hopkins, he became a University Fellow there. Before receiving a doctorate degree, however, he had an opportunity to go out to the University of Wisconsin and work in their college extension program. The concept of using the resources of a university in more ways than the formal cloistered setting of a four-year course of study was new, and its implementation appealed to the young Powell. Returning from Wisconsin, he enrolled at the Wharton

School of Finance in Philadelphia and also continued his university extension work from that city.

It was in 1895 that he decided to become a minister. During the intervening years he had left the Methodist church, in which he was raised, and become an Episcopalian. Ordained a deacon in 1897 and a priest of the Episcopal Church in 1898, he was the rector of St. John's Church in Ambler, Pennsylvania, for the next six years. In 1904 he was called to be rector of St. John's Church in Northampton, Massachusetts. St. John's sits in the middle of the Smith College campus, and presented him with a different mix of worshipers in his congregation from the suburban Philadelphia church. It was during the years in Northampton that Dr. Powell first became acquainted with the new phenomenon of Christian Science, as well as the healing effort called the Emmanuel Movement within his own Episcopal church.

Probably because he was alert to all the trends in American life as America moved through a period of exuberant growth just before the First World War, Powell became interested in the subject of business ethics. In 1912, he left the ministry to take a new chair at New York University in Business Ethics and Economics. After a year in New York, he was named President of Hobart and William Smith colleges in Geneva, New York, where he remained until the end of World War I. However, his activities were again broadening. In 1917 he made a trip to Europe to observe for himself the impact of the war on education there. His access to notable figures in both Britain and on the continent attests to his reputation in those years as educator and public figure. In the 1917–18 year he also served as vice president of the American Association of Colleges.

Resigning his college presidency in 1918, for the next seven years Powell lectured and wrote on education, democracy, and problems associated with America's role in the emerging postwar world. He was a frequent contributor to *The Review of Reviews*. He and his wife together put out one book on patriotism which sold more than 500,000 copies. Powell went on the lecture circuit; in fact, the 1920s probably witnessed the height of popularity for the phenomenon of public lecturing, which was gradually supplanted by radio and later by television. Powell estimated that he had lectured in one state alone — Indiana — more than one thousand times. Most of his lectures had to do either with education or America's role in the world — "The Rebuilding of the World," "The Melting Pot," "The Deeper Meaning of the War," "A Spiritualized Democracy." One, "America's Greatest Woman," was about Mary Baker Eddy.

From his Northampton days onward, Dr. Powell had been working to get a clearer concept of the meaning of Mrs. Eddy's life. He had published a highly critical book about Christian Science in 1907, but even then his writing showed his attraction to some of what he knew of Christian Science and his desire to be fair to it. It seems clear from the lecture title that by the early 1920s he had already come to have the view of Mrs. Eddy which he shows in this biography of her written a decade later.

After the lecture tours came the church again, but an entirely different kind of church experience awaited him. In 1925 Dr. Powell became rector of St. Margaret's Church in the Bronx. Even in the 1920s the Bronx had become a melting pot and was in trouble. It was undoubtedly the challenge of a different kind of ministry which brought

Powell back to this particular form of "educational" experience once again. He worked for ten years, until his retirement in 1935, to make St. Margaret's a meaningful institution to the local residents. Describing these years in his book *The Better Part*, Powell wrote:

> Anchored to the historic faith, St. Margaret's is as comprehensive as New York itself, where, if anywhere the compass, both of faith and practice, is well boxed. This parish is the Church in miniature. We use in worship the same Prayer Book as other churchmen use throughout the land. At every service we read the Bible, which Immanuel Kant long ago described as "the greatest benefit which the human race has ever experienced. . . ."

Yet it was in the midst of these years of serving a new parish that Dr. Powell felt impelled to write his biography of Mrs. Eddy. Why? The immediate reason must be that he was impelled to answer, even if obliquely, the picture painted of her in the book which had just been published. Behind this impelling event, however, lay at least two other larger facts. Dr. Powell had himself begun with a negative attitude toward Mrs. Eddy. However, his knowledge of the Emmanuel Movement in his own church and his own, at times, impressive experience with the power of prayer to heal, had led him intuitively to understand Mrs. Eddy's life in a way that no one, so long as he held to a wholly materialistic view of life, could ever expect to grasp. Spirituality was a reality to this man of the cloth; he had already gone some part of the distance Mrs. Eddy had traveled, so he had at least some firsthand knowledge both of the journey's requirements and ultimate rewards.

The other underlying fact is just as important: the near universality of Dr. Powell's outlook on life. A man as sure of himself as Powell must have been — consider the two round trips he made between the world of education and the ministry, with the lecture years added in as a kind of third career — could not be completely confined to any single institutional outlook, even one as broad and generous as that which the Episcopal Church encompasses. When there was talk of a possible heresy trial because of the Eddy biography, he was unperturbed, possibly aware of Jesus' advice to be wise as serpents and harmless as doves. He said to The Christian Science Board of Directors, "You will find that if I have to face anything of that sort I can be silent in a great many ways. I don't notice things. Mrs. Powell often says: 'That is how you escape so many things; you don't notice it until it is all over.' "

As for his universality, much of Dr. Powell's interest in the 1920s had been directed to establishing greater church cooperation. His biographer and close friend, Charles Mac-farland, was head of the Federal Council of the Churches of Christ in America. Powell, seeing the good in Christian Science, was concerned at a chasm he saw opening between Christian Science and the other Christian churches. Perhaps that chasm had been there from the start, but its perpetuation was something he felt should not be allowed. He felt that he could interpret Mrs. Eddy's lifework in such a way as to make others understand, as he already did, that she and her discovery were solidly in the Christian mainstream. That is a view which may still not be shared by a majority of other Christians, but certainly the work of Dr. Powell was a major factor in maintaining that position by someone outside the framework of the Christian Science church organization.

Dr. Powell's universality also led him to feel, perhaps

more than he explicitly said, that Christian Science was something too large for the Christian Science church alone. He did not deny the need for the institution Mrs. Eddy had set up to guard the purity of her discovery, but he also saw the need for Christian Science to leaven the teaching and practice of the other Christian churches. This is not as curious as it may sound to ears today, if one stops to recall that Mrs. Eddy herself at first hoped the other churches would adopt her teachings. Her own intentions had not been to start another, rival, denomination, but to bring the Christian church back to its beginnings, which had included the element of healing.

With this background, it is not difficult to understand the great interest there was in 1930 when the Powell biography appeared. For, not only was this written by a minister of another denomination, but by a public figure whose writing and lecturing had already made his name well known to the American public for more than a decade.

Most of the text of this edition remains unchanged. The chapters which locate the book in 1930 remain, as they give a portrait of how the Christian Science movement itself appeared at that time. There are a number of minor corrections which have been made, as for instance where Dr. Powell had an incorrect date. The most substantial change is at the end of Chapter Two, where some letters believed at the time to have been written by Mrs. Eddy in her youth have since been found to have been the letters of another "Mary B." This has necessitated the addition of a few connecting sentences, indicated by brackets in the text.

The original footnotes remain at the back of the book. Additional footnotes have been supplied only where the lapse of time seems to require some explanation. It is

quaint to read that Christian Scientists will give to their
church even if they cannot afford a radio, or that the automobile has become a competitor to Sunday church-going;
those comments need no explanation. But particularly where
names are used which are no longer familiar, some identi-
fication has been supplied. Dr. Powell was not a name-
dropper! His frequent use of names, however, suggests a
combination of factors — as a minister, he was used to
quoting others, when appropriate, in his sermons; as the
public figure he was, he was well acquainted with many of
the people whose names he mentions; and others are simply names that were as familiar in 1930 as is Ted Koppel
or Margaret Thatcher in 1990. In a very few cases, new
footnotes also indicate additional sources the reader may
want to consult for further material on the same reference
point.

Dr. Powell's characterization of Mary Baker Eddy is his
own. It is undoubtedly sincere, and he has correctly captured the broad thrust of her life. For a Christian Scientist
reading this biography today, it may be helpful to point out
that Dr. Powell purposely chose not to comment on every
event in her career, most importantly omitting many of the
crises she had with various people who figured in the early
history of the Christian Science movement. He was not
unaware of facts, but he felt that to tell her story in a reasonable length, he had to let the reader see the forest and
not each gnarled tree in that forest. That Mrs. Eddy had
trials along with every forward step she took, there is no
doubt; but it was her vision of her mission in life that sustained her, and it is that vision which he tries to portray in
the picture he decided to paint of her. This coincides well
with Mrs. Eddy's own statement in the Christian Science

textbook, "The discoverer of Christian Science finds the path less difficult when she has the high goal always before her thoughts, than when she counts her footsteps in endeavoring to reach it. When the destination is desirable, expectation speeds our progress."

When this biography first appeared, a friend of Powell's asked him what Mrs. Eddy was really like. Powell replied:

> In her 55th year she wrote a best seller which next to the Bible is more devotedly read than any other book in the world; in her 70th year she saw the church she had established girdling the globe...; and in the third place, past 87, she established what many editors believe to be the best daily paper published in the United States.

The friend replied: "That is enough. Anyone in the world who did those three things — I am for her."

Lyman Powell spent his life in the service of others. The fact that he felt there was something in Christian Science that must be broadcast to a wider world than the official activities of the Christian Science church had yet penetrated led him to write this book. His appreciation for Mrs. Eddy and his understanding that Christian Science belongs within the mainstream of Christian practice give this book a permanent place within the annals of the Christian Science movement. His personal example, based on his understanding that all Christians share in seeking the spirituality which underlay the life and work of Christ Jesus (as well as the commitment to demonstrate one's Christianity in daily living), can encourage us all to build our own bridges of understanding and love with each other.

RICHARD A. NENNEMAN
Lincoln, Massachusetts, April 1991

Prologue

NOWHERE IS THANKS-GIVING DAY SO MEANingful as in New England where the day originated. To the Rector of St. John's Episcopal Church in Northampton, Massachusetts, Thanksgiving Day, 1906, proved to be unwontedly significant. Long more or less interested in Christian Science, this interest had a year before been accentuated by the discovery, which many other clergymen were making, that as a rule conventional Christians who came under the influence of Christian Science were likely to fall away from whatever church to which they might previously have been more or less attached, in order to give full allegiance to the new faith.

In American religious life there was then nothing quite so puzzling as this new phenomenon. Few outside Christian Science knew how to account for it, and not all within, even with the best intentions, appeared able to interpret it with understanding to the average man. The vocabulary of Christian Science sounded strange in his ears. Its teachings required closer consideration than he could give them. The problems it presented were more intellectual than emotional.

They had to be thought out, and of course no clergyman could shift his thinking to anybody else.

In many a pulpit, sermons in explanation were preached which did not explain. The pulpit did perhaps the best it could in such a novel situation. But it rarely knew enough, and did not know it did not know. About the only thing concerning which the more thoughtful preachers agreed was that there were certain differences of opinion between Christian Science and other folds in regard to philosophy and theology; and between Christian Science and medicine radical differences in theory and practice which it appeared useless to attempt to reconcile.

The Rector of St. John's preached no specific sermon on Christian Science. When in the pulpit he mentioned it at all, it was usually in casual praise. He had another way — in his opinion more effective — of dealing with a situation for which nothing in his theological training could prepare a minister in that day to deal. Having a church at the center of the biggest women's college in the world, and a considerable representation of "gown" as well as "town" in his congregation, the Rector of St. John's wrote for his flock alone, a booklet in which he set forth what he believed to be the virtues as well as the defects of a faith which, for practical purposes, had suddenly emerged above the American horizon.

The booklet appeared on November 15, 1906. It began with the comparison, which the author still deems sound, of Christian Scientists with Apostolic Christians:

> Some of the purest souls alive today are Christian Scientists. They have done much good. They have helped the sick, reclaimed the prodigal, brought surcease to many a sorrow, tempered men's asperities and given a sense of unity and harmony where before were disunity and discord. To

an age grown weary and impatient of dogmatism, ...
Christian Scientists have brought something of the warmth
and glow, the freshness and the spontaneity, the poise and
the sincerity, the gladness and the otherworldliness which
suffused the Apostolic age and made it all alive with spiritual power. If Christianity is true, it is joyously, stupendously
true. It is so true that all other truths in life seem but partial or secondary by its side.

The early Christians gave proof at every turn that theirs
was a faith somewhat like this. They "did eat their meat
with gladness and singleness of heart." They lived above
life's fret and turmoil. They won and kept the peace which
passeth knowledge. They endured whatever came their way,
as seeing Him who is invisible. They lived for Jesus Christ,
and him alone. Knit together "in one holy bond of truth
and peace, of faith and charity," they went out to win the
world to Christ. ...

Christian Scientists have many of the marks of Apostolic
days upon them. Some of them are a protest ... against the
worldliness and the ecclesiasticism which afflict the church,
and the materialism and meanness which constitute a continuous menace to the world. They furnish men proof positive and peace-bringing — that where there is a will there
is a way to live the spirit's life against all odds.

In response to a copy of the booklet sent in courtesy to
the Committee on Publication[1] of The First Church of
Christ, Scientist, in Boston, a letter of acknowledgment written in a kindly spirit was received in Northampton, on
Thanksgiving morning. Its closing paragraph begins: "It is a
mystery why you clergymen do not recognize the beauty of
Christian Science and recommend it unreservedly to your
followers."

Scarcely had the Rector finished his Thanksgiving dinner

before he was dictating an eight-page letter in reply so indicative of the author's attitude at the time that it is here quoted freely:

> To say that I am interested in your letter is to speak with moderation. I am delighted with it because its friendliness and open-mindedness make it possible for me to hope that you and I may have a freer and a franker talk about the subject . . . than newspaper columns permit.
>
> . . . I do believe that the spokesmen for Christian Science are trying to make their position clear to the great world. . . . I gladly express abhorrence of all that business of a month ago when an aged woman's privacy was so rudely invaded to make newspaper "copy." I . . . yield to no one in my admiration for the singular purity and nobility of many Christian Science characters, and in my sincere gratitude for the great good that has been done. May I go farther and say that every day my conviction deepens that God has called Christian Science to do a work of more significance than can possibly be foreseen?
>
> There are three contributions Christian Science is making to the world . . . :
>
> 1. It is turning the thoughts of men back to the power the mind *spiritualized* has over the body. The doctors have neglected this truth to a great extent, the Christian Churches almost altogether. Christian Science is forcing the truth on the minds of men, and in another decade, I believe, thanks largely to Christian Science, every church will emphasize what it now neglects.
>
> 2. It is turning men and women into Bible readers and thus bringing them as no other set of people are to the very source of spiritual life. Nothing can be more important than that, and no later than last Sunday I paid glad tribute in

my pulpit to Christian Science for this service and called my people to a new and more devout reading of the Bible every day.

3. It is restoring something of Apostolic spontaneity and serenity and devotion to an ideal and of attendance on church services to our time sadly in need of it; and of this too I spoke last Sunday to my people. It is this especially that makes me feel that God has a good and great work for Christian Science in this land.

Why then do we clergymen, as you inquire, "not recognize the beauty of Christian Science and recommend it unreservedly" to our followers? I will tell you ... in the same friendliness and frankness which characterize your good letter.

Then follows a detailed statement of the honest differences of opinion, as the Rector understood them, between the orthodox church and Christian Science in regard to the inner meanings of philosophy, the essentials of theology, and the significance of the sacramental system to which Episcopalians are committed. But points of agreement may, on wiser reflection, claim and reward close examination far more than absorption in dispute over differences. It was for these the Rector looked. He said, "I want to praise. I want to find some common ground on which we both can stand."

As the Rector was then writing much on new developments in religion for the *Review of Reviews, Good Housekeeping,* and also various weekly journals, he expressed the hope that it might be made possible for him to interpret Christian Science aright to the general reading public at a time when snap judgments were perhaps too frequent.

No more courteous reply could have been made to this

overture than the one received from the Committee on Publication on December 5, 1906, and the friendly relationship then begun has proved, at least to the author, advantageous, as through the years he has been making preparations, unconsciously but nevertheless steadily, for the writing of the present book.

That winter the *McClure's* articles on Mary Baker Eddy began to appear. On their face, they seemed to bear evidence of the same will to investigate which characterized the serials running, during the first years of this century, in the magazines, concerning the past of big business and big business men. "Debunking" was the order of the day, and for a time few knew but that it might be their turn next. The Rector's interest in Christian Science, already keen, was further whetted by a publisher's suggestion that he prepare a volume which would answer some of the questions which he had raised in his parish booklet, at a time when the average reader had little choice between books of adulation and of condemnation. He accepted the commission with a strong desire to produce something which would deserve the judgment actually accorded his work, when it finally appeared, by the *Springfield Republican:* "A fair-minded and judicial interpretation of Christian Science by one who is neither its assailant nor its defender."

In the course of his preparation for the writing of the book, he tried to check up by interviews and letters as many of the statements as possible then appearing in the press. On his quest he visited various places. The correspondence which, in some cases, he started, continued after the book was published, and today constitutes evidence the more convincing because the letters were sent avowedly to help the author to write with understanding. His correspondents expressed themselves the more spontaneously and freely because never once were they asked to make affidavits.

As a critic has written the author, much of the testimony of that period was one-sided. Out of the obscurity of small-town life, some of the witnesses — not all — emerged into a nationwide notoriety, the enjoyment of which they made no effort to conceal. Not in every instance, dryly observes a critic, were "they the kind of sources we would have chosen." Such as seemed accessible were reported to have been interviewed; sometimes also their affidavits were taken.

Just as the author was wondering how he could possibly discover witnesses closer to Mrs. Eddy and more competent to testify, he received on May 4, 1907, a courteous letter from the Committee on Publication in Boston, which opened the way for a discussion of some of the problems involved.

But the summer of 1907 was not a favorable time for the author to collect material. Growth within and public clamor without had thrust so many new and unexpected duties upon all persons in any way engaged in Christian Science work, that granting to such an insistent investigator as the author all the time and help he wished was physically impossible.

Besides, most of the materials now available were yet to be collected; for it was not until the latter part of 1907, that there began the systematic and comprehensive mobilizing of the data, which at first consisted of Mrs. Eddy's letters to church officers. No special need for the materials had been foreseen; or, for that matter, could have been. As always Mrs. Eddy's attention was concentrated on things she counted of more spiritual import than the compilation of information concerning herself. Some of the letters, which perhaps the author might have seen, had come without expectation of their publication; and the mere routine of getting from various quarters permission for their use in a book would have taken time and care not then available to a staff already overworked.[2]

Although the "Next Friends Suit" did not come up in court until August, 1907, the action had months before been brought, and through the entire spring preparation to meet it was taxing every heart and mind in any way concerned. Owing to complete and inevitable failure to understand the conditions surrounding Mrs. Eddy, the author was persistently pressing her people for definite, even documentary, information; to which he added the request that, in company with the venerable Edward Everett Hale, he be allowed at her convenience to pay a call on Mrs. Eddy.

The hesitation and reluctance which the Committee on Publication showed to take steps for the granting of a request which seemed to the author altogether reasonable, he did not understand. In much of his writing, his habit had always been to go in every instance to the supreme source. Diplomatists and United States Senators, Presidents and Prime Ministers had opened wide their doors to him. In preparing, shortly before, his *Historic Towns of New England,* such men as President Charles William Eliot, Colonel Thomas Wentworth Higginson, Edward Everett Hale, and a score of other eminent New Englanders had personally assisted him.[3] Why Mrs. Eddy's door should be the only one in all New England which would not open to him, puzzled the author.

Now he understands. The circumstances that year were beyond even Mrs. Eddy's control. Long one of the busiest

women in the world, Mrs. Eddy had already been obliged
to write her Boston representative, "I shall not be subject to
interviews and you must not subject me to them. My time
is worth more for good than to risk its *misuse* or to be so
used by others." [4]

In due season, the author's book appeared. The preface
opened:

> Christian Science has long engaged my interest. For years
> I discouraged none who sought its healing ministry. The
> undiscriminating censure visited upon it in apparent igno-
> rance or prejudice made no impression on me. The desire
> Christian Scientists were constantly expressing to be judged
> by their fruits seemed to me to be both Christian and
> scientific.

In the copious notes of reference to his sources at the end
of the book, the statement was inserted that he had "spared
no effort to find all the evidence there is." He took pains
also to announce that he would stand ready to revise the
book, should new evidence come to light at any time to
make revision necessary in the interest of truth.

During the years that followed, his appreciation of Christian Science grew, along with his amazement that no presentation, fully documented and satisfying to critic as to
public, was in print touching a woman who had a record
to her credit of more extraordinary and benignant things in
life than any other woman in the history of the world. He
had in fact to wait until 1930 to find that Mrs. Eddy, with
characteristic wisdom, had once observed that neither the
time nor the person had come to write her life story.

The year 1910 brought to the author's eye many editorial
appreciations which were evoked by Mrs. Eddy's passing. As

he now looks back across the twenty years which have since intervened, he believes he then took a distinct step forward in understanding her personality and achievements.

Selected the next year by the editors of the Schaff-Herzog Encyclopaedia of Religious Literature to write a judicial estimate, to be published midway between articles of commendation and of criticism of Mrs. Eddy and her faith, his article closed with this paragraph:

> The public has no longer any disposition to deny that from the standpoint of achievement Mrs. Eddy stood alone among the women of the world. . . . Mrs. Eddy and her followers have identified themselves as have no others in the world with the religious and the philosophical revolt against materialism.

World War I broke and furnished the most convincing demonstration in the history of the world of the unspeakable ravages to which wrong thinking may lead. More people than ever began to realize that there is something in Christian Science, as one critic had observed, "wholly gracious and beautiful." Significantly enough he added: "It would be difficult satisfactorily to explain why or how or by what argument that power should be nonexistent in Christians now."

As America in 1917 was on the brink of World War I, the author again wrote for publication:

> In the last ten years Christian Science has certainly encouraged daily Bible reading, until now Christian Scientists are probably the most assiduous Bible readers in the world. They still avoid antagonisms. They keep singularly serene. They average high in otherworldliness. It looks as though . . . they were endeavoring to make the most of the spiritual reality which those who study far into the movement easily discover.

While overseas, a little later, to observe the effect of the war on English and French educational institutions, and during the two or three years that followed speaking in hundreds of places throughout the land, the author never lost a chance to add new impressions to the old of Christian Science. Everywhere he found the same devotion to things of the spirit, the same inconspicuous efficiency, and the same loyalty to the woman of their love and faith.

Moreover, his community contacts in such places as Mountain Lakes, New Jersey, where he had a suburban home, taught him to expect Christian Scientists to be found on the right side of public questions, from the education of the young to the reclamation of the old. In fact, more than once he had hearty cooperation from individual Christian Scientists in what are ordinarily termed ministerial duties, complicated in those days by the social dislocations and the family smashups which the War had brought.

By 1921 when he received an invitation to contribute the article on "Science and Health" to the *Cambridge History of American Literature,* he had become convinced that there was too much constructive achievement to the credit of Mrs. Eddy to withhold full credit from her longer. "Christian Science," he therefore wrote, "is really its founder's creation. Where she got this idea, or where that, little matters. As a whole the system described in *Science and Health* is hers, and nothing that can ever happen will make it less than hers." [5]

Of Christian Scientists his closing words ran thus:

> With allowance for those in every religion who do not try to live up to its highest teachings, they measurably avoid friction and irritation and preserve considerable serenity and otherworldliness amid temptations which many of us seem unable to resist. They have to their credit a widely read

daily paper which for editorial ability as well as excellent
news service ranks among the best journals in the country.
Finally, as the years go by, it is thought by many that
Christian Scientists seem to be increasingly disposed to
emphasize only the outstanding virtues which their book
teaches, and in consequence to bring forth "the fruit of the
spirit — love, joy, peace, long-suffering, gentleness, goodness, faith, meekness, temperance; against such there is no
law." [6]

During the decade which opened with the appearance of
the *Cambridge History,* America soared to the pinnacle of
material achievement. Power both to earn and to enjoy was
increased. The hours of labor were reduced. Comforts multiplied. The so-called hostilities of nature shrank, and her
benevolences increased. The standard of physical fitness rose
until it became bad form to enjoy ill health, or even to talk
of being sick. Speaking of symptoms ceased to be an indoor
sport except in institutions tarrying overlong in the past.
Death lost much of its terror. Too ostentatious mourning
gravitated into the discard. The Christian Science phrase "to
pass on" began to dispute popularity with the word
"dying," long associated, too long indeed, with the dark and
dismal.

Developments during this same decade in the academic
world of science took place, which, to say the least, were
hardly anticipated. Millikan began to strip the "atom" of its
coating.[7] Eddington denied "actuality" apart from consciousness. Haldane made the individual mind a part of that
"absolute or unconditioned mind," which was in the
thought of St. Paul when he stated that "in him we live,
and move, and have our being." Kirtley F. Mather of Harvard observed last April, as reported in *The Churchman,* in

a Boston parish meeting, that "scientists are more and more coming not only to acknowledge the existence of spiritual forces, but to give all phenomena a spiritual interpretation." But Christian Scientists had long been holding to the familiar phrase of Mrs. Eddy: "There is no life, truth, intelligence, nor substance in matter. All is infinite Mind and its infinite manifestation, for God is All-in-all." [8]

For better or for worse, religion, as well as science, began to feel the urge to restate its position. Defining God went on as energetically as ever. If God has not at last been defined to death in many a theological camp, most of us may perhaps take to heart the warning which Goethe gave to Eckermann:

> Dear boy, what do we know of the idea of the Divine; and what can our narrow conceptions presume to tell of the Supreme Being? If I called him by a hundred names like a Turk, I should yet fall short and have said nothing in comparison to the boundlessness of his attributes.[9]

Two preachers who grew so discouraged that they left the ministry this year past would seem to illustrate some adverse consequences of these unsettled conditions. One is a Presbyterian, two years out of seminary and still in the middle of his twenties. The other is an Episcopalian in the maturity of middle life and, until the other day, rector of a conspicuous church in New York City. The reasons for their withdrawal appeared in two popular magazines.[10]

After one year in the ministry, the younger man withdraws because, to cite some of his words:

> I am muckle sick of the optimistic slush with which the pastors are lulling their congregations to sleep by congratulating them upon their Christian piety and assuring them

that God loves them. I am also sick of all this talk about
the hunger of the human heart for "pure religion and
undefiled." The attempt to interest men in the church by
feeding them chicken dinners belies this theory. Why can't
we say quite frankly that the great majority of moderns care
nothing about the church or Him it represents? Why don't
we confess that the statistics showing forty million Christians in this country are a monumental joke? The religious
longing is ineradicably carved upon the human heart, say
the philosophers. Very beautiful, but untrue. I fear it is a
desire for "weenie" roasts and bowling-alleys rather than for
religion.

The more mature man has become convinced that the
Protestant reformers of the sixteenth century blundered in
substituting preaching for worship; that the recent rapid
subsidence of church going leads logically to the closing of
the churches; and that, with little prospect of developing a
spiritual technique, which will help the individual every day
as well as Sunday to be aware of God, Protestantism will
soon be over the abyss.

As between the two diagnoses submitted, the author is
unable to accept either. Anxious about many things, he is
not anxious about God. Conscious of human limitations, to
the author every new problem is nothing more than a new
challenge to wrest a solution out of the unknown; to find
in an enlarging understanding of the revelation which
Christ Jesus gave of God the solution of all problems, old
and new.[11]

But, no matter what the risk in too elaborate defining,
each mind must still give its account of God. It must state
the reason for the faith within it. The ability to do so
always depends on having firsthand faith, on knowing God

firsthand. Many of our intellectual interests we may pass on
to others. Some we may refer to a "Committee of the
Whole." But, in the higher life, each must know God with
the heart. If we doubt we have a heart, we have to grow
a heart to know God, to know God intimately near as well
as infinitely far. The business, therefore, of growing a heart
is always pressing. Nobody can grow a heart for anybody
else. The only way to prove that we have grown a heart is
to submit to the universal test found in Edna St. Vincent
Millay's verse:

> The world stands out on either side
> No wider than the heart is wide;
> Above the world is stretched the sky, —
> No higher than the soul is high.
> The heart can push the sea and land
> Farther away on either hand;
> The soul can split the sky in two
> And let the face of God shine through.
> But East and West will pinch the heart
> That cannot keep them pushed apart;
> And he whose soul is flat — the sky
> Will close in on him by and by.[12]

Divisions among Christians have lost God from many a
heart. That is why men like Bishops Brent and Manning,
Doctors Burris Jenkins and Macfarland (the latter having
recently rounded out twenty years of executive direction of
the Federal Council of Churches), in season and out, have
called Christendom to get together on at least a working
basis. That is why as long ago as November 12, 1906, Mrs.
Eddy wrote Dr. Hamilton Holt, then Editor of *The
Independent*,[13] now President of Rollins College, Florida: "I
love the prosperity of Zion, be it promoted by Catholic, by

Protestant, or by Christian Science, which anoints with
Truth, opening the eyes of the blind and healing the sick.
I would no more quarrel with a man because of his reli-
gion than I would because of his art."

History has been a succession of revelations of the Highest, flashing forth when the night looked blackest. And so
today as yesterday:

> I know of lands that are sunk in shame,
> And hearts that faint and tire;
> And I know of men who ask not fame
> Who would give their lives for the fire.
> I know of hearts that despair of help
> And lives that could kindle to flame,
> And I know a Name, a Name, a Name
> Can set these lives on fire.
> Its soul is a brand, its letters flame;
> I know a Name, a Name, a Name
> 'Twill set these lives on fire.[14]

When the resurgence of critical interest in Christian Science came a year ago, the author was invited, at a New
York luncheon table, to speak out his opinion of the situation. His reply to the friends who made the request, one of
whom had been editor of the Christian Science periodicals
and was himself the writer of several books, was an outright
declaration that the time had come for the spokesmen of
Christian Science effectively and finally to lift discussion out
of the lowlands of controversy, to the heights of general
understanding. To one he observed:

> You ought to write a book based on the hitherto unused
> materials which your church must have, and for all time lay
> some of the smaller bothers and misapprehensions which

every little while reappear. The climate has changed. The public is weary of controversy. Christian Scientists have done too many fine things to be disturbed so often by vexatious disputation. Bring it to an end the only way you can.

Almost chapter by chapter, the author blocked out the book he thought the times require. As the group broke up, each going his own way, it was assumed that such a book would soon be written by some one belonging to the fold with access to the abundant sources, which have of late been assembled by the authorities of the church. In due season, arrangements were made for a conference between the author and The Christian Science Board of Directors in Boston, consisting of Mr. Edward A. Merritt, Mr. William R. Rathvon, Mrs. Annie M. Knott, Mr. George Wendell Adams, and Mr. Charles E. Heitman. His vision of the book which he believed should be written could now be thrown on a somewhat larger canvas than was possible at a luncheon table. After several discussions, in which all present shared, agreement seemed to be general that the time at last had come to supplement the writings of the generation past, based on partial knowledge as they had to be, by a life-size portrait of Mrs. Eddy, for which the many new facts available might furnish the material. Such a book would have to be free from pettiness. Controversy would not be sought. It ought not merely to be based on original sources but also to be written with such simplicity and engaging freshness as would make it readable to all.

While humanizing Mrs. Eddy, this book would naturally not neglect to make much of the extraordinary foresight shown in her constructive work of instituting, organizing, and administering a movement which grew so fast as to attract the world's attention in her lifetime and to hold it since her passing on. Every incident accepted for inclusion would be chosen with relationship to this larger purpose, and nothing intentionally overlooked which would help to give Mrs. Eddy her proper place among world builders.

As the discussions developed, the conclusion slowly emerged that in order to interest and inform the public outside, in addition to those within Christian Science, the book would better be written by one without the fold and yet who had given proof that he possessed a good general understanding both of the movement and of its originator.

By a process of elimination, finally the task fell to this author. The Board of Directors generously promised him free access to the rich sources committed to their care, and also to respond to any proper requests for assistance that might be necessary in the execution of the task. No pledge was asked by the Directors of him, and he gave none.

Before reaching a final decision, he talked over the matter with friends in New York and elsewhere. They agreed with him as to the desirability of such a book, and predicted general interest on the part of the public in it. Dr. Albert Shaw, whose monumental life of Lincoln — now appearing — is a model, tersely advised, "Tell the story as though it never had been told before."

As, at last, the author approached his task, he felt that his background of twenty-five years of deepening appreciation of the significance of Christian Science and of the personality of Mrs. Eddy should be an asset. On the other hand, his conviction seemed warranted that, with access granted to the colossal collection of original materials — the most valuable part of which, for the author's purpose, had been collected in the last few years — the hour had struck for the life-size portrait of Mary Baker Eddy to be made.

On both sides, there was risk. The author might disappoint the Board of Directors. Every writer knows that between having a vision and projecting it on paper, a wide gulf yawns. Almost anything can happen to obscure a writer's insight, or to divert him from his course. Many a book has been marred by listening overmuch to counsel in its preparation. Many a book has been dwarfed by refusing counsel altogether. Even after investigation begins, conditions may not prove as favorable as they at first appeared. Sometimes the sources disappoint. They prove less important on close inspection than they promised in the distance, or they turn out so amorphous, so unordered, so impossible to classify, that they are unworkable. But whatever difficulties arise, once an author assumes his task, his is the inescapable responsibility to see it through in his own way.

On the other hand, the Board of Directors, through no fault of its own, might disappoint the author. More than once Mrs. Eddy herself had been misunderstood. Starting out possibly with good intentions members of her own household had, now and then, turned into foes. Furthermore, a part of the failure in those early days to grasp her meaning, was due to the novelty of her teaching. She humorously reported that on one occasion asking all those in her audience to stand up who had understood what she said, not one stood up. Since Mrs. Eddy passed on, the directorate, now representing her, have not always found their course clear or their task easy. The responsibility to direct the movement, to care for the flock which Mrs. Eddy mothered so wisely, rests upon their shoulders, and they must take no unnecessary risks.

But, if the task could be performed with the understanding of all concerned, it might be worth doing. The book would then, perhaps, do its bit to instill public confidence in a group which too few outsiders realize train themselves with the same meticulous care to live the higher life as the "track" man trains for his "meet," or the pianist practices for his concert appearances.

Certain conditions, on both sides, would naturally be observed. The author must be left untrammeled in his work. His habits of intellectual creativeness which for years had been developing must be respected. His time must be conserved. In spite of his marked social instincts, he had for a season to deny them indulgence. Financially, he had to be independent. The book was to be his book. If evidently official or inspired, his chief purpose in writing it might be defeated. On these terms the author set about his task; and as he nears its close, he gladly testifies that the faith pledged to him has been kept. He has been permitted to consult everything necessary to the understanding of the subject. Nothing has been withheld to which he sought access. By day as well as night, he has come and gone, as suited his convenience, on these errands of research. Unvarying courtesy has been shown him. There has been no infringement of his personal integrity or of his financial independence. All necessary aids have been at hand.

Being somewhat familiar with some of the greater libraries of the world, from the British Museum to the Library of Congress, the author cannot speak too highly of the originality, resourcefulness, efficiency, and unselfish service rendered by the Christian Science staff. No place does he know where a book of this type could have been done with such ease. In many excellent libraries, an investigator counts it no hardship sometimes to wait long for an important document to be placed before him. In the preparation of this book, the author cannot recall an instance in which what he has required has not been, without delay, forthcoming, so excellently organized is the entire department, so carefully ordered are the rich materials of which they take tender and intelligent care.

Since a biography is rarely written as completely as this from original sources, the reader may care to hear something of them. He will recall — if he has read to this point in the Prologue — that it is almost a quarter of a century since the author began without prevision to collect the materials out of which this book has grown.

Obviously his acquaintance, at first, was confined to those not close to Mrs. Eddy. No others then appeared accessible. As the years elapsed, his acquaintance widened, his correspondence increased with those who could speak with much authority, and the source of the materials grew on which to base the judgment which he was gradually forming. Now, as he nears the completion of a task which he began a quarter of a century ago, he finds that, in all probability, he has known, in one way or another, more of those on both sides qualified to testify concerning Mrs. Eddy than anybody else in the same period. All this time the author has been an ordained Episcopal minister, intensely interested in his Church, and with voice and pen often speaking for it beyond the range of his own parish.

His more immediate approach to the task began by making the personal acquaintance of The Christian Science Board of Directors, their many helpers, and also others able and ready to assist him. Many who knew Mrs. Eddy in the last years of her life, or their descendants, or even their neighbors, furnished him much information not before available.

The more important places where Mrs. Eddy lived were visited, and of her last home at Chestnut Hill a somewhat careful study was made. The many books she read, and marked, were examined; and the more important of them for his purpose were turned into abstracts for effective use.

Written recollections from almost all who ever knew her well were supplemented by talks in person with many of them, some of whom by request came from afar to see the author. Judged by the standard which courts apply to human testimony, these new witnesses have proved trustworthy. Intellectually alert, as those associated with Mrs. Eddy had to be, they are naïvely loyal to her memory. Yet without collusion, often indeed never having met or corresponded, their testimony is substantially free from contradictions.

The general correspondence of the movement, the copies of Mrs. Eddy's letters, the letters others wrote to her, and the multitudinous other materials occupy large fireproof vaults.

Her original letters, amounting to more than fourteen thousand, a large proportion of them written with her own hand and many of special value only recently added, are mounted in ninety-four large volumes having a general index, cross references, and a subject index in concordance style. Bound in fine leather, specially imported from England, the volumes are approximately fifteen inches by twelve inches in size. They are kept in a moisture-proof vault, specially fitted for them. The temperature of the vault is maintained at from sixty-six degrees to sixty-eight degrees in summer as well as in winter, and all other known precautions to safeguard such treasures are taken.

The preserving of the letters is done by a special process, in some respects original. Before its mounting, each letter is placed in a bowl of water and thoroughly soaked. Then it is stretched out even on a zinc board and covered with a coating of paste. Next it is set in a large sheet of special grade paper cut out to form a frame. Then it is hung up on a line like clothes to dry.

After drying, the letters are put under a heavy press with wax paper between the sheets to keep them from adhering to each other, and large pasteboards beneath them for protection. Then the press is clamped down and they are left there for twenty-four hours. Upon removal silk sheets are placed on either side of the letters, and, to prevent fraying, tissue strips are used to cover the edges where silk and paper meet. Once more they are dampened and pressed until they remain absolutely flat. Afterwards they are assembled in signatures, sewn to make volumes each of about one-hundred pages, and are ready for the binder, who comes to the church offices to do his work.

The leather for the binding is of the best blue-black levant, and the volumes are hand-tooled.

Approaching the volumes in The Mother Church vault, the designation on the back reads as follows:

MARY BAKER EDDY	MARY BAKER EDDY
Letters and Miscellany	Letters and Miscellany
Vol. 54	Vol. 55
Nos. 7526–7652	Nos. 7653–7824

Looking back with reverent appreciation of this rare privilege of studying the life of a notable religious leader, as reflected in this mass of unusual detail over which he has pored both day and night, the author vividly realizes how necessary such sources are in any writing on this theme.

In fact, to attempt to do a biography of Mary Baker Eddy without steeping the mind in this material would seem as futile as to attempt a biography of George Washington, without recourse to the Library of Congress and the fourteen volumes of letters edited by Ford and containing the recollections of Washington's friends.

In the nineties at Johns Hopkins University, the author had the good fortune to hear Woodrow Wilson give the material in lecture form of more than one book which he was afterward to publish. He recalls with special vividness his many talks with Woodrow Wilson about the materials for *Division and Reunion,* which covers our national history beginning with Andrew Jackson and ending with the close of the first century under the Constitution. Woodrow Wilson still a boy in the South was a loyal Southerner when the war was on between the States. In the course, however, of spending his college days in the North and later, after he took his Ph.D. at Johns Hopkins, of teaching successively at Bryn Mawr, Wesleyan, and Princeton, with six weeks of lecturing every winter at Johns Hopkins, many of his earlier prejudices against the North died out. Without the loss of his love for the Southland, he thought and spoke and wrote increasingly in terms national, once calling his students to:

Be strong-backed, brown-handed, upright as your pines;
By the scale of a hemisphere shape your designs.

Writing his preface after he had finished work on the manuscript of *Division and Reunion,* Woodrow Wilson showed that he was keenly sensible of both the advantages and disadvantages which lay in his Southern bringing up and his Northern contacts. In the closing sentence of that preface, after a modest admission that his work might contain imperfections, he stoutly laid claim to impartiality; for, he said, "Impartiality is a matter of the heart, and I know with what disposition I have written."

Lyman P. Powell
1930

— 1 —

A Challenge

*J*ESUS BROUGHT THE
UNDISTINGUISHED AND
the handicapped good news. "The blind receive their sight,
and the lame walk, the lepers are cleansed, and the deaf
hear, the dead are raised up, and the poor have the gospel
preached to them." [1]

No news could then have been more welcome to these
millions, ever with us, of neglected ones. All the centuries
up from the *Egyptian Book of the Dead,* that earliest religious book in history, to Nietzsche, contempt for the average man and fawning deference for the inhumanly unhampered superman have been the rule. Rarely have the sick,
the sinful, and the dying heard any good news other than
the good tidings which Jesus brought of a heavenly Father
who cares[2] for every one of us, poor as well as rich, young
as well as old, who numbers every hair in every head, and
lets no sparrow, however tiny, fall unnoticed to the ground.

To the early Christians this radically different understanding of themselves which Jesus brought to them was news
too good to keep. They simply had to pass it on. They had
no time to stop for argument. To every challenge to engage

in disputation they turned a deaf ear. Served with a summons to explain, they quoted the man after his sight had been restored who ended inquiry with the reply, "One thing I know, that, whereas I was blind, now I see." [3]

Christian Science proclaims itself a bearer of the same good news. Christian Scientists could not keep it to themselves if they would and would not if they could; for many of them have experienced in their own persons transformations similar to those of apostolic experience. They have been emancipated from grievous illnesses — not only physical, but also moral and mental. If they were to hold their peace, it seems to them as if "the stones would immediately cry out." [4] That is why their Wednesday evening service is anticipated by them weekly with delight and attended with singular devotion at a time when midweek services in other churches are either struggling for existence or have expired altogether.

There is a challenge here which Christian Science offers to the world, and no longer can it be evaded. In fact, ridicule, flaw picking in this tenet or in that of Christian Science, sometimes tumultuous controversy spiced with outworn gibes, no longer satisfy a reading public every day growing more sophisticated and also better informed.

The sincere testimony offered by thousands and thousands of responsible people the whole world round that they have found joy and peace, healing and a higher aim in life in consequence of their adherence to this faith must now be regarded seriously. Whatever opinion the reader may hold of the theology of Christian Science, the evidence is now overwhelming that for innumerably many, Christian Science works. It meets for them the pragmatic test which Professor

William James[5] in 1907 set up that "True ideas are those that we can assimilate, validate, corroborate, and verify."

It would be a poor compliment, indeed, to the reader if the author did not invite him in this noncontroversial book, written by one not a member of the Christian Science church, to join in a clear-eyed look on at least a few representative testimonies out of the many now available. No other course is open. The evidence is not to be dismissed. It is not negligible. The witnesses are people of social, intellectual, and spiritual significance.

Dr. Laurence McK. Gould, who was second in command to Rear Admiral Byrd in the recent Antarctic Expedition, sent these arresting words:

> In the physical world one may endure the hardships of exploration with some confidence that he will receive at least a modicum of approval and appreciation. In the world of things not material this is much less likely to be true. Too often the explorer or pioneer here receives but scant sympathy and seldom lives to see his visions become realities. Probably no person who pioneered or explored beyond the margin of the conventional in this world ever lived to see such abundant and widespread fruitage as did the Founder of Christian Science — Mary Baker Eddy. And each day finds this movement just a little bit at least more widespread than it was on the preceding day.
>
> Christian Science is an incontrovertible fact and no one can think to interpret or even understand the trends of modern religious thought without giving serious attention to it. To accurately appraise anything is in part to delimit it and that can scarcely be even attempted in the case of Christian Science. The Christian Science church with all its affiliated institutions comprehends this movement only in part. The essential philosophy of this faith has found its way into the

thought and attitude of many Protestant churches and there is no measuring its boundaries. This widespread and lasting fruitage is the greatest evidence of the essential soundness of Christian Science teachings.

The next is Philip Kerr, sometime secretary to Lloyd George and now Marquis of Lothian, who has recently written for this book:

Many spiritually minded men and women throughout the ages have found their way to the direct knowledge of God and have taught that knowledge to their fellow men. But Mary Baker Eddy has done something in the field of religion which is unique. Through her study of the Bible and of the words and works of Christ Jesus she has not only given us the full definition of the nature of the living God but she has also analyzed the origin and character of that evil or materialism from which humanity has never yet been able to escape and has shown us how we can destroy it and so prove our birthright as the children of God. Later ages will recognize that the writing of *Science and Health,* after Mrs. Eddy had demonstrated the truth of the teachings it contains by healing the sick, redeeming the sinner, and raising the dead as no one had done since the days of Jesus, was the turning point in human history. For it has given to mankind in a form which all can understand the Science which will enable it to destroy utterly every phase of evil, sin, sorrow, sickness and death and thereby bring into our experience in all its purity, beauty and loveliness that perfect world which Jesus described as the Kingdom of God. In this age of preoccupation with the cares and pleasures of mortal existence the unique significance of Mrs. Eddy may not be generally discerned. But posterity will recognize her as the greatest woman who ever lived upon this planet.[6]

Next is a word sent in June, 1930, by Viscount Astor, of interest on its own account and also because of the admiration felt for Lady Astor in her own land:

> Youth, science, intellectualism, modernism, challenge theology; and theologians are not able to give a satisfying answer to the very reasonable questions the world of today insists upon putting. As a result Christianity has lost both adherents and influence.
>
> Compared with this admitted loss the growth and the increasing membership of Christian Science is phenomenal. This is doubly remarkable in a conservative country like Britain with its Established and Free Churches and their great position and tradition. What is the reason for this phenomenon?
>
> Christian Science is logical. Given certain premises which are accepted by all Christians the conclusions of Christian Science are inevitable. The natural scientist, too, who is not an atheist can find in Christian Science a philosophy which fits in with many modern views of the Universe. Lastly, suffering humanity finds in Christian Science a remedy.

Across the years comes drifting the memorable testimony of the Seventh Earl of Dunmore, written in 1907:

> I never knew the meaning of real happiness until I became a Christian Scientist. Amusements, relaxations, tastes, and pursuits that seemed to me in the old days the only things that made life worth living, I now know had never the true ring of happiness about them; they afforded me but a spurious kind of satisfaction, which I, in my ignorance of what life really means, mistook for happiness. The world that one day appeared to me so full of what I mistook for happiness and joy, would the very next day appear to me to be gloomy and miserable, full of doubt and discord; whereas

today there is no shadow of uncertainty over the world as revealed to me in Christian Science, but a lasting sense of peace, sunshine, happiness, and love. Even money troubles can have no power to disturb the equanimity of the Christian Scientist, once he has brought himself to realize that God — and not man — is the source of all supply.

American visitors to Cambridge remember well the distinguished Master of Trinity College, Dr. Montagu Butler. His widow, daughter of the late Sir James Ramsay, is the next witness:

> Every day they live, Christian Scientists are indebted to Mrs. Eddy. Through her writings their whole outlook on life and experience of life has been changed. She has enabled them to find convincing proof of the truth of Christianity as taught by Christ Jesus, and has shown them how it may be applied and lived today. She has solved enigmas, for an answer to which they had searched in vain in other directions.

Count Helmuth von Moltke, of Berlin, expressed himself as confident that "the Christian Science movement is safely anchored through God's protecting wisdom and love."

Up in Sweden, where Christian Science is growing apace, Count Sigge Cronstedt, of Stockholm, adds his voice:

> The more I have the privilege to study Christian Science and to practice what I have learned therefrom, the more I humbly and gratefully acknowledge and appreciate the immense importance of the life work of Mary Baker Eddy.

There is a plentiful supply of impressive confessions from American sources which vie in appreciation with these European ones. As a businessman Mr. J. M. Studebaker, Jr., of the Studebaker Corporation says:

Although I am not as yet a member of the Christian Science church, I have for many years seen members of my family benefited by the teachings of this wonderful work. I sincerely feel that Mary Baker Eddy, as the Discoverer and Founder of Christian Science, has given to the world through *Science and Health with Key to the Scriptures* and her other writings, a complete statement of truth which is healing and bringing comfort to every sincere thinker.

For men who "go down to the sea in ships," Commodore John M. Orchard speaks:

Our Master's message, "Go and shew John again those things which ye do hear and see," impels this witness to my grateful appreciation of the work of our revered Leader, Mary Baker Eddy, Discoverer and Founder of Christian Science and author of its textbook, *Science and Health with Key to the Scriptures.*

In my own experience, simply through earnest study of the Bible in connection with *Science and Health,* old age glasses were permanently discarded.

At one time the ship under my command was enabled to carry out instructions which necessitated entering a harbor through a channel having outlying rocks and no navigating aids, in spite of dense fog and strong irregular currents.

More than all this is the peace and poise with which Science touches every phase of right endeavor and points it to higher, happier attainment.

Among educators Professor Hermann S. Hering,[7] sometime on the faculty of Johns Hopkins University:

Christian healing is an essential element in Christian living, although not generally so considered. From the inception of Christianity, however, only a few have accepted fully

Dedicated in 1895

This picture hangs in the Directors' room for which purpose Mrs. Eddy presented it.

our Master's teachings, caught their spirit, and manifested
this Christ-spirit in healing works, notably the early Christians who, during the first three centuries of the Christian
era, did such marvelous healing, and led such self-sacrificing
and consecrated lives.

Dean William E. Masterson, of the College of Law, University of Idaho, arrests attention with his words:

A thorough and unbiased study of the life of Mrs. Eddy
reveals a woman of great personal charm, rare culture and
learning, a purity of life and purpose, unsurpassed unselfishness, and the profoundest wisdom and spiritual discernment
and understanding. She is, doubtless, the greatest prophet
and benefactor that mankind has ever had, with the exception of Christ Jesus. I am convinced that she came according to prophecy and that through her there has been
revealed and restored to humanity the comforter which St.
John declared would be sent "from the Father." Such a revelation could come only through the noblest and purest type
of womanhood. Subsequent to this discovery, which she
later named Christian Science, her life was one unselfish
and tireless effort to reduce to human comprehension and to
establish among men this Science as a practical and healing
religion. This she did by means of her teaching, her writings, and her church and the manifold channels of its activity. Such was her unswerving devotion to a cause in which
her faith remained fixed and unshaken. Only those who
have observed the beneficial effects of the application of this
science to the lives of others or felt its benign influence in
their own lives can properly appreciate Mrs. Eddy and her
mission and justly appraise her work in its relation to
human welfare.

A former physician, Dr. Walton Hubbard, of Los Angeles, California:

My experience covering a period of nine years in the practice of medicine, followed by the practice of Christian Science, has proved to me that the results following Christian Science treatment are incomparably better than those following the use of material means.

For the stage, Mary Pickford:

We are adjured to count our blessings and I count among my greatest, the clearer spiritual vision that has come to us in the light of Mary Baker Eddy's interpretations of the teachings of Christ Jesus. Facing a material world and preaching a doctrine of spiritual thought, she stood practically alone and matched her humanity and vision with a high courage that, in itself, should be an inspiration to all of us.

Corinne Griffith:

Mary Baker Eddy is the greatest benefactress the world has ever known, and even to those not interested in Christian Science, the clean-minded, honest influence of her life and works is bound to be felt.

Conrad Nagel:

Mary Baker Eddy has given to the world a religion that is demonstrable and practical, and offers every human being a thorough and complete solution to any and all problems that may present themselves. I have many times discussed Christian Science and Mrs. Eddy with most of the foremost people in the motion picture industry, and find that they all have the greatest admiration for her and for her teachings. I have found that, while not members of any Science church or even avowed Christian Scientists, the heads of several of the biggest organizations in the motion picture industry have many times turned for help to her teachings.

Religious people outside of Christian Science, and naturally differing widely from those inside, are more and more bestowing upon the good news which Christian Science proclaims appreciative recognition. A few of the more commanding out of a multitude of such tributes are selected for citation here.

In one of the Encyclical letters issued to the Bishops and Clergy of the Anglican Church by the late Archbishop of Canterbury, Dr. Randall Davidson, to begin again overseas, one finds the sentence:

> There is much in Christian Science which ought to be found within the Church, where it would be supplemented by truths which in Christian Science are neglected.[8]

The new Archbishop of York, the Most Reverend and Rt. Hon. William Temple, in his book entitled, *Essays in Christian Politics:*

> There is no doubt that we have in the church neglected the connection that does exist between faith and health, and it is largely because of that that Christian Science, for example, has been able to gain so many adherents; for the practice of Christian Science has brought incalculable benefit to many people.

One of two London clergymen who have spoken with unusual clearness, the Reverend Edward T. Vernon:

> God used Mrs. Eddy for a special revelation, and there is, indeed, no reason why this should not be so. No just person can fail to admire her as a religious leader. She has founded a great church, and, let us say it frankly, brought

great blessing on countless lives.

The second, Dr. John Shaw:

I am not a Christian Scientist, but I believe in what I should regard as the essential tenet of their creed, and which I might sum up in the words, "The Lord's hand is not shortened, that it cannot save."

Ireland will be represented by the Reverend Richard W. Seaver of Belfast:

We owe much to Christian Science for emphasizing the fact that "thoughts are things," and insisting upon our power and our duty to manage thought as the root of action.

Returning to the United States, the following admission is made by the new Episcopal Bishop Coadjutor of St. Louis, the Right Reverend William Scarlett:

Christian Science has made the church aware it has overlooked a great power and it has set the church to thinking of healing.

But even more to the point are the words of the Reverend Dr. Elwood Worcester because he established the Emmanuel Movement, which is largely responsible for the development of the new interest in spiritual healing observable in the Episcopal Church:

The doctrines of Christian Science, for example, have been denounced, ridiculed, exploited times without number, apparently with as much effect as throwing pebbles at the sea checks the rising of the tide. Preachers, physicians, editors of powerful journals, philosophers, humorists, unite in pouring contempt upon this despicable superstition, very much as Juvenal, Tacitus, and Celsus mocked at nascent Christianity, but in spite of them it lives. While most other religious bodies are declining or barely holding their own, it grows by leaps and bounds. All over this country solid and enduring temples are reared by grateful hands and consecrated to the ideal and name of Mrs. Eddy. And this strange phenomenon has occurred in the full light of day, at the end of the nineteenth and at the beginning of the twentieth century, and these extraordinary doctrines have propagated themselves not in obscure corners of the earth, among an illiterate and a fanatical populace, but in the chief centers of American civilization.[9]

The Reverend Dr. Charles F. Potter describes Mrs. Eddy as "the most compelling figure in American religious history."

The late President Charles William Eliot, eminent in the field of education, in his customary downright and forthright way once observed that "Christian Science is good Christianity."

President Edward S. Parsons, of Marietta (Ohio) College, gives this explanation of his good opinion:

> The Christian Science churches have been crowded because they have been in a real sense the church of the living God. They have somehow persuaded people that there is a living God, whose strength is in a real way at their command; that not merely the past, but the present and the future, are the field of God's control and action, and that because He is, there can be nothing fundamentally wrong with the world.

Doctors, too, are beginning to show less reluctance in admitting that Christian Science has good undeniable to its credit:

Dr. William Mayo, of Rochester, Minnesota:

I have sent people to Christian Scientists and they have got relief.

Dr. Copeland Smith, of Chicago, in a radio sermon described Christian Science as:

The opening of a window to the winds of Heaven. It is the mightiest protest yet made by the human spirit against the blatant materialism of the present age.

Dr. Richard C. Cabot, of Boston:

Christian Science has done a great deal of good.

The attitude of the press is no longer so adversely critical as it used to be. Even twenty years ago, Isaac Marcosson could describe Mrs. Eddy as "a striking character, who must be reckoned with in any estimate of the women who have made history."

Thomas L. Masson:

They pay their bills, erect beautiful edifices ... heal diseases according to the teaching of Christ, and, owing to the strict discipline of keeping their minds pure, are exceedingly prosperous.

The Editor of the *Daily Journal-Press,* of St. Cloud, Minnesota:

Whatever opinions one may have had regarding the doctrine of this church, it must be admitted that its members are splendid, patriotic, law-respecting people.

Judge William G. Ewing:

Christian Science is the Christian religion pure and simple, a religion of works, a nearer approach to the ministering religion that Jesus taught and practised in the accomplishment of his mission to the world than men have known for seventeen hundred years.

Many of the women who have made places for themselves since the freer entrance of their sex into American public life are giving serious thought to Christian Science. Mrs. Alvin T. Hert, sometime Vice Chairman of the national Republican Committee:

> The constantly increasing preaching of health by various religions is proof of the truth of what Mary Baker Eddy taught. The lives of Christian Scientists expressing this truth are a benefit to mankind which people generally must acknowledge.

Mrs. Mabel Walker Willebrandt, recently Assistant Attorney General of the United States:

> The world is now far enough removed from controversy over Mrs. Eddy as a personality to recognize her wholly spiritual conception of the universe and human personality as a world force making toward the betterment and happiness of individual lives, control over adverse environment, and the purification and elevation of even material and human aims and activities.

The Editor of the *Christian Herald,* Stanley High, who was once a member of the staff of *The Christian Science Monitor:*

> From my own observation and my own contact with these friends, I am convinced of the very rich fruitage that Christian Science is bringing about in the lives of many people.

Cecil B. DeMille, of the Metro-Goldwyn-Mayer Studios, Hollywood, California, who is not himself a Christian Scientist:

> Mrs. Mary Baker Eddy is one of the great benefactors of mankind. She has given to the world one of the great religions. She has interpreted the life and teachings of Jesus of Nazareth in a manner to prove a blessing to many hundreds of thousands of souls. She has carried the light of truth into many dark places. She has perhaps done more to fulfill the words of the Great Master, himself, than any individual of recent centuries.

Mark Twain's final reversal of his previous judgment may come as news to many:

> Christian Science is humanity's boon. Mother Eddy deserves a place in the Trinity as much as any member of it. She has organized and made available a healing principle that for two thousand years has never been employed except as the merest kind of guesswork. She is the benefactor of the age.[10]

Although subject all through its history to ridicule and criticism so unreasonable as sometimes to cross the line of persecution, Christian Science has gone steadily on its way. In fact, opposition at the fiercest has stimulated its growth. In three years alone, following the hue and cry of 1907, the Christian Science churches built and paid for almost doubled. The following dates are stepping-stones in its development:

1875, *Science and Health* was published.
1875–1876, The Christian Scientist Association was organized and services were held under its auspices in Lynn.

1879, church organized in Boston under a charter.

1892, church organized under unique statute of Massachusetts and with twelve First Members.

1892, the number of churches and societies was 155.

1907, the number of churches and societies was 646.

1910, the number of churches and societies was 1212.

1930, the number of churches and societies is 2451, as well
as 39 university organizations.

Those who expected that when Mrs. Eddy passed on (in 1910) Christian Science would soon begin to dwindle and in the end disappear will note that, from 1910 to 1930, the increase in the number of churches, societies, and university organizations has averaged between five and six a month, and that for ten years past one new church has been dedicated, and paid for, every week.

To those who ask in good faith, "What are representative Christian Scientists like?" the answer is, "Quite like other people." They smile, but not vacuously. Recruited some may be from the discard and the graveyard as well as from the membership rolls of the churches but they never laugh unnaturally like Lazarus in O'Neill's play. They seek peace with all men, because they start with peace in their own hearts. If they look prosperous that can scarcely be surprising since poverty, like sin and sickness, is to them an illusion and, in accordance with Professor William James' well-known law, they tend to become what they believe they are. Christian Scientists are so busy minding their own business that they do not have, and show no disposition to make, any time to interfere with the business of their neighbors. Taught by their faith that "the powers that be are ordained of God," they of course obey their country's laws. Such bad habits as have not already been crowded out by the adoption of this new interest, the economy of Christian Science is designed to correct.

> Moderate tasks and moderate leisure,
> Quiet living, strict-kept measure, —

it is this which Scientists desire. Never are they noisy or disorderly. They do not fret, nor cry aloud. Drink they regard as an evil, and fleshly. Tobacco is also taboo. Many of them shun coffee and tea. To Christian Scientists the inner dynamo of the God-life furnishes all the energizing man requires. That without any official compulsion they vote "dry" goes without saying. Contact with the sensational in the newspapers is avoided by the habitual reading of their own dignified daily, which the Rt. Hon. H. A. L. Fisher[11] calls "one of the best-informed journals of our time."

In books ephemeral in content, they take little interest. Their reading taste is kept fine by employment upon a literature of lasting worth. None show more liking for good music than Christian Scientists. They travel, and enjoy it, as do others. For small-town gossip, they substitute an interest in world affairs by which they have become internationally minded and intelligent friends of world peace.[12] While the difference between Christian Scientists and other Christians may appear slight, what difference there is matters. It is often an actual redistribution of the emphasis in human relationships.

Dr. Joseph Wood Krutch observes that, with some of the main trends of scientific thought now headed toward religion and of theological thought toward science, the two may pass each other on the road and not know it.[13] But

Christian Scientists believe they have the answer to the riddle. They are openly committed to a mutual and peaceful interpenetration of religion by science, and science by religion, and they would gladly see all Christians of whatever fold commit themselves to the same.

"The love of Christ in the human heart ... creates a new, vast world," says the Reverend John S. Bunting, "in which the spirit of man may live and move." [14] Christian Scientists make such constant daily endeavors to live in that world that many of them, with St. Paul, might say without exaggeration, "For to me to live is Christ."

All this awareness of God, this demonstration of the power of God to transform, this devotion to the Bible, this absorption in the Christ, is the product of what may perhaps be called a priesthood of democracy, fostered now through almost three generations. Christian Science makes every man responsible for his own inner life. Helps he may have, not substitutes. If he is to attain the higher salvation which expresses itself in perfect health of body and mind, he must "work out [his] own salvation." [15]

Never can the dubious privilege be his of referring back to a date, immediate or remote, when he was converted, and of letting it go at that. He cannot live on a mere date. The manna on which his inner life is fed has to be gathered fresh every day. Nor has he any preacher to whom he can look to keep up his morale. For there is no place in Christian Science for any human preacher. "The Bible and the Christian Science textbook are our only preachers," states the *Christian Science Quarterly*. The Readers appointed to read the Bible and the textbook at the Sunday services hold office as a rule no longer than three years. No Christian Science church is given any chance to grow dependent on the personal popularity of any man, or any woman. A reminder to "have no ambition, affection, nor aim apart from holiness"[16] rings ever through the teachings of Christian Science. The springs of its democratic priesthood must be replenished from the everlasting hills.

Nor can the Christian Scientist shoulder off his personal responsibility on to any "group." The obligation Jesus laid on Nicodemus rests likewise on him. "Ye must be born again" is an experience every Christian Scientist must undergo. Everyone must heed this necessity, or forfeit his Christian Science birthright.

Has one a bad temper? He must conquer it. Is his mind unclean? He must clean it out. Is he inordinately ambitious? He is the one to use the curb. Is he avaricious? That is an obnoxious form of selfishness which is taboo. A Christian Scientist supports his church whether or not he can afford to keep a car, to have a radio, or even to go much to the movies.

Without pulpit "begging," without resort to church suppers, without any kind of money-raising by indirection, Christian Science has solved the problem of church support. Its members give to their church for but one reason, gratitude. The loosening of the purse strings has sometimes been called the test of faith most commonly — in college student parlance — "flunked." Christian Scientists when subjected to this test — one of several — rarely fail to pass it. Loyal Scientists give generously to their church because of an almost universal belief that their church has bestowed upon them something beyond money, beyond price. The love of Christ constraineth them.[17]

But the method used in raising the budget by The Mother Church is businesslike. The revenues needed are obtained from a nominal per capita tax of not less than one dollar a year, paid by each member; from the Sunday offerings; from the net profits of The Christian Science Publishing Society; and in part from the profits on the Founder's writings which go for special expenses in promoting the Cause of Christian Science. In addition, the Board of Directors invites contributions for the support of the remarkable philanthropic institutions[18] in operation under Christian Science auspices and for other benevolent causes such as cooperation in relieving distress of famine, fire, or flood. But in no case is the need felt of any strident call for aid; a simple announcement in its periodicals suffices. The money required comes. Indeed, the amount desired is often oversubscribed.

The grateful show their gratitude in every way they can. Christian Scientists are thankful for the healing which soul and mind and body usually receive. Sharing in the expenses of carrying on its enterprises is to them the most natural thing in the world. The Christian Science priesthood of democracy are glad to accept the full measure of their responsibility, and by their gratitude to let the world perceive that they lay it on themselves.

Simplicity is the outstanding characteristic of the Christian Science organization. The Mother Church (The First Church of Christ, Scientist, in Boston) is the hub. Out from the hub radiate spokes so numerous that the organization may appear complex to some outside who do not understand the centralizing character of the hub.

The organization consists of The Mother Church and its branches — either churches, or societies — located at all points where enough Christian Scientists have collected to be organizable. A group few in number is formed into a society, and then when its growth warrants, into a church.

At colleges and universities the members of the faculty and the students who are Christian Scientists may form and conduct an organization. The rank and file of the membership are protected from all sense of isolation by the dual privilege habitually exercised of membership at the same time in both The Mother Church and the branch church near which they chance to live. To insure this amalgamated dualism, but even more to sustain the vital relationship of branch to vine in full vigor, no branch church or society can be formed until a certain number of the petitioners for the establishment of a local organization have already become members of The Mother Church.

The *Manual* of The Mother Church, which contains its By-Laws and related deeds and documents, is both the Constitution and the fundamental law of the denomination. The Directors act within its scope. It sets forth the constituent departments and agencies of The Mother Church, including The Christian Science Publishing Society, and provides briefly for the conduct thereof. Branch churches and societies are formed under the *Manual,* which gives general directions for their government. From first to last, however, each church is a democracy, and makes its own by-laws. Provision for the discipline, if need arises, of a member of The Mother Church, also, is made in the *Manual.*

The Founder of Christian Science specifically provided the method to be used for the general supervision of her church, after she should pass on. In accordance with the provisions of the *Manual,* which she prepared, the affairs of The Mother Church are in the hands of The Christian Science Board of Directors. In Mrs. Eddy's lifetime the Directors were nominated by her, elected by the Board, and finally accepted by her; now the Board fills its own vacancies. Besides exercising full administrative responsibility over the congregation of The Mother Church in Boston, comfortably filling an edifice which will seat about five thousand, and over a large local Sunday School, the Board oversees the business of the denomination as a whole, taking final action on all applications for Mother Church membership from the entire field, appointing or electing the officers of The Mother Church and the editors and manager of The Christian Science Publishing Society. They certify the accuracy of the list of those qualified to act as practitioners, published in *The Christian Science Journal,* appoint the lecturers, edit their lectures and supervise their work. In the largest sense theirs is the responsibility to guard the integrity of Christian Science and to take whatever measures they consider best, always in line with Mrs. Eddy's instructions, to make it known to the public. Almost identical in personnel with the Trustees under Mrs. Eddy's will, who pass on all questions relating to the issuance of her writings, the Directors establish the policies and exercise a close supervision over all the other literature of Christian Science published by The Christian Science Publishing Society, including its daily newspaper. William P. McKenzie, Fred M. Lamson, and James E. Patton are now serving as the Trustees of The Christian Science Publishing Society, created by a Deed of Trust executed by Mrs. Eddy in 1898 to carry on the business of the Publishing Society. It regularly publishes the *Christian Science Quarterly, The Christian Science Journal* (monthly), the *Christian Science Sentinel* (weekly), and *The Christian Science Monitor* (daily), besides several periodicals in other languages.

Every Christian Science church has a Sunday School

which is carefully conducted. The large enrollment which is the rule is to the outsider one of the surprises of Christian Science. The teaching adheres strictly to the fundamental principles enunciated in the Ten Commandments and the Sermon on the Mount, and does this so intelligently that parents not interested in Christian Science — or for that matter in any religion — send their children as years go by in increasing numbers to Christian Science Sunday Schools solely for the effective spiritual training they receive under teachers above the average.

The work of instruction for adults is so regulated as to make it available to all interested. There is a Board of Education which selects, instructs, and certifies authorized teachers, subject to the approval of The Christian Science Board of Directors. Selections from the lists of the qualified are made somewhat on a geographical basis so that in all countries there may be teachers conveniently situated to respond to every call for class instruction in Christian Science. Class teaching is particularly desirable for Christian Scientists who wish to practice healing as a vocation. The relation between teacher and pupil usually becomes close, and is strengthened by the annual association meetings and by the opportunities afforded for special consultations.

The Christian Science Board of Lectureship is composed of men and women of culture and distinction. They can hold their own in any company. Dignified, gracious, immaculately dressed, they speak with a serious effectiveness, which is free from all strenuousness and emotion. They do not extemporize. Every lecture, before it is given, has to be approved by the Board of Directors. They interest. They instruct. Year by year their work has grown, until today it covers not only the English-speaking world but also the Continents of Europe, Africa, South America, Australia, portions of Japan and China, and many islands of the sea. During the past year two hundred twenty-eight lectures were given in Great Britain and Ireland to 262,000 people; on the Continent to 75,500 people, eighty-seven lectures of which fifty-eight were in German, five in French, and four in Dutch. In Australia, New Zealand, Tasmania, China, Japan, and the Philippine Islands and Hawaii, sixty-four lectures were delivered to 53,000 people. In the United States, Canada, Mexico, West Indies, Bermuda, and the Canal Zone, 3412 lectures to 2,829,000 people. For the first time, a beginning was made also in South America. A total of eight lectures with an attendance of 1920 were delivered in the larger cities of Argentina, Brazil, Chile, and Uruguay.

In general, attendance on the lectures and enthusiasm for them increase as the following typical report would seem to indicate:

I have just returned from a lecture tour of four months which has taken me all over England, Scotland, and Ireland, Paris, Geneva, Zurich, and Berne, Switzerland. . . .

The audiences throughout Great Britain, with possibly two or three exceptions, have been the largest the Scientists have ever known. An idea as to the numbers of non-Scientists attending the lectures can be gained from the following: in the city of Birmingham we had at the lecture twenty-three hundred people. Certainly not more than eight or nine hundred in that audience were students of Christian Science and the rest were, therefore, inquirers.

The crowds in London were so great and so many people were unable to gain admission to the lectures that six of the churches decided to give a joint lecture in the Royal Albert Hall. I lectured there in 1920 to an audience of six

The Mother Church

View of The First Church of Christ, Scientist, in Boston, as it looks today.

or seven thousand people which only comfortably filled the great auditorium. At the recent lecture the place was packed to the roof with an audience estimated between nine and ten thousand and a thousand or more were said to have been turned away. It was a most inspiring experience.

The Committee on Publication has grown from one, functioning from Boston as a center, until now every state, every country, where there are Christian Science organizations has its committee. Their responsibility is to give correct information through the press concerning Christian Science, and also to correct misapprehensions proceeding from other authorship appearing in print. It would be impossible to over-estimate the service to Christian Science rendered by these committees. Developed for educational purposes, the Committees on Publication have become the medium of better understanding between the public and Christian Scientists.

Much missionary work is done through literature distribution committees, maintained by the local churches and societies. Copies of periodicals used and new are donated by Christian Scientists and are dispensed in various ways. They penetrate to parts of the world where human missionaries could not travel. Railway stations, fire stations, hotels, theaters, and other public places are equipped with containers kept supplied with literature, which thus falls under the eyes of those interested who might not always care to be interviewed. Quantities of *Christian Science Monitors* are put on board ships for the crews at the large ports.

To overpraise *The Christian Science Monitor* would be difficult. It never exploits crime or scandal. Disaster is only an incident in its reports of the day's news. Unhampered by partisan politics or by fear of financial losses, the *Monitor* acts as the purveyor of world information to its readers with such a fine sense of proportion as to be substantially accurate and informing without becoming dull. Nearly half of its readers live two thousand miles and more from Boston, where the *Monitor* is published. The teeming highways of the world are rapidly becoming the streets where dwell its subscribers as well as the channels of its news.[19]

The establishment of the Christian Science Benevolent Association Sanatorium in Chestnut Hill[20] marked a step of policy in advance of larger import than at the time could have been foreseen. Mrs. Mary Beecher Longyear, of Brookline, Massachusetts, generously presented to the church, of which she has long been a member, a tract of twenty acres on beautiful Single Tree Hill; and the Directors, in accepting the gift, announced the enterprise in the *Christian Science Sentinel* of October 7, 1916. The characteristically modest notice that funds were needed met with an immediate response from all parts of the world. This enabled the sanatorium to be ready for its first guests on October 1, 1919. Approximately one hundred sixty-five can be cared for besides the necessary attendants or associates, including the staff of Christian Science nurses for whom a training school is maintained. The Assembly Hall, where services are held on Sunday morning and Wednesday evening, seats three hundred people. A temporary haven which offers practical assistance toward the healing of sickness and the removal of distress, it has brought peace in a genuine Christian spirit to thousands of deserving people from all corners of the earth. And this year a similar institution has been established on the Pacific Coast.[21]

The same benevolent purpose of looking after Christian Scientists in need and providing a proper environment for them which led to the establishment of the sanatorium at Chestnut Hill has inspired the Directors of The Mother Church to provide a home for elderly Christian Scientists, whose length of service in the Cause, good works, or other special circumstances furnish good reason for giving them a comfortable home. Pleasant View, where Mrs. Eddy lived from 1892 to 1908 at Concord, New Hampshire, was chosen for the site — Mrs. Eddy's home having been torn down years before. Again Christian Scientists were informed through the church's literature about the plan. Again the responses were adequate. The building, which was ready for use on July 15, 1927, is a beautiful structure of Georgian architecture, containing one hundred forty-four bedrooms, and is now occupied by more than one hundred residents from various places.

Like the sanatorium, the Pleasant View Home has beautiful reception rooms, sun parlors, and assembly hall, a well-equipped library, and besides all this some sixty acres of farm land. Farm buildings also and a commodious dairy have been erected and equipped; and milk, as well as vegetables and fruit in season, is thus supplied. This Pleasant View Home does a great deal more than simply shelter some aged members of the Cause. It supplies them also with discriminating care and comfort, artistic surroundings productive of such a happy spirit that they live together like one big harmonious household. Its table — and the same is true of the sanatorium — would do credit to the best hotel.[22]

With no paid preachers, Christian Science does a successful pastoral work. The Readers preach the only Christian Science sermon heard, when on Sundays they read aloud the Scriptures and their textbook. The lecturers aim to explain the larger meaning of the movement and its message to honest inquirers outside, as well as seekers of a still better understanding within Christian Science. It is the office of the teachers to train the smaller groups. The practitioners treat those sick in mind as well as body. They carry everywhere they go the comfort and the consolation of a faith which makes God real to men, leads many to the way-showing Jesus, and turns them into daily Bible readers.

To many now starting on pilgrimage through this volume, Christian Science may already appear to be — as it actually is — simply a reassertion of Christ's teaching that God is Love and Spirit; and that Love and Spirit are adequate to master sickness, sin, and death. All that Christian Scientists have to do is to live up to the teachings to which they are committed and to be loyal to the Founder, a woman who never rose too high to pray in all humility:

> Shepherd, show me how to go
> O'er the hillside steep,
> How to gather, how to sow, —
> How to feed Thy sheep;
> I will listen for Thy voice,
> Lest my footsteps stray;
> I will follow and rejoice
> All the rugged way.[23]

— 2 —

A Rich Girlhood

APOLEON HAD GONE AT LAST BEYOND AMBI-
tion's lure, and family talk in many a New England home
was turning toward the slavery issue just emerging above
the horizon, when Mary Morse Baker was born to Mark
and Abigail Ambrose Baker on July 16, 1821, at Bow, New
Hampshire.[1]

More farm than village, Bow, five miles from Concord,
then had its own schools and its meetinghouse. As elsewhere in New England, home was reinforced by school and
church, as it rarely is in these days when the community
bus carries children from many a mile round to the central
school of the township, and the Sunday paper keeps at
home most of those whom the automobile does not whisk
entirely out of range of worship.

Mary Baker's parentage was New England to the back-
bone, substantial, intelligent, and very religious. The devout
mother[2] was preparing both in mind and soul for the coming of her baby girl, and an understanding neighbor joined
her in frequent prayer and Bible reading all through the
months before the birth of Mary Morse Baker.[3]

Mark Baker,[4] on his part, led his family in daily devotions and in energetic argument for the church, then over-inclined to Calvinism. It is, therefore, not surprising that in her mature years Mrs. Eddy should have written:

> From my very childhood I was impelled, by a hunger and thirst after divine things, — a desire for something higher and better than matter, and apart from it, — to seek diligently for the knowledge of God as the one great and ever-present relief from human woe.[5]

It was altogether natural too that in her more intimate talks with friends in later years she should indicate that the goodness and mercy which followed her all the days of her life manifested their presence so early that memory all but failed her when she endeavored to recall their consoling ministries.[6]

One dedicated, like Mary Baker, from her birth to the religious life, would early learn to pray; and when her mother read to her from the Bible that Daniel prayed three times a day, for spiritual good count she prayed seven times a day, chalking down on the shed wall each prayer in succession, for a while as a settled habit.[7] When young as Samuel, she, like Joan of Arc, heard voices; and only those will minimize the incident who fail to catch the purport of the reply of Joan to the question put by King Charles, "Oh, your voices, your voices. Why don't the voices come to me? I am king, not you."

Joan: "They do come to you; but you do not hear them. You have not sat in the field in the evening listening for them. When the angelus rings you cross yourself and have done with it; but if you prayed from your heart, and listened to the thrilling of the bells in the air after they stop ringing, you would hear the voices as well as I do." [8]

But Mary Morse Baker was never a theorizer, even while still in pinafores. She was practical as a little girl, and there is on record an early instance of her putting to quick test the immediate availability of prayer. As her mother was bathing Mary's temples to allay the suffering from a fever, she bade Mary pray. The prayerful obedience was followed by "a soft glow of ineffable joy," and the fever quickly subsided.[9]

From the first little Mary Baker wanted and expected to become "somebody." There is evidence that a sense of mission early lodged in her consciousness. As in the cool of many a summer evening in her latter years, she loved to recall for those whom she knew best treasured incidents of the past, she once half humorously described how her sisters used to take her when a tiny child to school with them, and how they would set her during the luncheon hour on a table and would say, "Mary what are you going to do when you grow up?", to which she would reply, "I will write a book." [10]

Not merely did the little girl with blue eyes and chestnut curls say that she expected some day to write a book, she also began to make ready for the task by reading and by thinking. To her most brilliant brother she said, "I must be wise to do it"; and her pastor, evidently a man of insight, predicted for her "some great future." [11]

Evidence abounds that from the first her mind was quick and active. At a time when social usage encouraged girls to be frail of body, or at any rate to appear to be ready on occasion to faint in full accord with all the proprieties, patterns of "the lass with the delicate air," such an alive and acquisitive mind as Mary Baker's was apt to overtax the body. Nor was the strain lightened by her habit of taking her books home from school and putting them under the pillow in her little trundle bed.[12]

In later years she often referred to these disturbances of her childhood. Whether they indicated an inherent delicacy or the wideness of margin in vigor between mind and body which made her an easy victim to casual discomforts, it was soon found that the noise and confinement of the country school, which she attended with her sisters, wore on her so seriously that her father promptly heeded the family physician who advised, "Do not doctor your child, she has got too much brains for her body; keep her out of doors, keep her in exercise, and keep her away from school all you can, and do not give her much medicine." [13]

Although as a rule mention of her health was incidental with her, as in a letter written at the age of fourteen to her brother George, always there hovered in the background of her thinking an oppressive sense of the precarious equilibrium of adolescent life which had to wait for larger understanding of ways and means of stabilizing till the coming of such men as G. Stanley Hall and S. Weir Mitchell.[14] In *Doctor and Patient,* published in 1888, Dr. Mitchell, already foremost nerve specialist in the land, wrote that "no one knows women who does not know sick women"; and to the end of his distinguished life, he sometimes seemed anxious lest colleges for women should one day prove over-hazardous to their nerves.[15]

The mind of little Mary actively responded to its first strong stimulus when only nine years old. Her brother Albert was home from Dartmouth College — from which he was to graduate in 1834 — on his first vacation. Mary adored Albert. He was her knight without fear, above reproach. Nor was she the only one to find in Albert Baker a youth of unusual promise. A political rival later said of

him that "gifted with the highest order of intellectual powers, he trained and schooled them by intense and almost
incessant study throughout his short life." [16]

The Dartmouth freshman of twenty and his sister of nine
found each other on his first vacation. He knew things and
books as yet beyond her reach. Her girlhood ecstasy spared
no words to make him understand her joyous pride in him,
her purpose to deserve his pride in her. "I must be," she
said, "as great a scholar as you or Mr. Franklin Pierce." [17]
But there is some reason to believe the brother received as
well as bestowed. One of Mrs. Eddy's girlhood friends at
least implied in a letter written years later that Albert early
shared his sister's feeling about the supremacy of the
spiritual.[18]

No wonder then that Albert's good-by to Mary as he
turned back to college should take the form of earnest
counsel to apply herself to her Lindley Murray *Reader,* with
which she was later to become as familiar as with the
Westminster Catechism, which her orthodox father and her
godly pastor would make sure she learned.[19]

Before me as I write are the very copies of Lindley Murray's *Introduction to the English Reader* and the *English
Reader* itself, which Mary Baker read and marked and
inwardly digested at the early age of nine.

While eighteenth-century writing is admittedly inferior to
Elizabethan literature, it is at least serious and substantial,
more worthwhile than much of the bad art and worse ethics which compel attention today on every newsstand, in
every railway train. Even in these high days of up-to-
dateness, many a boy and girl could fare worse than at the
hands of Lindley Murray.

Going with Mary Morse Baker on the journey she took
when she was only nine years old through Lindley Murray's

books one finds much of interest. These books which were published respectively in 1803 and 1813 at Alexandria, Virginia, open with "Rules and Observations for Assisting Children to Read with Propriety." Then follow select sentences, some of them expressing sentiments as wise as those of Francis Bacon. Interesting narration, sound moralizing, vivid description, sustained dialogue, and "promiscuous" pieces make up the rest.

For those expecting to find little Mary at the age of nine an infant prodigy moping over the pages of Spinoza and Leibnitz, it is perhaps worthwhile to recall that Emma Willard was only that very year making her first trip to Europe to get acquainted with the old world thinkers, and that Mary Lyon's dream of a real educational institution for women was not to take form for some six years yet in Mount Holyoke Seminary, in turn waiting more than fifty years to become Mount Holyoke College. Mary might perhaps have been reading Emerson; but Emerson was still young and too busy getting married and starting his preaching career at the Second Church in Boston to be writing anything.[20]

On closer inspection the author notes in these two books of Lindley Murray's, no fewer than forty of the better known writers of the eighteenth century quoted, sometimes at great length. Out of a total of four hundred thirty-eight pages in the two books, Goldsmith has twenty and one-half pages, Addison twenty-one, Pope nine and one-half, Cowper seven, Hume five and one-fourth, Thomson ten and one-half, Cotton eleven and one-half, Milton four and one-half, Samuel Johnson seven and one-half, Young four, Wordsworth three, More three, Lord Chesterfield three, Benjamin

Franklin two, Robertson four; with some shorter contributions from Socrates, Horace, Sallust, Cicero, Marcus Aurelius, Plato.[21] All through the two books the Bible appears in the King James Version or in paraphrase.

In these sophisticated days the choice might fall on more diversified passages from eighteenth-century literature than little Mary Baker read; but they would not perhaps be more representative of eighteenth-century writing. Most significant is the evidence that she did read and reread them until they were so deeply embedded in her memory that sometimes they reappeared automatically in her own later speech and writing, possibly, as is familiar to all acquainted with modern psychology, unconsciously to point a moral or adorn a tale.[22]

Her marginal markings in the books reveal three of her girlhood tastes in reading:

First, she was always interested in everything about the social niceties. She dwells much on Chesterfield's canons of good breeding. Her pencil often marks such sentences as "Awkwardness can proceed but from two causes; either from not having kept good company, or from not having attended to it." [23] Her love of preciseness in speech, which several near her in later years have emphasized to the author and her many letters before him as he writes confirm, appears in this passage:

> To begin a story or narration, when you are not perfect in it, and cannot go through with it, but are forced, possibly, to say in the middle of it, "I have forgotten the rest," is very unpleasant and bungling. One must be extremely exact, clear, and perspicuous, in everything one says; otherwise, instead of entertaining or informing others, one only tires and puzzles them. The voice and manner of speaking,

too, are not to be neglected. Some people almost shut their mouths when they speak, and mutter so, that they are not to be understood; others speak so fast, and sputter, that they are equally unintelligible. Some always speak as loud as if they were talking to deaf people; and others so low that one cannot hear them. All these, and many other habits, are awkward and disagreeable, and are to be avoided by attention. You cannot imagine how necessary it is to mind all these things. I have seen many people, with great talents too; and others well received, only from their little talents, and who had no great ones.[24]

Second, a fine balance of interest in the moral and the spiritual at the early age of nine is one of the surprises which her copies of Lindley Murray give us. Already the Bible was the Book of Books to her. It furnished her many a precept on which she relied for self-direction in her personal contacts. The sentences from Proverbs which follow, not merely marked, but also numbered with her pencil, are commended to the consideration of the adolescent of today:

> He that hath no rule over his own spirit is like a city that is broken down, and without walls.
>
> Happy is the man that findeth wisdom. Length of days is in her right hand; and in her left hand, riches and honor. Her ways are ways of pleasantness, and all her paths are peace.
>
> Faithful are the wounds of a friend; but the kisses of an enemy are deceitful. Open rebuke is better than secret love.

Third, at an age when a girl's interest is usually confined to dolls, little Mary was beginning to take a lively interest in patriotic matters. Lindley Murray goes back to the time in which the Louisiana Purchase was sowing the seeds of discord over slavery. It was a year before Abigail Ambrose

Province of
New-Hampſhire,

BENNING WENTWORTH, Eſq;
Captain-General and GOVERNOUR in Chief, in and over His
MAJESTY's Province of *New-Hampſhire* in NEW-ENGLAND, &c.

To *Joſeph Baker Gentleman* Greeting.

BY Virtue of the Power and Authority, in and by His Majeſty's Royal Commiſſion to Me granted, to be Captain-General, &c. over this His Majeſty's Province of *New-Hampſhire,* aforeſaid ; I do (by theſe Preſents) repoſing eſpecial Truſt and Confidence in your Loyalty, Courage and good Conduct, conſtitute, and appoint You the ſaid *Joſeph Baker* to be *Captain* of the Foot Company in the Place commonly called known by the Name *of Suncook* in *Colo. Zacheus Lovewell Regiment*

You are therefore carefully and diligently to diſcharge the Duty of a *Captain* in leading, ordering and exerciſing ſaid *Company* in Arms both inferiour Officers and Soldiers, and to keep them in good Order and Diſcipline ; hereby commanding them to obey you as their *Captain* and your ſelf to obſerve and follow ſuch Orders and Inſtructions, as you ſhall from Time to Time receive from Me, or the Commander in Chief for the Time being, or other your ſuperiour Officers for His Majeſty's Service, according to Military Rules and Diſcipline, purſuant to the Truſt repoſed in You.

Given under my Hand and Seal at Arms, at Portſmouth, *the Thirtieth Day of May in the Thirty first Year of the Reign of His Majeſty King* GEORGE *the Second,* Annoq; Domini, 1758

By His EXCELLENCY's
Command
Theodore Atkinson Jnly

B Wentworth

Governor Benning Wentworth Appoints Joseph Baker Captain
of the Foot Company of Suncook, New Hampshire.
Joseph Baker was Mrs. Eddy's great grandfather. He married
Hannah Lovewell, daughter of the famous Indian fighter, John Lovewell.

Baker was praying for her unborn baby that Maine, neighbor to New Hampshire, was admitted to the union as a "free state" and Missouri also came in, but on terms so questionable that John Quincy Adams read in the historic Compromise of 1820 the "title page to a great tragic volume."

A family of consequence,[25] the Bakers read the papers of the day, particularly the *New Hampshire Patriot and State Gazette,* and talked over what they read in the living room.[26] Mary listened in and also joined in. Young as she was, she read the papers both for herself and also to the household. From her little trundle bed at night, as Mark Baker puzzled over the latest news from Washington, Mary would call out, "Father, I know what you are doing: you are reading the newspaper," to which he would reply, "Hush, child, and go to sleep." Then she would say, "I'll read it to you," and though she could not yet pronounce the longer words, she satisfied her father.[27]

These two books of Lindley Murray have much to say concerning slavery of every sort. The verses of Cowper and of Addison on the subject were elaborately marked by this little girl. For books published in Alexandria, Virginia, before the Missouri Compromise, the four articles Lindley Murray quotes on slavery, significant enough in themselves, become more so as one reads the following paragraph with the marginal pencilings of Mark Baker's daughter:

> It may not be improper to remind the young reader, that the anguish of the unhappy negroes, on being separated for ever from their country and dearest connections, with the dreadful prospect of perpetual slavery, frequently becomes so exquisite as to produce derangement of mind, and suicide.

If already, as she tells us in her writings, Mrs. Eddy took to verse more readily than to prose and thus laid herself open to the criticism that her verse was stilted and bathetic, it may not be amiss to remind ourselves that the same things are still said of Dryden and of Pope, whose "couplet," however, was to remain the model for imitation by succeeding poets until well along in the nineteenth century. All through her life, the strong impression which measured speech thus early made on the girl's mind endured. But it was John Dryden, and not Mrs. Eddy, who wrote such couplets as:

> Him of the western dome, whose weighty sense
> Flows in fit words and heavenly eloquence.

It was Alexander Pope, and not Mrs. Eddy, to whom belongs the couplet:

> His soul proud Science never taught to stray
> Far as the solar walk or milky way.

The conclusion to which these small particulars cumulatively point is that Mary Morse Baker was having a normal girlhood. She was the social center in every youthful neighborhood gathering. She loved and quarreled and made up with her sisters and brothers, and with her other boy and girl companions. She read much, and often "took her pen in hand." One of her first written verses was occasioned by the removal of her family from Bow to Sanbornton Bridge. She found parting with her young friend, Andrew Gault,[28] such sweet sorrow that in Popean style she left for him this farewell verse:

> Hard is the task to take a final leave
> Of friends whom we shall see ah! never
> With unaccustomed grief my bosom heaves
> And burns with latent fire forever.
>
> A vernal fe[e]ling thrills my very breast
> And scarce the accustomed word is spoken
> We firmer grasp the hand still loath to part
> And wish that grasp might ne'er be broken
>
> But go — those finer feelings riven
> Which through my bosom shot
> And with thee take this flower of Heaven
> The flower forget-me-not.[29]

Sunrise at Bow

Down the road, now overgrown, Mary Baker and her sisters
trudged to the schoolhouse where she spoke her determination to write a book.

From a painting by James F. Gilman.

In letter writing more clearly than in verse making, Mary Baker revealed her girlhood self. The earlier letters, in common with other letters of the time, appear somewhat self-conscious here and there. The spelling at the first is markedly informal, as is evident; so too was the spelling of George Washington until the end.[30] Now and then the characteristic sense of more or less complete isolation apt to be the experience of the sensitive adolescent is revealed along with its conventional concern about her health. But taken in their entirety, the letters which she wrote between her fourteenth and her sixteenth year throw sufficient light on that formative period in her life to convince a keen appraiser like Isaac F. Marcosson that they represent a "find of genuine historic value." [31]

Her first letter extant — the second she says she ever composed — was written September 7, 1835, at Bow to her brother, George Sullivan Baker, whom she loved to call "Sullivan," then living at Wethersfield, Connecticut. It simply expresses the affection of a fourteen-year-old girl for an older brother and her eagerness to have his counsel in all her concerns.

> There is one thing if I have not improved it aright I have lerned from expperience to prize more perhaps than ever I did *before* that is *Dear brother* the *friendly advice* and *council* you was ever giving me and the lively interest you ever manifested in my welfare but now when I sit down to my *lonely* meal I have no brother Sullivan to encourage me as formerly — but there is no philosophy in repining I must extend the thought of benevolence farther than selfishness would permit.[32]

The next letter, dated May 2, 1836, from their new home (then Sanbornton Bridge, renamed Tilton in 1869) to the same brother refers to him as "brother S. at Conn." and also makes mention of the more gifted Albert:

My Dear brother

We have just finished our morning vocations, and I am engaged in the sweet emplyment of writing (or rather talking) to brother S. at Conn, and to comply with good *ton,* I shall first enquire for your health, spirits, and the like of that, hopeing time sill continues to glide smoothly as in former years, it continues to do so with us only when we are obligeed to ride in a *wagon* and then it is rough. . . . I hope after I read the book you sent us, I shal becom some what more civilized in my presant state of ignorance I cannot express the gratitude I feell for the presants you sent us by Mr. C., they meet a weelcom recepttion you may depend, although I should much rather have seen the original. You cannot imagin the disappointment I felt on receiveing your letter that you should not return, but I hope it will not be long before I shal again see you, do not disappoint me but come and see us if you cannot stay. We received a letter from Albert not long seince, he informed us he had written to you but had received no answer. Mother wishes to be remembered to you with all the kindness of parental love, but none more sincerely than your Sister

Mary.[33]

Another letter which was written to "Sullivan," December 20, 1836, is alive with happy references to those she loves. The election of Franklin Pierce to the United States Senate calls forth proud comment on the prospect of even closer relations between Albert and the future President. After a reference to the illness of her "Uncle Baker," she runs on about affairs in this fashion:

We attended a party of young ladies at Miss Hayes last
evening she was truly sorry our Brother from Conn. was
not there, but she is soon to be married and then the
dilemma will close as it is your fortune to have some
opposeing obstacle to extricate you. Oh brother I wish I
could see you, and I hdly think Abby and I would be as
sleepy as we wer the last night you spent with us; but
could amuse ourselvs (if not you) by telling you things that
would excite laughter if nothing more, but when are we to
realize this this happiness? I am impatient to learn soon
verry soon I hope: but if we are not to see you soon, to
hear of your health and prosperity is a pleasure that none
but those to whom we are most nearly can experience. But
I must obey Mothers motto to be spry — and hasten to a
close with executing her commissions to give her love to
Sulivan — hoping you will receive the same from us all
not forgetting to tender it to Mr. Cutchins.

Write soon Dear brother and excuse the *unpardonable sin*
of our writing so often but do retaliate if you have any
resentment in writing to us. Pardon all mistakes for I am in
hast and accept the well wishes of yours truly

Mary M. Baker.[34]

Spring was in the air when April 17, 1837, Mary, now
near sixteen, writes "Sullivan" a long letter, more illustrative
than ever of her widening interests and her growing sense
of humor. She says:

> . . . it is a little funny, I will give you an abridged sketch
> of a gentleman recently from Boston, now reading medicine
> with a doctor of this town, a *perfect complet gentleman I met
> him a number of times at parties last* winter he inviteed me
> to go to the shakers[35] with him but my superiors thought it
> would be a profanation of the sabbathe; and I accordingly
> did not go. But I have since then attended a wedding with

a Mr. Bartlett he was goomsman and I bridsmaid; we had
a fine time I assure you.

Referring to her sister Martha's illness she adds — as
though foreseeing later years, "I should think her in a confirmed consumption *if I would admit the idea,* but it may
not be so, at least I hope not."
To "Sullivan" the news may not be altogether welcome
that "Father has been speculating of late, . . . he has swaped
your favourite horse with Mr. Rogers. And he thinks it a
fine trade."
The writing master is urging the Baker girls to join his
village class, writes Mary, "but Martha is not able and *I*
have not wherewith." And she closes her long letter thus:

> Write soon dear Brother and give me all the good advice
> you can for yours is the genuine growth of experience don't
> forget but remember the solicitation of your affectionate

Mary[36]

G. Stanley Hall's words,

> that bright girls of good environment of eighteen or nine-
> teen, or even seventeen, have already reached the above-
> mentioned peculiar stage of first maturity, when they see the
> world at first hand, when the senses are at their very best,
> their susceptibilities and their insights the keenest, tension at
> its highest, plasticity and all-sided interests most developed,

would appear from the letters to be presented next an
almost photographic likeness of Mary Baker at that age.
Her interest in books is now spreading and deepening.
She writes her friend, Augusta Holmes:

My dear Augusta, Have you Surwalt's gramar? If so, would you do me the favour to loan it to me for a short time? I am told it is easier than Levizac's — at least if it is not I shall have the *horrors* worse than last evening — *after you left* are you well, and did you return safely? but answering echo must reply to this. Much love to Abi- As ever your aff

Mary

P.S. In looking over some books yesterday I spied an essay I think must be *yours* will forward it the first opportunity.[37]

Even in inviting Augusta to a "party" Mary's eagerness for books vies with her enthusiasm for the party. In a post-script longer than the invitation she writes: "You will please to bring along with you that favourite book of mine, — entitled, *Forget me not,* I have not had an opportunity to send to Concord for one yet." [38]

[Mary's interests included all those concerns normal to a maturing young person: acquaintance with the popular culture of her time, an awareness of the young men from among whom she might find her future husband, and, always in her case at least, of the claims that God made on her to live a devout Christian life.][39]

A Methodist revival was held in Sanbornton Bridge in 1843, when Mary Baker was twenty-one years old. Mary was interested, but evidently had her doubts in some instances as to whether conversion had gone beyond the talking stage, for she wrote:

... the *marvelous* James Smith! Your *crazy correspondent* was correct, so far as pretensions warrant; he professes to have religion, and so far succeeded in *exhausting* that interesting and exalted subject, I grew weary and retired.

She hastens to describe the meetings themselves as "very interesting." Entertaining friends and relatives — the Bakers had many — who drove in from miles around to attend the daily services, involved Mary and her family in much "extra labor." She hopes Augusta will forgive her for neglecting to write oftener, and would have her know that almost all her acquaintances are now rejoicing in the hope set before them of higher aims and nobler joys.

> The sceptic's scoff, and the ribaldry of the multitude is scarcely left among us. I will mention some of your particular acquaintances who have experienced a change indeed since you were here *Esqr. Cate & wife,* Mr. Curry, wife, and *two daughters* Mr. Wingate. *N. Atson.* J. Tilton Mr. BARTLETT, Mr. Carr & wife My sister, Mrs. Tilton; with a hundred of others, I cannot mention, and with whom I am unacquainted. Would that you were here to witness with me this changed scene! tho I *fear* for *some,* I rejoice with *many,* whom I doubt not possess the "pearl" which is priceless And do you not also rejoice with me if it were but for *one* sinner that hath repented? Doubtless as you feared, there are some who have deceived *themselves* by "zeal without knowledge" — But methinks we have less to fear from fanaticism, than from stoicism; when a question is to be decided that involves our weal, or woe, for *time* and *eternity.*[40]

[In the summer of that same year, she made her first real visit to another town, Haverhill, New Hampshire. This visit included a stay with her friend Augusta Holmes, and exudes the enthusiasm most young people feel when away from home for the first time.] She was then, as a cousin in later years recalled, frail and fair with "brilliant blue eyes, cheerful, hopeful, enthusiastic,"⁴¹ as this letter's account of the many impressions made on her will show:

My dear Brother:
   Since I left you I have made it a religious duty to obey you in *all things*. And today, according to promise, write you the order of exercises since Wednsday — I reached here about 6 o'clock P.M. was the only passenger inside, and such a *sky-rocket* adventure I never had; some times I really thought I was at least *midway* between heaven and earth, till the driver's shrill whistle, or a more tolerable road would restore my senses; Mr. Hale is the very most polite good natured driver in the *whole world* (As *I have seen it all*) and was very kind to me on your account I suppose — You cannot know how *lame* and unwell I felt *yesterday;* Augusta would sleep with me the first night, and kept me awake so long after we retired, I did not rest much, if any, that night. Yesterday in the afternoon, we both took off our dresses and went *to bed* — I rested some, and to-day am as well as usual — have *not been any where.* Augusta and *all* want me to stay here until commencement And then attend with them, but there is so much to excite me here, and such a teazing etiquette in this vill. it is not best for my health And I go to L. tonight — *God bless you*

Mary⁴²

[Earlier that year she had written to Augusta to "say something nice" to "Mr. Dickey" in her name.]⁴³ She admitted to being willing to share with her friend the high responsibility of "making cold hearted man raise his standard of female excelence, still higher." ⁴⁴ We do not know who Mr.

Dickey was, or to what degree Mary was beginning to think about marrying. In any case, it was only to be a few more months before she herself would become a bride. Her suitor from afar, George Washington Glover, had identified his own "standard of female excelence," and was heading her way.

— 3 —

Finding Herself

*T*HE CHRISTMAS SPIRIT WAS ALREADY IN THE air when Mary Baker was given in marriage to George Washington Glover on Sunday, December 10, 1843. The wedding guests, from Concord and Boston, as well as from Sanbornton Bridge and from the surrounding country, came in sleighs to the little farmhouse, a mile and a half from the town. All the other Baker children were there, Samuel, George, Abigail, and Martha, except Albert, whose lovable character and whose brief career of rich promise had kept the family grief green for two years.

Samuel brought his wife, Eliza, from Boston. From Concord came Martha with her husband, Luther C. Pilsbury. Abigail, more sure of herself than ever because six years before she had made the best marriage in the Baker family, brought her husband, Alexander H. Tilton. The father's and the mother's cup of joy was now full with the sight of the family they had founded starting well in life.

Mary Baker looked her best. Past twenty-two, she was drawing near to wifehood.[1] George Glover was no stranger. Collaterally related and once of Concord, he had learned the building trade in Boston with Samuel Baker, and for four years had been making for himself a place in Charleston, South Carolina.[2] On a former visit to Boston he had run up to Tilton with his friend, Samuel, and had left his heart with Mary Baker, who was ten years his junior. An impetuous wooer,[3] scant delay intervened till the day when the pastor of the Baker family, the Reverend Corban Curtice, made the two one.[4]

The wedding night was spent at Concord, and the next day the bride and groom drove up to Bow for a fitting farewell to the birthplace of the bride.[5] Then Mr. and Mrs. George W. Glover set sail from Boston for their new home in the South. There were no domestic storms to mar the honeymoon, but the ship did run into heavy weather, and on Christmas Day the gale was so severe that even the captain became alarmed.

Mrs. Eddy in her later years related to Miss Shannon, Mr. McKenzie, and Mr. Tomlinson this almost tragic experience. She told them how after she and her new husband knelt in their cabin and prayed to God to save them, in a short time the wind subsided and she, as always in a crisis, gave God the credit. The captain also was so impressed with the sudden cessation of the storm that he called it "a miracle." [6]

Young Mrs. Glover was not the first bride — nor yet the last — to find a sea voyage little conducive to the happiness of the honeymoon. A penciled note in Mrs. Eddy's handwriting on the margin of her old scrapbook records that she "was hopelessly seasick." The letter of counsel which her mother had given them to ponder when halfway on their voyage, she was scarcely in a mood to read with the storm adding its aggravation to her discomfort. But of her husband she writes, "When I grew better" I "saw the tears wet on his cheek," as he read what her mother had given him under seal to be opened "when we were midway on our journey South."

Normal mothers are torn between tears and smiles when they see a daughter whom they love passing into the most complex experience which ever comes to a woman. But they rarely show the tender forethought of Mrs. Glover's mother in counseling the man to whom she gives her daughter to take heed of Mrs. Sigourney's verse, popular in those days on both sides of the Atlantic; and we of these more prosaic times may perhaps overlook the sentimentality of a less sophisticated age.

> Deal gently, thou, when, far away,
>   'Mid stranger scenes her feet shall rove,
> Nor let thy tender cares decay —
>   The soul of woman lives on love;
> And should'st thou, wondering, mark a tear
>   Unconscious from her eyelid break,
> Be pitiful, and soothe the fear
>   That man's strong heart can ne'er partake.
>
> A mother yields her gem to thee,
>   On the true breast to sparkle rare —
> She places 'neath thy household tree
>   The idol of her fondest care;
> And by trust to be forgiven,
>   When judgment wakes in terror wild,
> By all thy treasured hopes of heaven,
>   Deal gently with my darling child.

Then, as now, the approach from the sea to Charleston was attractive. Josiah Quincy of Boston who made the same trip not long before this left record in his diary:

This Town makes a beautiful appearance as you come up to it, and in many respects a magnificent one. I can only say in general that in grandeur, splendor of buildings, decorations, equipages, numbers, commerce, shipping and indeed everything, it far surpasses all I ever saw, or ever expect to see in America.[7]

And the Philadelphian Owen Wister, in his *Lady Baltimore,* called Charleston "the most appealing, the most lovely, the most wistful town in America."

Not even in Boston, or in Philadelphia, was the pursuit of culture for its own sake keener than in Charleston, when Mrs. Glover arrived. Had she stayed long enough, Mrs. Glover might have been admitted to *The Southern Review,* then the leading literary journal of the South. Or she might have made the acquaintance of Edward Malbone whose miniatures on ivory were already taking high place in the world of art.[8] She might even, had she remained long enough, have been invited to attend one of the concerts of the St. Cecilia Society, the most exclusive social club in all the land. Save for the fact that John C. Calhoun was in that same year to leave for Washington to become Secretary of State to President Tyler, she might, after establishing herself securely in Charleston society, have contemplated the possibility at least of measuring swords over the question of slavery with the man then dominating South Carolina.

Mary Baker Glover chose to turn as usual toward the moral, and this meant the particular issue to which her attention was most sharply called by her transfer to Southern soil. Already in her Tilton life, she had observed the slavery question dividing families. Her father was a Northern Democrat who, like Franklin Pierce, was in favor of letting slavery alone. Still mindful of her early training in the

Lindley Murray[9] *Reader* — the influences of which in her life have often been overlooked — Mary Baker Glover took a stand stoutly against slavery. As practiced in Charleston it only deepened her conviction that slavery was too wrong for talking to make it right. The simplicity of the negroes appealed to her, and their religious earnestness touched her heart. It is on record that she once drove up to a little chapel where negroes were at worship and listened to them express "their trust in God and Jesus Christ their only Saviour from slavery." [10]

There may be room for differences of opinion concerning some other of Mrs. Eddy's views; but nobody who knows whereof he speaks can question that from childhood until the day she looked out for the last time from her Chestnut Hill window this woman believed with all her heart and soul that "All God's Chillun's Got Wings."

Never in her long life was Mary Baker Eddy content to stop with anything so unaggressive as mere opinions. Her opinions soon climbed up into convictions. Quick to catch the point, she never remained long the noncommittal spectator cautiously and objectively weighing evidence. She soon became the passionate and prophetic proponent of profound conviction. No grays crept into the warp and woof of her mentality. The scarlet thread of spiritual conviction ran conspicuously and unweariedly through all the thinking of the fourscore years and nine of her extraordinary life.

But there were circumstances during those first weeks in Charleston by which the young bride from the North was somewhat handicapped. Her husband for a newcomer was a man of some consequence; for in barely four years he had built up a business already past the stage of promise, and "possessed real estate of considerable value." [11] Among these

assets, however, were a few slaves, readily accepted in payment of debts at a time when slaves passed as "current
coin." [12] His wife would have had her husband free his
slaves at once but he had lived in Charleston long enough
to be well aware of the difficulties in the way. Not only
was there local condemnation with which to reckon; there
was also a State law, passed in 1820, before Mrs. Glover's
birth, which forbade the formal freeing of slaves except by
special act of Legislature. Though the ardent young wife
could not but admit that her husband had no power in the
circumstances to do her will, one thing at least to her
seemed possible and that she did in spite of all the admo-
nitions of expediency. Under a pen name she pointed out
the inherent wrongness of slavery in a local paper which
drew from its rival a query, not at all courteous, as to the
identity of "that damned Yankee" [13] who had come to
Charleston to rob people of their property. Thus early giving evidence in the South, as had been her habit in the
North, of living up to her convictions, she clinched the
point as soon as the passing of her husband gave her the
sole power so to do by letting her slaves "go free without
any formal act of emancipation." [14]

February 1844 found her accompanying her husband on a
business trip to Wilmington, North Carolina, where much
rebuilding was necesssary following a severe fire in the city.
In June he was laid low by yellow fever. During his illness,
the young wife assisted by brother Masons — for he was
highly regarded as a Mason — attended his sick bed.

With loving hands she could do so little, but she prayed
ceaselessly; and to such purpose that it drew from the doctor the remark that George Glover would have died earlier
but for his praying wife.

The dying man's last words were a pathetic plea to his

brother Masons to see his wife safe to her home in the North.[15] Faithful to their trust, they laid their brother's form to rest with the full Masonic ritual in the cemetery of St. James' Episcopal Church at Wilmington. During the weeks that followed they gave the grieving widow tender care while, with their counsel, she salvaged what she could of her husband's estate, informally allowed the slaves, now hers alone, to go free, and under Masonic escort made the journey to New York where her brother, George, was waiting to greet her.[16]

In August Mrs. Glover was once more under the Baker roof. For her, romance was at an end. No care her childhood home could give was compensation for the piteous completeness of her loss. The tender grace of a day that was dead would never come back to her. In a nature so vital as Mrs. Glover's, love would awake again. This was as inevitable as it was desirable. The life urge was not buried. The life urge cannot be. It knows no grave. But the men who came into her life in after years never evoked what she gave George Glover during those six months of happy expectation that their marriage would run the usual appointed course, with children playing round, with home ties growing stronger, and sweet responsibilities heavier.

Motherhood was near. Her whole being was making ready for it. As the autumn opened she said good-by to that high spot which Charleston represented, in the verse:

> For trials past I would not grieve,
>   But count my mercies o'er;
> And teach the heart Thou has bereaved,
>   Thy goodness to adore,
> Thou gavest me friends, in my distress,
>   Like manna from above;

Earliest known picture of Mrs. Eddy
This picture was photographed from a daguerreotype,
made in Mrs. Eddy's young womanhood.

> Thy mercy ever I'll confess,
> And own a Father's love.[17]

Born September 12, 1844, her son was named George Washington Glover, II, for his father. Childbirth all but plucked life from her body. For a time her family gravely doubted whether she would survive. Not even her stout-hearted father thought she would ever regain strength enough to nurse her child and bring him up. In his own arms Mark Baker carried little George to a nursing mother at a neighbor's home, where shortly before one of twins, newly born, had died, and Mrs. Glover's baby was therefore welcome.[18]

Recovery from this, her first and only childbirth, was long delayed, and during this period Mary Baker Glover herself needed as tender care as any baby. Mahala Sanborn, the blacksmith's daughter, became her faithful nurse. Even so, Mark Baker, whose heart was as big and active as his mind, used for hours at a time to hold his nerve-racked daughter in his arms and rock her gently to and fro, enforcing silence in the house; and with rare forethought taking the precaution to deaden the clatter made by passers-by, he strewed the road outside with straw and tanbark.[19] If in her girlhood there had been clashes of will between the strong-minded father and the even stronger-minded daughter, now in her extremity there was nothing left but the devotion of an anxious father and the confident dependence of a frail daughter on a father's strength.

The story of those years of widowhood can be quickly told. Mrs. Glover, try as she would, and did, found herself not vigorous enough to care for the little boy she had brought into the world and always dearly loved.[20] He was left too much for his best interest to the company of his good nurse and her indulgent associates. Attractive and precocious, in the circumstances his spoiling was inevitable.

Changes, too, were taking place in the Baker home. Mark Baker, growing every year more prosperous, now built a comfortable house in Tilton and moved his family to town.[21] George Baker had located in Baltimore, married and planned to start a branch of the successful mills owned by Abigail's husband in Tilton. About the time Mrs. Glover might have given the measure of care which one so frail would naturally bestow on the child she loved, her mother, whom they all adored, fell ill and after six months passed away. Mrs. Glover sat down the morning after, November 22, 1844, and wrote to her brother George:

> My Dear Bro':
>
> This morning looks on us bereft of a Mother! Yes, that angel on earth is now in Heaven! I have prayed for support to write this letter, but I find it impossible to tell you particulars at this time. She failed rapidly from the time you saw her, but her last struggles were most severe; her physician spoke of it as owing to so strong a constitution. Oh! George, what is left of earth to *me*! But oh, my Mother! She has *suffered long with me,* let me then be willing she should now *rejoice,* and I bear on till I follow her. I cannot write more. My grief overpowers me. Write to me.
>
> Your affec' Sister,
(Signed) Mary.
>
> Died last night at half-past seven o'clock; will be buried next Saturday. I wish you could be here.[22]

The coming into the home next year of a stepmother left the young mother in an awkward predicament. There was no room any longer in her father's house for the frail young widow. When a stepmother comes, even one as kindly as was Elizabeth Patterson Duncan, there is rarely room in any home for such a charge. The situation was not to be evaded. Something had to be done about it. Mrs. Glover had no private means. She had flung away her only potential assets when in Charleston at the call of conscience she had freed her slaves. She was not well enough to earn a living for herself. She did the best she could. She wrote for the weekly papers; but this, as usual, brought a precarious income. Earlier she had tried teaching, but teaching proved to be a makeshift — a poor one at that.

Her sister, Abigail, expressed a willingness to receive Mrs. Glover into the comfortable Tilton home; but as she had a somewhat younger boy of her own there seemed no room even in that ample house for little George, who had in consequence to go with Mahala Sanborn, by this time Mrs. Russell Cheney, to live in North Groton, forty miles away.

Mrs. Glover had no alternative. If her life with her generous, but dominating, sister did not prove satisfactory to either, perhaps it could not be. The situation was impossible. No family roof is wide enough to cover long an adult dependent of different habits and ideals. Mrs. Glover, still frail in body, often confined to her bed, was, however, mentally independent and spiritually resourceful. Beholden, of necessity, for bed and board to Abigail, Mrs. Glover saw no reason for subservience also to her sister's intellect. There had never been a time — no matter how young she was — when she had not done her own thinking. She knew no reason why, amid the new conditions, she should not continue to think for herself.

In the nation, the irrepressible conflict was steadily moving on to its climax. Down in Washington, Henry Clay was now espousing the adoption of the Compromise of 1850 to avert open war. Daniel Webster, who was born and spent his earlier life in Salisbury, about five miles from Tilton, threw in his lot with Clay, and made his Seventh of March Speech not without the forlorn hope of inducing the South to help him to the nomination for the Presidency.

Many a substantial home became a hotbed of discussion. The Tiltons one day turned a community reception, given in their home, into a political discussion. Graceful and attractive in spite of her delicate health, Mrs. Glover assisted Mrs. Tilton in receiving. But she kept out of the discussion until one of the guests openly insisted on hearing what she thought concerning slavery. She replied, with her Charleston days in mind, that the South as well as the North suffered rather than benefited from the continuance of slavery and its spread to other States; that the election of Franklin Pierce would involve the whole country in fiercer and more menacing disputes; and that victory for him would therefore be good neither for the North nor for the South.

With the Tiltons and the Bakers siding with the Northern Democrats, and in a community so divided that some of its members as late as 1865 illuminated their homes when news came of Lincoln's assassination, Mrs. Glover's words created consternation. Mrs. Tilton is reported to have said in protest, "Mary, do you dare to say that in my house?"

"I dare to speak what I believe in any house," [23] was the decisive reply she received, uttered with dignity.

Mrs. Tilton, with that strange disposition observable in some families to force on blood relations the adoption of group opinions, a policy which in friendship's circles is tabooed by conventional courtesy, would have constrained her sister to think as well as live like her. But during the three years that followed, Mrs. Glover held her own in all their repetitious discussions, even though that course could scarcely have promoted household harmony. Mrs. Tilton's persistence, however, lasted to the end; for when she reached threescore years and ten she wrote her sister, by that time famous, a letter so little to her credit as to be hardly fair to quote, to which Mrs. Eddy replied:

> How my heart goes out to you in sorrow that you are not filling the last pages of your life with better thoughts, motives, and aims. May our dear Father forgive you and fill you with the sweet peace that I find in His love.

Through the long nine years that followed the experience of childbirth, Mrs. Glover suffered from ill health, which persisted almost unbroken until she was in middle life. The symptoms were different from the earlier adolescent disturbances. All through her correspondence until well on into the sixties mention of these symptoms now and then recurs as a matter of course. The nervous agitation which her father had quieted by taking her into his arms, her sister endeavored to allay by putting up a swing in her bedroom, forerunner of the chair swing in which in later years at Pleasant View she liked to sit on summer evenings, rocking back and forth, while passing in review for the entertainment of her house friends various episodes of her earlier days.

Seldom after George was born can she be said to have rested well. She suffered from pangs of indigestion traceable to the stomach, as well as to the intestinal tract. Incidentally it may be mentioned that graham bread and rye pudding were in those days the staple foods in her diet.[24] But it was the persistent pain she habitually located in her spine which indicated that something may have gone wrong when George was born.

In spite of all her physical distress, however, Mrs. Glover often participated in church and other social life. She obviously had rare social charm. Of a certain John M. Burt she had occasion to write[25] as though the coupling of his name and hers in village gossip had gone too far to please her. James Smith[26] seemed disposed to seek her heart through the pious pathway of the consolations of religion. But, persistent and pervasive as he was, she never took him seriously.

John H. Bartlett, however, made more headway in his suit. In her letters years before to Augusta Holmes, she had habitually underscored his name. In opening his campaign, March 21, 1846, for her heart, he presented her with the conventional autograph album of that day, fondly indicating in the opening pages his hope that she will remember him "when friends near and dear are far away." [27] Some sort of understanding between them for a time existed, with reservations on her part. She was not the woman to make a marriage that would leave out of the home she craved the boy for whom the Tilton house was never big enough. Winsome as young Bartlett was, she never could be sure that he could furnish the conditions necessary for the proper bringing up of her young son. For that matter, he had doubts himself; for in his acceptance of what looked like a dismissal, he indicated that he agreed with her as to his financial outlook, and he called heaven to witness that he would insist on nothing that did not appeal to her feelings and in addition promise family support.

Some of the reasons why Mrs. Glover, June 21, 1853, married Daniel Patterson are not difficult to give.

The Cheneys were, not long afterward, to take young George far away with them. Meanwhile, Mrs. Glover, as she found living through those days of humiliating dependence on her strong-minded elder sister increasingly irksome, was trying to find a way to keep her young son at least within hailing distance. Abigail was so immersed in her unceasing efforts to bring up her boy, Albert, to be a "gentleman" that she felt she had no right to let him play daily with his somewhat rougher and more boisterous cousin. There was something to be said on both sides. There always is. But it is scarcely open to discussion that real home life was not to be expected in an atmosphere too often charged with controversy and perhaps acrimony.

That herein lay an impelling motive for Mrs. Glover's second marriage is, also, indicated by the removal of Dr. and Mrs. Patterson, after their first two years of married life in Franklin, during which her invalidism continued, to North Groton in order to be near her son.

The very happiness, in fact, of Mrs. Glover's brief wifehood, so shortly ended, had made her eager, as is usual with normal people, for a closer comradeship and a more intimate understanding than she was now experiencing in these years of isolation. The sentiments expressed in a lengthy letter she had written in 1848 to Martha D. Rand (who married George Baker in 1849) might be said to speak for the entire period of her widowhood:

Now dearest Mathy, I am alone to-day. The family are all at church, and solitude, and silence, reign supreme, meek dwellers in the old chateau. Two things well calculated to

influence memory to bring up the light of other days, when
"we two have met" — Alas! for the bye-gones in memory,
would that I possessed the power of Magic, to command
the delicate spirits of fancy to reproduce the dear reality,
that would bring you to my side, — where in one fond
embrace of affection I could clasp thee to my lone heart, so
weary of solitude I have half determined this very moment
to throw aside my pen and wait to *weep.*[28]

Apparently Dr. Patterson was well equipped to comply
with some of the conditions required to satisfy the lonely
widow. He was big, handsome, healthy — such a Beau
Brummel as was never seen before in Tilton. Confidence in
himself was another asset which would appeal to Mrs.
Glover's need for a strong arm on which to lean. Incidentally, too, he was a relative of Mark Baker's second wife.
His wooing proceeded apace. He soon convinced her that
no honor in his estimation could possibly equal the right he
craved to help her in the care of George. To Mrs. Glover
he became the one person in the world who seemed to
understand her invalidism and to be qualified to make her
well, if he might have the chance which marriage would
afford to keep her under close professional as well as loving observation.[29] On his side, he evidently believed that if
she could once be taken out of the depressing conditions in
which she was living she could certainly be restored to
health and happiness. He confided to Mrs. Tilton his conviction that Mrs. Glover's suffering was due as much to
separation from her boy as to any possible organic or func-
tional disorder. Mrs. Tilton, therefore, had the right to feel
that she was acting in her sister's interest as well as in her
own in encouraging a marriage which would take out of
her home an invalid not of her immediate family.[30] Mrs.

Glover's father was not so easily convinced. He endeavored to impress on Patterson, whom he did not wholly trust, the gravity of the double responsibility which he would be assuming, for a wife who was a sick woman and a stepson, self-willed like all the Bakers, and in addition already showing at the age of nine, the unhappy results that usually follow being "handed about" from babyhood.

In this marriage Mrs. Glover's heart did not go freely with her hand. But at last, almost desperate, her personal tragedy deepening, she accepted the bewhiskered, broadclothed, silk-hatted suitor in kid gloves. Looking back in 1892, across the years to this decision which she made in 1853, and its disappointing consequences, she wrote, "My dominant thought in marrying again was to get back my child, but after our marriage his stepfather was not willing he should have a home with me." [31]

The years she spent as wife to Dr. Patterson proved as drab as any years could be for a woman always virile in mind, no matter how her body failed her. In the two years passed at Franklin the income of the itinerant dentist was disappointing but adequate. The two lived in a modest house and kept a cow. Selling his horse, Patterson evidently gave up his dental itineracy for a local practice. Neither her mind nor her body found health in this second marriage.

She yearned more than ever for her boy; and it was this, on her part, that took them in 1855 to live in North Groton.[32] Now her liege lord, obliged to add the running of a sawmill[33] to his dental work in order to make both ends' meet, showed himself more reluctant than before to take in little George. Therefore, when the Cheney family moved to Minnesota in 1856, they took twelve-year-old George with them. At seventeen, when the Civil War broke out, he joined the army and went South to fight for the freedom which his mother had for years been preaching both with voice and pen.

For several years in Groton, her sole attendant was a girl incapacitated by her blindness and, like herself, unwanted in the average home. Often depressed as well as ill, sometimes, as this companion — dear to her through many years — wrote in 1911, Mrs. Patterson would grow violently impatient under the goad of nervous irritation with the blind girl's uncertain movements, but "immediately came and put her arms around my neck and said that she was sorry." [34] A wife's ill health and a husband's broken promises due to his conspicuous inability to make a living, to pay even fifty cents on the dollar of the obligation he had expressly assumed to make a home for a stepson as well as for an ailing wife, were not contributory to that happiness in marriage which is dependent on generous reciprocity. The neighbors began to talk about the inharmony in the Patterson home, and the "blind girl," looking back long afterwards, admitted sadly that "they often quarreled." [35]

One of the many children who loved Mrs. Patterson through all these years wrote in 1916, when she was then an aged woman:

> My blind sister Myra Smith (Myra Smith Wilson) worked for Mrs. Patterson, consequently I was at the house two or three times each week She was ill nearly all the time and would lie in bed, with a book for her constant companion but when I came up to the bedside she would lay aside her book and pat me on the head and say "Oh you dear little girl. You are worth your weight in gold. I wish you were mine."

Every pleasant day my sister would wrap Mrs. Patterson up and draw her out on the piazza and when she was too tired to stay longer out of doors would draw her into the house & she would retire and rest.

When she was ready for breakfast she would ring the bell and my sister would cook a rye pudding to be eaten as a cereal. When she ate pie it had to be made with a cream crust as she could eat no fatty substance. One of the greatest pleasures of the children was to carry in the earliest berries and wild flowers to the "poor sick lady" but they did not call when Dr. Patterson was at home for we were all afraid of him.[36]

Dr. Patterson soon tired of the inconveniences to which a husband with a wife of "nerves" must, at least, try to grow accustomed. Nor could she on her side continue in heart to "honor" one who kept his promises no longer than it was convenient. There were scenes. The husband's absences from home grew more frequent and lengthy than his scant business required.

Things went from bad to worse. The mortgage on the Groton house came due, and the holder resorted to law to collect the past-due obligation. Mrs. Tilton was importuned to come to her sister's rescue. The foreclosure which followed sank Mrs. Patterson into the deepest depths of humiliation. As her sister drove her down the mountain side while hard-hearted persons tolled the church bell in celebration of his failure, Mrs. Patterson broke into tears, and the "blind girl" who stumbled after on foot wept bitterly in sympathy for the woman whom she truly loved.[37]

There followed a superficial resumption of home ties. The doctor made some effort to keep the home together. The unhappy couple boarded with a Mr. and Mrs. John

Herbert at Rumney Station. Mrs. Patterson turned all but
hopeless, and Dr. Patterson took her to a little house in
Rumney Village. Then, early in the Civil War, he went off
to Washington, commissioned by the Governor of New
Hampshire to distribute a fund from that state among
Union sympathizers in the South. He left his wife without
money, and also without food.

With customary carelessness, straying in March, 1862, too
near the Confederate lines, Dr. Patterson was captured and
sent to Libby Prison in Richmond, and later transferred to
the prison in Salisbury, North Carolina, from where, on
April second, he wrote his wife the following letter in
which he expresses the lively hope that God will find her
food and shelter and seems also to hope that some
way may be found to salvage for him the inconsequential
boots and traveling bag he had left behind in Washington
and to commandeer the interest of their Congressman,
T. M. Edwards, M. C., in effecting his release:

Dear Wife

You will be amazed to learn that I am in prison in the
confederate States prison, but it is so, I was taken one week
ago today. Give yourself no uneasiness about me. I have
found very gentlemanly officers and friendly gentlemen as
fellow prisoners, But God alone can tell what will become
of my poor sick wife with none near to care for her "but
God who tempers the wind to the shorn lamb" will care for
you, I have no care except for you — I left my travelling
bag and a new pair of boots at 381 Pensylvania Avenue
Washington at Mrs. C. W. Heydon's — perhaps you had
better write to our representative in congress T. M. Edwards
M.C. and ask him to see that I am exchanged if there is
any exchange of citizens — I became somewhat acquainted

with him while in W. if you write to me direct by way of
Fortress Munroe and put on a confederate state stamp
which I will enclose if I can find one, and also a United
States one, I would send you some money if I thought it
safe, and I would write more but fear if too long it will not
pass, it will have to be sent unsealed as yours must also,
write short and plain or it will be burned perhaps instead
of forwarded — My anxiety for you is intense but be of as
good cheer as possible and trust in God

> Your Affectionate Husband
> D. Patterson.[38]

To occupy her mind there was news coming almost every
day from the battlefields, and Mrs. Patterson rose to her
intellectual best in interpreting to the Kidders and other
friends the deeper meaning of the war. Then too, spiritualism, mesmerism, and other psychical phenomena were on
the air and in town talk as much as radio today. Mesmer
had died, but mesmerists were everywhere in evidence. A
certain Charles Poyen had been talking in places where
Mrs. Patterson later was to live, of the "Power of Mind
over Matter," and had made ready for the publication in
1837 of his book on *The Progress of Animal Magnetism in
New England*. What Braid had done in England to make
mesmerism popular, Grimes was doing in New England,
and Dods and Stone, Andrew Jackson Davis, and Warren
F. Evans were to follow him.[39]

How much more widespread was the interest in these
related subjects than is now commonly believed may be
inferred from the fact that the Boston Medical Library today
contains ninety-three books dealing with animal magnetism,
and the Boston Public Library has over one hundred, of

which seventy-seven bear a date previous to 1870. Of mag-
netizers or mesmerists there were almost three hundred
listed in Boston, and in every New England town lectures
and séances were the "movies" of that day. Not a few were
reading *The Magnet* and *The Mesmeric Magazine* — for mesmerism had even its own magazines.

But Mrs. Patterson was too broken in body, too wounded
in spirit, too troubled in mind to find such interests more
than superficial and temporary. A lonely, forsaken woman
often too weak to stand on her feet, confined day after day
to her bed, already long suffering from the spinal trouble
which made her a "helpless cripple," [40] Mary Glover Patterson, in the nature of the case, was not likely to be as much
occupied as some of her neighbors with mesmerists or sitting in as often at séances.

More likely she was praying with the Psalmist: "Out of
the deep have I called unto thee, O Lord; Lord, hear my
voice." She, who in childhood at her mother's knee, had
listened with joy to the Bible stories about the healing of
the sick, was now promising God sometimes during her
years in North Groton — as thinking backwards at Pleasant View she once remarked — that if He would raise her
up to health she would give her life to the help of the
sick.[41]

Of her mother, the Reverend Richard S. Rust wrote that,
to her entire family, Abigail Ambrose Baker was "a living
illustration of Christian faith." [42] Mrs. Eddy also recalled to
a friend that once when a heated discussion with her father
about everlasting punishment brought on her a fever, it was
her mother's comforting exhortation to "lean on God's
Love" [43] that drove down her temperature. Always in her
brilliant daughter's thought, Mrs. Mark Baker was associated

with God and health, with love and goodness; and when in 1849 the mother passed away, Mrs. Glover, following her habitual impulse to express in verse[44] her deeper feeling, wrote:

> Supporting faith be mine below,
> Life's parting words to greet;
> Thy mantling virtues o'er me throw,
> Till child and mother meet.[45]

At the time her brother George was seeking Martha Rand in marriage, his widowed sister wrote:

> Let us ever remember, there is One "who careth for us" — too wise to err, too *good* to be unkind. On Him may you rely, and find a Father and a friend. Yes, dear Mathy, this is my only consolation, *unworthy* as I am — and tis the greatest I can recommend to those I love.[46]

Three months before her marriage to Dr. Patterson, she made it clear that what Mrs. Tilton, outclassing the new husband in power to bend others to her will, had failed utterly to do, he need not so much as try to do; for hers was a "fixed feeling that to yield my *religion* to yours I could not." [47]

Throughout this period she was, says Mrs. Turner, "a very spiritual woman." [48] In the Congregational Church at North Groton Mrs. Patterson frequently responded to the call to offer prayer in public, and her prayers were long remembered as uplifting and helpful. All through her life there surged such a tide as never seemed to ebb of consciousness of God, a sense of absolute dependence on Him. Her most recent critic of distinction admits that:

> Prayer, meditation, eager and puzzled interrogation of the Bible, had claimed from childhood much of her energy, so

that those who met her in later times were conscious of a certain quiet exaltation, such as may come to a woman nursing a secret spiritual advantage.[49]

In spite of her ill health, of which the sign manual was an evident nervousness of manner which caused some to regard her as "peculiar," [50] Mrs. Patterson, as she entered her forties, was a very attractive woman.[51] She had a grace of manner the more appealing, because of her habitual neatness and exquisite taste in choosing and in wearing clothes. A frailness unmistakable and apparel indicative of poverty were much in evidence, when Mrs. Patterson came to P. P. Quimby's office in the International Hotel at Portland, Maine, in October, 1862. The young George Quimby — he told the author so himself in 1907 — helped her up the stairs. "She was too feeble," wrote her sister-in-law, Mrs. Mary A. Baker, who went with her, "to go unattended."

P. P. Quimby was Mrs. Patterson's last hope. She had heard of him a year before, for stories were in wide circulation of his magic cures. People reported that he used no medicine and was particularly helpful in afflictions of long standing. Her husband was so impressed that on October 14, 1861, he wrote Quimby:

> My wife has been an invalid for a number of years; is not able to sit up but a little, and we wish to have the benefit of your wonderful power in her case. If you are soon coming to Concord I shall carry her up to you, and if you are not coming there we may try to carry her to Portland if you remain there.[52]

The next May, after her husband had been transferred to the prison at Salisbury, North Carolina, Mrs. Patterson herself wrote Quimby:

Mary Baker Eddy

From a tintype thought to belong to the period 1864–67. Waiting to be photographed, Mrs. Eddy quieted a crying child and then their picture was taken together.

I have entire confidence in your philosophy as read in the circular sent my husband Dr. Patterson. *Can* you, *will* you visit me at once?[53]

She then thought that all the ways to Portland were closed to her. Mrs. Tilton believed Quimby to be a quack and the reports of his cures greatly exaggerated. She would not lift a finger to help Mrs. Patterson get to Portland. Mrs. Tilton did, however, agree to finance her sister if she would consent to go to Dr. Vail's Hydropathic Institute at Hill, New Hampshire, and there take the water cure. In no position to make terms, obliged to accept the best that she could get, and therefore scarcely in a mood to receive help from any water cure, Mrs. Patterson arrived at Hill as summer dawned in 1862. She found few of the patients were settling down to profit by Dr. Vail's care. Reports of Quimby's wonderful cures at Portland, coming day after day, sowed the seeds of unrest and of longing in the minds of the unfortunates at Hill. Now and then a patient would slip off to Portland to see Quimby. When one of them, Julius Dresser,[54] returned visibly improved, Mrs. Patterson became sure her very life depended on seeing Quimby. A letter she wrote to him in August, 1862, runs:

Dear Sir: I am constrained to write you, feeling as I do the great mistake I made in not trying to reach you when I had more strength. I have been at this Water Cure between 2 and 3 months, and when I came could walk ½ a mile, now I can sit up but a few minutes at one time. Suppose I have faith sufficient to start for you, do you think I can reach you without sinking from the effects of the journey? I am so excitable[55] I think I could keep alive till I reached you but then would there be foundation sufficient for you to restore me — is the question. I should rather die with my

friends at S. Bridge, hence I shall go to you to *live* or to
them to *die* very soon. Please answer this *yourself*.[56]

The more her physical ailments challenged her resolution,
the more determined Mrs. Patterson was to have her way.
The little sums of money which Mrs. Tilton kindly sent her
now and then for "extras" she hoarded until she had
enough to pay her fare to Portland.[57] She came expecting
much — altogether overmuch — and in consequence she
responded quickly to the treatment she received. As with
kindly eyes and sympathetic heart, Quimby looked into that
wan, worn face, his friendly understanding went out to her
in a consuming desire to do all he could for her. His diagnosis in itself increased her faith. He told her that she was
"held in bondage by the opinion of her family and physicians," and "her animal spirit was reflecting its grief upon
her body and calling it spinal disease." [58] His assurance that
she would soon be well was accompanied by his usual
manipulation of the head to generate the flow of healthy
electricity, on which he laid great stress.[59]

Encouragement to expect recovery Quimby furnished with
persuasive forcefulness. With her flaming faith the patient
helped herself while she thought she was only helping
Quimby to help her. The change was instantaneous. Her
pain and weakness disappeared. A sense of comfort and
well-being stepped into their place.[60] Within a week she
says that without help she climbed the one hundred eighty-
two steps to the dome of the City Hall.[61] And in this
whole experience she furnished, though she was not to realize it until 1866, a new illustration of the words Jesus
spoke to the woman healed after twelve years' illness, "Thy
faith hath made thee whole."

At last the prayers of years seemed to be answered.

Though her healing was not permanent and she soon suffered a relapse,[62] she told others of the change that had come over her; and to Quimby, almost two years later, she wrote: "I have often repeated the first instance of my salvation to wondering hearers, and if when we are converted we should strengthen our brethren how ought I not to preach." [63]

Out of the thirty-four hundred cases[64] which Quimby treated in those last two years at Portland only one at once felt any obligation to pass on the healing gospel. Mrs. Patterson did not delay. She was not content merely to be healed. She would know how the healing was effected. With becoming modesty and characteristic deference she wrote the *Portland Courier* that "At present I am too much in error to elucidate the truth." [65] She would know all before she ventured to apply any. That was Mrs. Patterson's way. That was why at last she traveled far in heavenly healing.

During those autumn weeks of 1862 she haunted Quimby's office. She asked him questions. She read all the notes accessible to those in whom Quimby showed some interest. She studied his method. He was impressed by her, as by no other patient. More than once, he buoyantly remarked, "She is a devilish bright woman." [66] As weeks went by, Mrs. Patterson grew greater in his estimation, which once led him to remark to another patient: "This is a very wonderful woman and in comparison I am the man, but Mary is the Christ." [67]

After her three weeks in Portland with her daily talks with Quimby, she went back to her sister's home. Mrs. Tilton was so impressed by the change in Mrs. Patterson, that she took her son Albert to Portland and put him under

Quimby's treatment for alcoholism; but to no purpose. The boy knew not how to make himself the vehicle of the curative forces which his aunt's faith alone had so promptly brought to her, and which she then in turn too generously ascribed to Quimby. But even that benefit was only temporary. When she turned back to Tilton, Mrs. Patterson soon grew ill again. She reported to Quimby that the spinal trouble had returned, and with it the chronic indigestion.[68] But faith like hers was not readily put down. In the spirit in which the Fourth Gospel describes Christ as "the true Light, which lighteth every man that cometh into the world," [69] she once inquired in print, "Is not this the Christ which is in him?" When in January, 1866, Quimby passed away, she paid this tribute to his memory:

> Rest should reward him who hath made us whole,
> Seeking, though tremblers, where his footsteps trod.[70]

What Quimby by his own method did for many, none would undervalue. Generous as usual, Mrs. Patterson overrated his method and underrated the efficacy of her own abounding faith. Not only did he, with his vitality, encourage her to expect much but he also confirmed and deepened her conviction — already larger far than his, had she only known it — which she had had since 1844, that the Christ has a message for the body as well as for the soul, and that Jesus knew whereof he spake when he once observed, "If ye have faith as a grain of mustard seed . . . nothing shall be impossible unto you." [71]

But Mrs. Patterson meant much to Quimby — more perhaps than he or anybody then could be expected to realize. Close contact of two such vivid personalities was bound to be significant to both. She was always about. This, George

Quimby, in his early manhood, resented. He was too young to understand; to have as yet, perspective. To him his father was a finished product. George was jealous for his father's reputation, and fearful lest the most arresting personality he had ever met might endanger it. That was the boy of it. To himself, of course, no man is ever finished.[72]

Seventeen years later, the interest which she was the first generously to show in Quimby, others one by one began to show. No evidence is more illustrative of her magnanimity than her appeal, soon after Quimby's death, to Julius Dresser — with Quimby much the last few years of Quimby's life — to "step forward into the place he had vacated. . . . You are more capable of occupying his place than any other I know." Nor could any answer be more illuminating than Julius Dresser's of March 2, 1866:

As to turning Dr. myself, & undertaking to fill Dr. Q's place, and carry on his work, it is not to be thought of for a minute. Can an infant do a strong man's work? Nor would I if I could. Dr. Q gave himself away to his patients. To be sure he did a great work, but what will it avail in fifty years from now, if his theory does not come out, & if he & his ideas pass among the things that were, to be forgotten? He did work some change in the minds of the people, which will grow with the development & progress of the world. He helped to make them progress. They will progress faster for his having lived & done his work. So with Jesus. He had an effect which was lasting & still exists. But his great aim was a failure. He did not succeed, nor has Dr. Q. succeeded in establishing the science he aimed to do. . . . No I wouldn't cure if I could, not to make a practice of it, as Dr. Q. did.[73]

In the period which followed it was Mrs. Patterson who kept green the memory of the unusual man, and but for

her supreme success Quimby would, as Dresser in 1866 predicted, long since have joined the forgotten failures of the
world.

Mrs. Patterson went away from Quimby with the same
faith in God she had when she came to him, and which
she was in a few years to make so effective in the healing
of the sick that in retrospect Quimby became to her scarcely
more than an interesting episode.

Certain phrases which developed in their frequent conversations were to stick in her vocabulary for a while. Of them
in February, 1899, she wrote:

> Quotations have been published, purporting to be Dr.
> Quimby's own words, which were written while I was his
> patient in Portland and holding long conversations with him
> on my views of mental therapeutics. Some words in these
> quotations certainly read like words that I said to him, and
> which I, at his request, had added to his copy when I cor-
> rected it. In his conversations with me and in his scrib-
> blings, the word science was not used at all, till one day I
> declared to him that back of his magnetic treatment and
> manipulation of patients, there was a science, and it was the
> science of mind, which had nothing to do with matter, elec-
> tricity, or physics.
>
> After this I noticed he used that word, as well as other
> terms which I employed that seemed at first new to him.
> He even acknowledged this himself, and startled me by say-
> ing what I cannot forget — it was this: "I see now what
> you mean, and I see that I am John, and that you are
> Jesus." [74]

Quimby never rose to the spiritual heights scaled by Mrs.
Eddy. However, with her habit of impressing upon other
minds what was dominant in her own, she gave Quimby
credit in full measure,[75] running over, for all she thought at

the time he did for her, but which it is now plain was the product of her own faith. But, as her understanding grew with ripening experience, she was soon filling old words and phrases with new meaning, then coining her own unquestioned terms to elucidate her system, and at last in obedience to the same persistent urge, writing the book.

She discovered Christian Science in a larger sense than ever Columbus discovered America. Hers was no peep at a new world and then a scuttling back to the old. Hers was that real discovery which consists of finding an age-old truth, settling in it, sharing it with others, and making the most of it for the redemption of the world from sickness, sin, and death.

This was essentially the discovery which Shakespeare made in drama when reading Plutarch, Holinshed, Sir Thomas More, and even Fox's *Book of Martyrs,* he sent characters singing down the ages who otherwise would long since have faded out of memory.

This was the discovery in government which the Fathers of the Constitution made, in 1787, when they gave us what Gladstone mistakenly called "the greatest work ever struck off at any one time by the mind and purpose of man"; of which James Bryce was then to say "there is little in that Constitution that is absolutely new, there is much that is old as Magna Charta"; and of which no less an authority than Sir Henry Sumner Maine with veracious accuracy ultimately said: "The Constitution of the United States of America is much the most important political instrument of modern times."

What did Mrs. Eddy owe to those who went before her?

The name at last she gave her teaching, Christian Science?[76] As early as 1866 Abraham Coles used the name

in verse, and earlier, in 1846, an English clergyman in a
lecture published in 1847. The Episcopal Bishop of Wisconsin, Dr. William Adams, had also, in 1850, published his
addresses on Moral Philosophy under the caption, "Elements of Christian Science." But his book was not yet to
come her way, and when it came, through the gift of a student, the book bore no relationship to Mrs. Eddy's faith.
Two years before, a friend of Dr. Oliver Wendell Holmes,
Mrs. Sarah Josepha Hale, followed her somewhat familiar,
"Mary had a little lamb," [77] with a more ambitious poem in
which the line occurs:

'Tis Christian Science makes our day.

But there is no evidence that the poem affected Mrs.
Eddy. Nor would the phrase Christian Science be now significant if it had had only such casual launching.

Did Mrs. Eddy get the title of her book from Quimby
who once spoke of the "science of health"? [78] Again, the
evidence is lacking that Quimby's phrase ever made on anyone a lasting impression. Of the thirty-four hundred whom
Quimby treated thirty-three hundred ninety-nine went their
way like the nine out of the ten cured of leprosy in the
New Testament. In 1902 Mrs. Eddy wrote that the title
came to her in the silence of the night, and not till six
months later did a friend find "science and health" in John
Wyclif's version of the New Testament, and bring it to her
notice.[79]

God as love, spirit, truth, and life is found in one version
or another of the Bible, and they are terms used in many
a theology long before the day of Quimby and his more
famous patient.[80]

As for the nothingness and erroneousness of matter, this

is an idea almost as old as human thinking. Before ever Gautama took his seat beneath the Botree, India was accepting it as a general concept. As early as four hundred thirty B.C. Democritus of Abdera remarked, "Man lives plunged in a world of illusion and of deceptive forms which the vulgar take for reality." Plato esteemed matter nothing, and mind everything.[81] Being without well-being is naught, "John the Scot" was teaching France in the ninth century.

In the years when Spinoza was resolving to remain a materialist "until the last king had been strangled with the entrails of priestcraft," [82] he was heading towards Mrs. Eddy's "Infinite Mind" with his talk of "Universal Substance." Berkeley came to the conclusion that apart from some mind to perceive it, matter would be nonexistent. Jonathan Edwards, rated by A. M. Fairbairn as "the highest speculative genius of the eighteenth century," could say that the "Material Universe exists only in the Mind." [83]

"The laws of nature" were to Kant "creations of our own understanding, acting upon the data of the senses." "Man has no body," wrote William Blake, "distinct from his soul." Lotze avowed "that matter is nothing but an appearance for our perception." Like the morning stars, the Transcendentalists all sang together of "the supremacy of mind over matter"; and Emerson required no urging to report that:

> Out of thought's interior sphere
> These wonders rose in upper air.

But before her views could run into a complete system Mrs. Patterson was again in need of help. In the early spring of 1864, she paid another visit to Quimby.[84] As late as 1904, Mrs. Eddy was able to recall a conversation with a fellow patient in 1864, in which she expressed her judgment that "Dr. Quimby is the most progressive magnetic doctor I ever knew, and back of it all there is a science that some day will be discovered." [85]

On this visit Mrs. Patterson was keener than ever to exhaust the possibilities in Quimby's teaching. No other patient ever took such pains to understand him. This was the more necessary because, as Horatio W. Dresser says, "he could not express his thoughts accurately. One searches his manuscripts in vain for a clear explanation of his method of silent cure." She talked things over afternoons with Quimby and sat up "late at night" writing down "what she had learned during the day." [86] All the time, at first unconsciously, she was reading into Quimby's teaching what had been growing in her own consciousness amid vicissitude and change, in loneliness and destitution. Beginning in those early days when she was no older than thirteen and yet used to "converse on deep subjects" [87] with her pastor, no one can go intelligently with her all those years from 1844 to 1866 without hearing now and then a lonely and heroic soul singing to herself:

> I shall arrive! What time, what circuit first,
> I ask not: but unless God send his hail
> Or blinding fireballs, sleet or stifling snow,
> In some time, his good time, I shall arrive:
> He guides me and the bird. In his good time![88]

Eager to practice what she had learned and was spiritualizing for herself, in the spring of 1864 she went to Warren, Maine, to try to complete the restoration, begun in Portland weeks before, of Miss Jarvis's health. Later in the year found her stopping at Albion, Maine, with Mrs. Sarah

G. Crosby, who in 1907 recalled to the author that on that visit Mrs. Patterson seemed as *"one* fired with the prescience of a great mission." Even in 1909, as she was near her passing, Mrs. Crosby tenderly observed:

> Many months Mary Patterson was a beloved guest in my home, — for I had a most unselfish love for her and deep sympathy with her, when in her poverty she came to me, — no money, scarcely comfortable clothing, — most unhappy in her domestic relations. Her only assets being her indomitable *will* and active brain.[89]

This, then, was Mrs. Eddy at the age of forty-three, her health improved but not yet all it should be; somewhat better friended than before, but still hard pressed to make a living; overrating in a grateful woman's way what she owed to Quimby, and looking vainly for a man to carry on his work, — and, when none appeared, carrying on herself till the hour struck when she could write with truth: "In. the year 1866, I discovered the Christ Science...."[90]

— 4 —

Building the Book

*T*WICE IN 1866, THE FIRST YEAR OF THE period when the book was building, Mrs. Eddy lived with Mr. and Mrs. George D. Clark on Summer Street, in Lynn. The names of the group of persons gathered round Mrs. Eddy in the Clark home and even the places where they sat at table are known, thanks to a diagram[1] prepared by George E. Clark, the son.

Mrs. Eddy

14

Mrs. Raymond 13	1 Hiram Crafts
Minot Raymond 12	2 Mrs. Crafts
George Clark 11	3 Mrs. Brene Paine Clark
John Bogart 10	4 Charles Porter
Nathaniel Brookhouse 9	5 Mrs. Porter
John S. Keyes 8	6 Wm. Wadlin

7

Joshua Sheldon

If there were not, in that friendly circle, any fisher folk, as among the twelve who surrounded Jesus, emphatically there were nineteenth-century equivalents — workers in the Lynn shoe factories, salesmen in shoe stores, a painter, and a teamster.

Mrs. Eddy sat at the head of the table. Wherever Mrs. Eddy sat, at any time, was the head of the table. The years which followed were abundantly to justify the soundness of judgment of Asa G. Eddy expressed in a letter written on August 5, 1880, that, as a matter of course, in any project success was certain only when Mrs. Eddy led the way.[2]

Records reveal to us how Mrs. Eddy looked in the days when her book was going through its final stage of preparation for the printer. Though entering the fifties, she still retained the complexion of her girlhood, the color coming and going in her fair cheeks, and her hair falling in a shower of brown curls around her face. Her blue eyes, as she talked, shone more brilliantly than ever. Says Mr. Clark:

> She usually wore black, but occasionally a violet or pale rose color, and I remember well a dove-colored dress trimmed with black velvet that she wore in the summer. She was a little above medium height, slender and graceful. Usually she was reserved though her expression was never forbidding. But when she talked, and she talked very well and convincingly, she would make a sweeping outward gesture with her right hand as though giving her thought from her very heart.[3]

Argument was frequent at that dinner table. Wherever fourteen New Englanders are met together serious discussion, and often actual debate, is likely to spring up. Young Clark, soon to go to sea, became at times apprehensive lest the pitch of intensity to which discussion was carried should lead to dissension. But courtesy invariably tempered feeling, and saved the day, much of the credit for which belonged to Mrs. Eddy. One of her friends thus drew her picture from memory in later years, "I can seem to see her now as she sat before us with that heavenly spiritual expression which lighted her whole countenance as she expounded the truth . . . her conversation was always an inspiration and instructive." [4]

Naturally, the talk sometimes turned to Quimby. At the Wheelers his name was often on her tongue.[5] During her stay with the Crafts family, in the winter of 1866–67, Quimbyism was not infrequently her theme. Notes in Mrs. Eddy's handwriting, which Hiram S. Crafts preserved, still exist, as proof that Mrs. Eddy was already thinking independently of Quimby, and identifying " 'the whole idea man' with the perfect man of God's creating." [6]

At the Wentworths she took advantage of the opportunity to add an introduction to *Questions and Answers;*[7] and as her two years with them drew to a close, her incessant talk concerning mind and matter bored some of the intellectually incurious members of the family.[8]

By 1871, she was leaving Quimby far behind, and no one was more aware of it than Mrs. Eddy herself. She was coming to realize the full import of his admission to her in 1864 that she had discovered something different from anything he ever taught, which now no open-minded investigator can doubt who has access to these comprehensively informing sources the author has studied and also to the author's extensive personal correspondence, supplementing his face-to-face talking with Quimby's son. During this same year, in writing to her friend, Miss Sarah Bagley, Mrs. Eddy's reference to some unknown person whom she described as "that *half*[9] scientist, a former patient of Dr. Quimby" [10] indicates this clearer understanding of herself. If further testimony were needed her severest critic of a generation ago conceded that "she had improved upon the original Quimby method and left it behind her";[11] while one of her most recent critics[12] affirms that: "In those eight years Quimby had ceased to be an entity" in her life.

In this connection her own observation late in life is worth consideration that for "a time (after 1866) she was somewhat hampered by the theories of Quimby." [13] Of aid, also, in plotting correctly the upward curve of her development is this other later statement:

> What I wrote on Christian Science some twenty-five years ago I do not consider a precedent for a present student of this Science. The best mathematician has not attained the full understanding of the principle thereof, in his earliest studies or discoveries. Hence, it were wise to accept only my teachings that I know to be correct and adapted to the present demand.[14]

The table talk at the Clarks was often of her fall in Lynn. It was one of the most significant experiences in Mrs. Eddy's significant career. Its consequences in dealing with the years that followed no one will minimize who cares to understand her extraordinary career. Starting from Swampscott anticipating a happy evening at a temperance meeting in Lynn, on Thursday, February 1, 1866, Mrs. Patterson had a hard fall on the ice, of which this account appeared the next Saturday in the *Lynn Reporter:*

> Mrs. Mary Patterson of Swampscott fell upon the ice near the corner of Market and Oxford streets on Thursday evening and was severely injured. She was taken up in an insensible condition and carried into the residence of S. M.

Bubier, Esq., near by, where she was kindly cared for during the night. Dr. Cushing, who was called, found her injuries to be internal and of a severe nature, inducing spasms and internal suffering. She was removed to her home in Swampscott yesterday afternoon, though in a very critical condition.[15]

Forty years later, Dr. Cushing, near fourscore years, recalled that he found Mrs. Patterson very nervous, partially unconscious, semi-hysterical;[16] symptoms not unusual in cases of profound shock. The next morning he gave her one-eighth of a grain of morphia as a sedative. Her response to this small dose was such as to indicate that she was not in the least accustomed to the drug; for she was so late in awaking from the profound sleep into which she fell that the doctor feared he had given her a larger dose than he had the night before intended. Incidentally, once when talking to the author he observed, "Probably one-sixteenth of a grain would have put her sound asleep."[17]

It was in the summer of 1907 that the author had a long talk as well as correspondence with Dr. Cushing, who was spending his last years in Springfield, near the author's Northampton home. Across the twoscore years he recalled with pride the days when he was a popular doctor and a man of social consequence in Lynn. His eyes brightened in describing the "spanking" team which he often drove on sunny afternoons along the Lynn speedway. He observed that one day he had prescribed for as many as fifty-nine patients.[18]

About the value of attenuated doses both of arnica and "belladonna to the two hundredth attenuation," he spoke with not a little gusto. Having spent a summer not many years before with Osler, the world-eminent diagnostician, later Sir William, of Oxford,[19] and helped him daily in the preparation of his still world-used book on *The Practice of Medicine,* and having also heard at length his well-known opinions about homeopathy, the author was not impressed with Dr. Cushing's missionary zeal for "attenuation" to the two hundredth degree of such drugs as arnica and belladonna.

Although of less importance than the spiritual consequences of the fall in Lynn, the former physical symptoms soon returned. Within two weeks Mrs. Patterson was writing Julius Dresser for mental aid to forestall a possible return of "the terrible spinal affection from which I have suffered so long and hopelessly." [20]

On June twenty-fifth, the Mayor of Lynn presented to the city government a communication from Mrs. Patterson:

> in which she states that owing to the unsafe condition of that portion of Market Street at the junction of Oxford Street, on the first day of February last she slipped and fell, causing serious personal injuries, from which she has little prospect of recovering, and asking for pecuniary recompense for the injuries received.[21]

But the fall did bring its spiritual revelation. She never in the years that followed doubted that it led her farther on the way to God. The Sunday following the fall, still prostrate in her Swampscott home from the accident, as she was reading the Bible narrative of how Jesus healed the palsied man, she experienced one of those rare visitations reserved for the religious discoverers of the race and thus describes it: "The lost chord of Truth (healing, as of old) I caught consciously from the Divine Harmony. . . . It was to me a revelation of Truth." [22]

Mrs. Eddy as she looked at Lynn
and Stoughton about 1867
(From a tintype.)

Her consciousness of God's power to heal, which had been ever growing brighter with the years, and had been enhanced by the idealizing faith which for a while she honestly believed that Quimby also had, was now at its full. She was sure, as the Rt. Hon. H. A. L. Fisher writes, that "a spiritual life transcending the human formed the ultimate basis of reality." [23] No matter what might happen to her in the years ahead, never again would she doubt the literal truth of the New Testament promise, "My grace is sufficient for thee."

Not that she understood it all at once. She was, in fact, to spend her life in plumbing its depths upon depths. In the calm of eventide in her swinging chair at Pleasant View, musing over this experience, she confided to a friend [24] that she had come to the realization that:

> ... she had been thinking about God, and it dawned upon her that it was the attitude of mind which she was in that made it possible for the divine power to heal her, that in some unknown way she had attained unto that consciousness of the divine Presence which heals the sick even as the natural musician without scientific knowledge touches the harmonic chords. [25]

Like Jacob at Peniel, with many a weary mile yet to trudge before his journey's end, Mrs. Eddy always afterwards felt that she could say, "I have seen God face to face, and my life is preserved." [26]

The way now began to clear for that complete concentration on her life work which was essential if the goal she set before her was ever to be reached. In 1862, poor and sick as she was, from her husband's brother[27] she borrowed thirty dollars, with which to try to bring about the release of her blundering husband from prison. In 1864, an effort was made, in all good faith, to re-establish a home in Lynn. But in his consort's dreams the husband sought and took no lot or part; for in the summer of 1866 he eloped with the wife of another man;[28] was divorced in 1873 for unfaithfulness; and in 1896 died at Saco, Maine,[29] in the poorhouse. But, long before this, he took on himself the full responsibility for the failure of his marriage, when to a friend he described Mrs. Patterson as "a pure, estimable and Christian woman," and added "that if he had done as he ought he might have had a pleasant and happy home as one could wish for." [30]

Already Mrs. Eddy was well along with the building of her book. But there was other building to be finished before the book could be completed. At this time, Mrs. Eddy was a disadvantaged woman. Between her fall in 1866 and the appearance of her book in 1875, more than once she lacked both friends and "where to lay her head." Her father had died in 1865. Not merely was her boy, now a grown man, gone to war, but there were years when she knew not so much as his whereabouts. Mrs. Tilton's doors at last swung open very grudgingly. Ellen Pilsbury, her own niece, had attended to that. Healed by Mrs. Eddy of a serious illness, Ellen went with her aunt to complete her recuperation at Taunton, where, like a typical Baker, she reacted against the plainness of the Crafts home and returned to Tilton with such sorry tales as ever after made the older aunt shut Mrs. Eddy out of her heart.[31]

There were times when Mrs. Eddy had to fight for her personal independence. Now and then every man's hand seemed to be against her. In 1890, she told her good friend, Miss Shannon, that for a time, while living in Lynn, she was annoyed almost beyond endurance.[32] No wonder that in a day when the law was often a woman's only protection from imposition, Mrs. Eddy sometimes felt the need of legal aid.

The situation grew acute. She was rarely free from grave anxiety. She became sensitive even to the thoughts which she believed were directed at her, and she wrote one to whom she had given confidence and who was failing her,[33] "won't you exercise *reason* and let me live or will you *kill me?* Your mind is just what has brought on my relapse and I shall never *recover* if you do not govern yourself and TURN YOUR THOUGHTS wholly away from me . . . won't you *quit thinking* of me."

She needed at her right hand someone who would ask nothing except the chance to help her carry out her larger purpose. And the man was there. Asa Gilbert Eddy was kindly, modest, unassuming, patient, sensible, methodical, reliable, no troublemaker, and "careless in nothing but his own comfort." [34] To some originality and considerable ability, he added a true man's instinct to defer to superior wisdom and to work with others. Into the expanding life of this unusual woman Asa Gilbert Eddy came unobtrusively. But here is her own story, written January 12, 1877, to a friend:

> Last Spring Dr. Eddy came to me a hopeless invalid. I saw him then for the first time, and but twice. When his health was so improved he next came to join my class (his residence was South Boston). In four weeks after he came to study he was in practice doing well, worked up an excellent reputation for healing and at length won my affections on the ground alone of his great goodness and strength of character.[35]

On New Year's Day, 1877, they were married, and a satisfying home was now hers which all her life she had been craving and sometimes seemed destined never to possess. Writes one who knew them well, "This home in Lynn was very simple in all its arrangements, but immaculately neat." [36]

On the death of her husband, June 2, 1882, she wrote to this same friend from the Vermont hills, whither she had gone in her bereavement:

> I can't yet feel much interest in anything of earth. I shall try and eventually succeed in rising from the gloom of my irreparable loss but it must take *time*. *Long* after I shall smile and appear happy shall I have to struggle alone with my great grief that none shall know if I can hide it. I think of you at the fort and always as little, or rather great heroes and pray that my coming shall be a joy and not a sorrow to you I know you will hail it but O! I hope I shall be more useful to you all than a *mourner* is apt to be. I shall never forget dear, dear Gilbert his memory is dearer every day but not so sad I think as when I left home. It is beautiful here the hills vales and lakes are lovely but this was his native state and *he is not here.*[37]

More and more the truth pressed home that she could never hope to build her book until she had first acquired an income on which to live; a sum at least above the margin of actual want. To this grilling task she set her hand while her spirit ranged the skies. Who shall say that it may not have been with these hard days in mind that she wrote in 1893:

> O, make me glad for every scalding tear,
> For hope deferred, ingratitude, disdain!

> Wait, and love more for every hate, and fear
> No ill, — since God is good, and loss is gain.[38]

If she was to write, she had to have a roof over her head, and food to eat. The Phillipses gave her shelter for a while, and in the Clark home there was good food, and happy company. Then, too, she earned a little by her healing work. Her first student was Hiram S. Crafts, whom she taught from the Bible and her manuscripts.[39] The pages of her notebook, which he retained, the first two of which are now before the author, are expositions of the first Gospel which are full of her reliance on God, and descriptions of the harmony and healing which she said outright would naturally result from such a faith. He paid her while they were fellow boarders at the Clarks; and, when he set up for himself as a practitioner, she went to live with him and Mrs. Crafts, first in East Stoughton, then in Taunton. At the Wentworths, where she stayed one and one-half years, in exchange for her "keep" she explained to Mrs. Wentworth her new method of healing and also allowed her to copy *Questions and Answers* together with her comments. But the time came when that was not regarded as compensation enough; and at last she was obliged to move on.[40] During one of the years of that long period while her book was building, she tells us that she moved eight times.

Never in the years from 1866 to 1875 was she happier than while with the Ellises,[41] spending many an evening with the family. Kindly Mrs. Webster at Amesbury, who was interested in spiritualism,[42] was hospitable to Mrs. Glover until her son-in-law came from New York and made conditions so impossible for Mrs. Glover that she moved to Miss Bagley's.

But always this woman of the book kept at her task.

Nothing else — not even a living — seemed so important to her. Some of her students paid her óne hundred dollars for ten lessons, and promised her a commission of ten percent on their future earnings.[43] This arrangement appeared necessary at the start; but it later proved to be unwise and was discontinued. Mrs. Eddy looked upon a contract as a contract even with her earlier students; as is evident from a letter which she wrote one of them July 28, 1869:

I learn from your own signature that you have retained a copy of those MSS. This was a fraud for which I must hold you or any other person responsible who should commit such an act. Now if you wish for a private settlement I will spare your feelings and charge you fifty dollars only for the copy; but if you do not wish to settle in this manner I shall certainly take measures to protect myself against such damage.[44]

Once in those early days when other helpers failed, Mrs. Eddy felt driven to invoke legal aid to protect her teaching in the well-known Arens' Case, and with success. Without her consent some suits were brought against students.[45] Richard Kennedy, her business partner from 1870 to 1872, however, told the author in 1907 that after their partnership was dissolved and her income was decreased she felt the pinch, and did the best she could.[46]

But her habitual policy is clearly stated in the *Church Manual:*[47]

A member of The Mother Church shall not, under pardonable circumstances, sue his patient for recovery of payment for said member's practice, on penalty of discipline and liability to have his name removed from membership. Also he shall reasonably reduce his price in chronic cases of recovery, and in cases where he has not effected a cure. A

Christian Scientist is a humanitarian; he is benevolent, forgiving, long-suffering, and seeks to overcome evil with good.

Poor as she was in those days, not letting her left hand know what her right hand generously gave, she often helped substantially both the worthy and also the less worthy. Mrs. Annie Macmillan Knott recalls the authentic case of a woman who for two years was counseled by Mrs. Eddy without charge. S. P. Bancroft[48] paid his three hundred dollars, which Mrs. Eddy promised to refund if he found he could not "demonstrate" what she taught him. And when James C. Howard was unable to meet his obligation, he received from his generous teacher a receipt in full, along with a check with which to buy an overcoat which he conspicuously needed.[49]

At last, after much experimenting, she came to the conclusion, confirmed by general experience, that people habitually value only that for which they pay. Just why she raised her price to three hundred dollars and later reduced her lessons from twelve to seven may never be known in full. There is reason to believe it was a wise decision, and that it was not made at the expense of her high standard. In a letter which she sent to Mrs. Clara E. Choate she declared, "I shall teach them as soon as they will study. The taxes, coal and repairs on building, and *book* have drained me. But not for that would I teach this Science."[50]

Years later she wrote:

> When God impelled me to set a price on my instruction in Christian Science Mind-healing, I could think of no financial equivalent for an impartation of a knowledge of that divine power which heals; but I was led to name three hundred dollars as the price for each pupil in one course of lessons at my College, — a startling sum for tuition lasting barely three weeks. This amount greatly troubled me. I

[handwritten note: Rec'd James C. Howard on the day of ... Dorel 1887 payment in full of all demands. Mary B G Eddy]

[handwritten note: Please dear Student accept the inclosed for an overcoat they are cheaper now and this will square our account ...]

shrank from asking it, but was finally led, by a strange providence, to accept this fee.[51]

To the impartial observer, nothing more surely indicates the prevision and administrative wisdom of the Founder than the financing of the Christian Science movement. The present situation in some parts of Christendom is intolerable. The shabby money-raising devices to which some churches resort which hark back to the time of Jesus when a settled income was not necessary, and when the poorest peasant in the region around Galilee, might, like the Pilgrim Fathers, "suck of the abundance of the seas, and of treasures hid in the sand," are out of place, archaic, adventitious, and distinctly hurtful to the larger cause. This is no plea to turn the minister into a man of wealth, but to save him from deteriorating into what a young man, who recently left the ministry at the end of his first year, describes as "the proverbial, down-at-the-heels, dispirited, sad-eyed parson."

Mrs. Eddy's views were products of a personal experience which had cost her much travail. Her belief never wavered that the truth she taught was for the rich, as well as for the poor. "Seek ye first the kingdom of God, and his righteousness; and all these things shall be added unto you," [52] was the basis of her economic counseling. She wrote, "Soul has infinite resources with which to bless mankind, . . . " [53] and in another place, "We are all capable of more than we do." [54] To one of her students, having "quite a financial struggle," Mrs. Eddy cheeringly observed: "Keep on in the work of Science and you will always be glad that you did. Know that you are fed and clothed by Spirit, and you will be fed and clothed and to the world it will be a miracle." [55]

In those dark days when, with the odds against her, she learned to make a living, she demonstrated that those who, in singleness of mind, seek the kingdom receive all the human things of which they have real need. The mind that is set on higher things draws to it the lower if only — like the sheaves in Joseph's dream — to do homage to the higher. That is why Christian Scientists look prosperous and are often prosperous. They seek the kingdom of God, and other things are usually added to them. God keeps His promises.

Mrs. Eddy had to protect her spiritual morale as well as win her economic independence. Sensitiveness over the attitude of public opinion toward the domestic differences with Dr. Patterson led her, unfriended and distressed as she sometimes was in her Lynn days, to turn back to the name Glover. The aloofness and censoriousness of her relatives cut her to the heart. The one sweet note of her earlier home was struck by her sympathetic stepmother who wrote her on a pale little postcard:

My own Dear Daughter

It is a long time since I have heard one word from you. Hope you are well and enjoying the light of God's countenance and surrounded with kind friends, a good Minister, and good society. I know you must miss your own dear relatives and former friends. . . . My love to yourself and all who are kind to you.

E.P.B.[56]

How to sheathe her sensitiveness from exposure to the world's venom took her many a year to learn. But she learned. Richard Kennedy[57] once said: "It was an unfortunate fact that Mrs. Eddy with her small income was obliged to live with people very often at this time in her life who were without education and cultivation."

A woman sharing the same house with her when Mrs. Eddy was busiest on her book, described her to Miss Emma C. Shipman[58] as "The purest minded woman I ever knew." But she added that she thought Mrs. Eddy a "crank." Asked to explain what she meant by "crank" the aged woman answered, "Mrs. Eddy wished the house kept so still," — a condition essential to intellectual creativeness which every educated household, where books are written, accepts without calling names.

But whether people understood her or not, Mrs. Eddy lived with them. "It was never her custom to keep apart from the family. She invariably mingled with them and through them kept in touch with the world." [59] Even in what in 1869 she called her "time of severest trial," she wrote:

My Father chastens in love, and I know if my physical frame endures I shall rejoice here for every tear I have shed, and ere long enter the lighted sa[n]ctuary, and cast off my crown won from the cross — at the foot of the throne, whither have gone through great tribulation such as have washed their souls in the blood of the lamb which is the spirituality of truth bleeding from the wounds of error.[60]

There were, however, some to give her loving sympathy. That summer of 1866, which she spent with the Phillipses at Lynn, Grandmother "Mary" and Mary Baker Glover — many years her junior — were so completely one in mind and heart that one time when "Uncle Thomas" came home and found them side by side on the sofa talking of the higher things of life, he remarked to his wife, "Hannah, do you see our two saints? There they sit together, the two Marys." [61]

Though personally and industriously building up a growing business, George Oliver was known, when Mrs. Eddy was at his house, deliberately and repeatedly to overstay his luncheon hour. Returning to his office, he never offered an excuse. One day, however, he did casually observe, "I would rather hear [her][62] talk than make a big deal in business."

Hiram S. Crafts, that first student in whose home she lived for some months, paid the last tribute to his teacher on December 20, 1901, in a renewed confession of loyalty to her teachings which covered all his later years.[63]

The Wentworths were a large household. During the two years from 1868 to 1870, when Mrs. Eddy lived in their home, now and again her relationship with some members of the family became somewhat strained — a not unusual experience. But what one of the sons, Charles O. Wentworth, remembered in 1909, when trivialities were fading out of mind, was that her "gentle, unassuming nature made her a peacemaker."[64] This confirmed his mother's judgment expressed in 1869 that "If ever there was a saint on earth it is Mrs. Glover."[65]

She had constant need of a full suit of armor for her natural sensitiveness. No sooner was she fairly launched upon her teaching enterprise than some of her first students — usually crude, frequently unteachable, and sometimes merely mercenary — began to make trouble for her. When to his amazement George Tuttle, home from a sea cruise to Calcutta, seemed easily to cure his first patient, he fell into a panic and nothing could induce him to try to repeat his experience. His brother-in-law, Charles S. Stanley, gave such free vent to his argumentative spirit in class that Mrs. Eddy, in the interest of her other students, had to dismiss him to make him realize that he was not the only student in the class.

A certain young bank clerk, Wallace Wright, would not — or perhaps in his crassness could not — for the life of him see how mesmerism and Mind Science differed. With retaliatory zeal he hurried into print to attack a teacher whom he did not understand; whereupon five of her larger-visioned students came to her defense. In consequence, young Wright disappeared from public view and also from history after making the somewhat premature announcement, on February 24, 1872, "that Mrs. Glover and her so-called science are virtually dead and buried."[66]

Of all those earlier students Richard Kennedy gave most promise. From 1870 to 1872, he was in partnership with Mrs. Eddy. Under her inspiring touch he was from the first a growing success as a healer, which at last left her free entirely to teach. At the end of two years, Mrs. Eddy had

six thousand dollars in the bank.[67] But young Richard
found the business obtainable by rubbing heads so satisfactory that he felt no desire to study under Mrs. Eddy what
she taught. Why bother about theory, so long as he could
make a good income from his practice. The more he used
those expert hands of his, the more he closed his agile
mind until, by mutual consent, on May 11, 1872, the partnership was dissolved.[68]

Daniel H. Spofford brought into Mrs. Eddy's life a more
mature and less ebullient personality. He won much success
at first in healing, and was also more or less helpful for a
time in the management of her growing interests. As the
months slipped by, however, his interest in her teaching did
not keep pace with her enlarging plan. As she turned more
to Asa Gilbert Eddy, she depended less on Spofford. Personal difficulties arose, and Spofford went the way of
others.[69]

In 1881 eight of her students — none of them at all
concerned about what she considered the real issue —
openly rebelled and put her leadership to a severe test. As
usual, Mrs. Eddy made appeal to rise above the pettiness of
personalities. Getting no response, she rallied to her side the
better disposed members, and as the event proved gave a
conclusive demonstration that she ruled, no matter what
might happen, in the little world around her. After that it
was clear that she would be able to cope with any crisis
which might arise.[70]

The spring before the book appeared in 1875, Mrs. Eddy
was living in a boarding house at Number 7, Broad Street,
Lynn. Still pursued by controversy and overtaken by much
contumely, she yearned even more intensely for the quiet
which a home of her own would probably provide. Leaning

one day from her window, she observed a sign "For Sale," fastened on the two-story frame house, with attic, at Number 8, across the street. She resolved that this should be her haven and on March 31, 1875, she bought the place for five thousand six hundred and fifty dollars.

But her income was not yet adequate to maintain so large a house. She was obliged to lease all but the front parlor on the first floor, and on the third floor the tiny upper bedroom under the sloping roof, in which during the months that followed, she completed the preparation of her book.

Number 8 was not a mansion. It, however, put a roof over her head. Fancy perhaps might see in its modest bow windows and little cornices above the windows tokens of the comforts and the beauty to be hers. The enforced wandering, which for years had handicapped and humiliated her, she now believed was near an end. Status, at last, she had — the security furnished by the owning of property. It was little enough, but that little was sweet to one who had known less. Number 8 might possibly, she dared to hope, one day bring her the condition "when an ounce of sentiment may save a ton of sorrow."[71]

At any rate a student of those days reports that he "never knew her so continuously happy as in that summer at Number 8." Sibyl Wilbur, too, says:

> The little place grew most attractive. The affectionate zeal of her students, many of whom she had healed from serious complaints or diseases and some of whom she had reclaimed from intemperate lives, made her gardens bloom, kept her grass-plot like velvet, and relieved the austerity of her parlor with decoration. Mrs. Glover's balconies were filled with calla lilies of which she was particularly fond,

and when she stood among them tending and caring for them with the sunlight sifting through the leaves of the elm, making splashes of green and gold upon her cool white gown, she made a picture of composure and purity.[72]

Not only in numbers, but also in love and loyalty, her students seemed to multiply. No service, at that time, appeared too great for them to render. Often they anticipated her unexpressed wish; and with them she shared her confidences and also took them to her heart. Some she addressed by endearing names. To many she opened a new heaven and a new earth. Letters written by students in their old age are on record in which words fail them to describe all that she had meant to them in the elysian days they spent with her.

To ensure her independence against all accident Mrs. Eddy needed not merely to triumph over the sordid and the commonplace with whom she overlong had been obliged to associate, but also to be drawn increasingly within range of the circles in Boston and in Concord devoted to those higher ideals and cultural interests congenial to her.

Certain phrases used by Emerson are faintly reminiscent of *Science and Health*. Those were the days when he was telling lecture audiences: "Mind is supreme, eternal, and one. . . . The universe is the result of mind." But we have Mrs. Eddy's own word dictated to a secretary that she never read Emerson till after her book was published.[73] Between Emerson and Mrs. Eddy there was a great gulf fixed. He was all for thought, and she for demonstration. He never fired her imagination, or awakened her enthusiasm. The Reverend Thomas Van Ness says:

I asked Mrs. Eddy one afternoon, when we were talking on the subject of her plans, whether she cared much for the teachings of Emerson. . . . Her reply was vague. The subject did not interest her and we soon drifted away from it, or rather, she did.[74]

But to Whittier Mrs. Eddy turned instinctively. He was more approachable and more responsive. Nine of his poems, in which she took a great personal interest, were put into the *Christian Science Hymnal*,[75] and to the end it was a joy to her to hear people sing:

> The healing of his seamless dress
> Is by our beds of pain;
> We touch him in life's throng and press,
> And we are whole again.

On one occasion when Sarah Bagley (in whose home Mrs. Eddy stayed in Amesbury) took Mrs. Eddy to call on Whittier, they found him "sitting before a fire in a grate (in July) coughing incessantly with hectic flush on his cheeks and scarce able to speak above a whisper." As she talked and showed a sympathetic interest over his indisposition, he brightened up and appeared to be much better. Of her visit Mrs. Eddy writes, "When I rose to go he came to me with both hands extended and said 'I thank thee Mary for thy call, it has done me much good, come again.' " [76]

For all his kindly reserve, Bronson Alcott had a sympathetic nature which appealed to Mrs. Eddy. Concerning slavery, their opinions were identical. After her book appeared and the storm of criticism broke, he introduced himself to her with this salutation, "I have come to comfort you."[77] For that reason, she sent him on January 14, 1876, a copy of the book, which he acknowledged in the pleasure-giving words:

Number 8, Broad Street, Lynn
Asa Gilbert Eddy seated at an upper window of the little house.

The sacred truths which you announce sustained by facts of the Immortal Life, give to your work the seal of inspiration — reaffirm in modern phrase, the Christian revelations. In times like ours so sunk in sensualism, I hail with joy any voice speaking an assured word for God and Immortality. And my joy is heightened the more when I find the blessed words are of woman's divinings.[78]

Twice he visited her in her own house at Lynn. He showed an interest in the class work, and indicated clearly that he had abundant reason for his confidence in her and in her followers.[79]

Again, on June 5, 1878, in company with the Reverend J. L. Dudley, Mr. Alcott was a welcome guest at a Christian Scientist Association meeting. Should the question ever arise as to whether Mrs. Eddy borrowed from Alcott, the author would refer inquirers to the minutes of the meeting, now in the files of The Mother Church, and reading thus:

After listening to questions & answers between teacher & class, Mr. Alcott presented his argument of the working of mind from Spirit down to atom & "vice versa." It was interesting to notice how near some points in the argument approached to the true argument in Science.[80]

At the Emersons and elsewhere in Concord in those days, there was much talk of Mrs. Eddy; and Mrs. Emerson, whose time usually was altogether occupied in balancing with her practical sense the unpracticalness of her husband, expressed a wish to meet her. Mr. Alcott often spoke to his daughter, Louisa M. Alcott, of *Little Women* fame, to Frank Sanborn and various Concord Brahmins of his new friend; and among them so little opposition developed to her teachings that he evidently believed there could be little of it also among people worthwhile anywhere.[81]

As the years passed, Mrs. Eddy won a place in Boston life, and met many Boston people. But by that time she was so engrossed in writing, in teaching, in building up her book and her church, and in multitudinous details of administration, that she had little time to spare for those occasions which have always given dignity and distinction to Boston society, and still give it a unique place among the cities of the land.

All those years when she was building up her health, her income, her equilibrium, she was qualifying more and more for building up her book. Her very hardships lent substance to her writing. She was coming up through much tribulation. As the Scriptures put it, "The earth helped the woman." Speculation about what might have been may be interesting, but it is scarcely worth the time and trouble. Yet had not Mrs. Eddy been so absorbed in building up her book from 1866 to 1875, when life was seldom kind to her, she probably would never have become infused with the heavenly courage to go on and on more soundly building up her health, her income, her equilibrium.

The work on the book, exhausting as it sometimes must have been, was her anchorage to reality when a lesser soul would have drifted to oblivion. Did she, like St. Paul, have to become all things to all men that she might save some? It was the honest toil she gave the book which taught her tact and courage. Was it necessary to pay attention to the spiritualistic rhapsodies of Mrs. Webster[82] in order to keep a roof over her head? She could bring herself to do it for the sake of the precious hours it would give her every day to write. Did she have to sit in at a game of cards to keep on good terms with acquaintances, when she so begrudged every minute stolen from her writing that to some she now and then appeared distracted, even cross? There was sure to be some hour of the day when, huddled in her shawl, with the house rocking in the wintry wind, she could be at her book. Were there times when, with children mimicking her, with adults insulting her and even threatening her with harm, her pride was wounded sore, and her heart was broken, by the cruel trivialities inflicted upon a woman striving to establish her spiritual security? Her book brought some relief from pain, and assistance to forget. Who shall say that it was not this absorption in the book which gave her power to rise above cold,[83] above hunger, above all the thousand stings of petty persecution to regions where nothing counts but Spirit, regions which sustain in the supreme conviction that nothing exists but Spirit?

For years Mrs. Eddy was working on her book. As her students more and more desired to see her teachings put in writing, she first fed them the familiar *Questions and Answers,* to which she was soon adding an Introduction — almost immediately to find its way into the text itself. By the summer of 1869 another booklet was ready — forerunning *Science and Health* — which later received the title *The Science of Man,* but at first evidently was called *Science of Soul.*

On June 7, 1869, from East Stoughton (now Avon) she wrote a Tilton friend of her earlier days:

I have just sent a work to the press for publication entitled — *Science of Soul* — I mean you shall read it sometime. I have written this and notes to the entire book of Genesis within the last year and this, besides laboring for clothes and other expenses with teaching I am worn almost out, have lost my love of life completely and want to go where the weary have a rest and the heavy laden lay down their burdens.[84]

The postscript to this letter further indicates that she was hard pressed at the time for money:

I am anxious to know why Dr. P. (Patterson) does not send me my annual remittance.

In February, 1872, she began to write what in her little notebook — in the author's hand — she calls *The Science of Life*. A little earlier (1870) she had put out *Soul's Inquiries of Man,* in which there are more touches than ever of Mrs. Eddy's individuality. While traces of her state of mind in the fast receding Portland days may here have lingered on, they steadily grew fainter until, at the very latest in 1875, she gave her students printed instructions they could not misunderstand to omit "manipulation"; after which Quimby's name was very rarely mentioned by her.[85] Perhaps, therefore, the author of this book was justified when he wrote, in 1921, for the *Cambridge History of American Literature* that "As a whole the system described in *Science and Health* is hers, and nothing that can ever happen will make it less than hers."[86] As though to confirm the author's judgment, which had for years been growing, the *New York Times'* review in 1922 of *The Quimby Manuscripts,* which appeared in 1921, adds:

It is a gigantic task which the editor of *The Quimby Manuscripts* has undertaken when he offers this loosely arranged mass of writings and reflections as not only containing the beginning of spiritual healing but also the origin of Christian Science. . . . *Science and Health,* whatever views may be held concerning it by individuals, has served to build up a mighty organization which could hardly have been reared on the uncertain foundations of the Quimby manuscripts.

Under the tiny skylight which, even that cool summer,[87] focused the hot rays of the sun uncomfortably on the head of Mrs. Glover, proofreading her first book at a time in life when many a writer has said farewell to his creative power, Mrs. Glover, in 1875, put the last touch on the first edition of *Science and Health*. To find a publisher was no easy task. She had long been trying. Nothing could be impossible to one who, more than a half-century before had prattled in the schoolroom "I will write a book," and had never quite lost sight of her high purpose.[88]

Mrs. Glover had already taken young George Clark[89] with her to Boston in search of a publisher, with no more to show him than the prospectus which she carried with her. Seeing no profits in an enterprise which might even today appear an unpromising business risk the publisher expressed the usual regrets. To publish the book would cost more than fifteen hundred dollars. Eight years later, three of Mrs. Glover's friends advanced the required amount, and the first edition of one thousand copies of *Science and Health* appeared on October 30, 1875. The bill for its production, which came the next day from the printers, W. F. Brown & Company, of No. 50 Bromfield Street, Boston, mounted to $2285.35, of which Mrs. Glover paid seven hundred dollars.[90]

The book now lies before the author, in its pale green cover and in a style of type usual at that time. As a piece of bookmaking it is somewhat like *The Bible Looking Glass, Fancy Fern, Nurse and Spy,* and also other books then popular. In appearance, it is no better and no worse. No

Boston, Oct 30 1875

Mr *Edward Hitchings of Geo. W. Barry.*
To W. F. Brown & Co., Dr.
Job, Card, and Book Printers,
No. 50 Bromfield Street.

(handwritten itemized bill; figures include) 100 00 · 31 70 · 14 64 · 697 41 · 72 60 · 17 00 · 10 00 · 45 200 · $228 5 35 · 700 · $158 5 35 · 500 · $1085 35

sooner was it off the press than Mrs. Glover was visualizing, in a letter written to a student,[91] a new edition, which she hopes will be an improvement on the first:

There are grammatical errors in Erata and some in the book doubtless that I have not touched ... and if you see them and are sure of what is right in the case correct them but *not* otherwise dont meddle with the punctuation but mark any doubtful cases so you can point them out to me. Our next printer should have a proof reader who is *responsible* for this.[92]

If this first edition bears some marks of a first book, Mrs. Glover at once began to remove them and continued to improve the successive editions until at last *Science and Health* became, next to the Bible, the "best seller" among serious books.

Like the Bible, *Science and Health* was published — as Mrs. Glover says in her first preface — "to do good to the upright in heart, and to bless them that curse us, and bear to the sorrowing and the sick consolation and healing." The style is well adapted to the end in view. Without sacrificing dignity, the language is often conversational. Developing out of her rich experience among plain people, the *Science and Health* of 1875, like the King James Version of the Bible, is easily "understanded of the people." Help does come to those who would be "upright in heart" when they read, "Every pang of repentance, every suffering for sin, (accompanied with reformatory efforts) and every good deed, atones for sin." [93] There is blessing for those whom the world would curse in such a glowing sentence as, "Love must triumph over hate." [94] Rightly understood, there is ample comfort for all who sorrow and who suffer in the seven words, "Mind, and not matter, embraces all suffering." [95]

Never was Mrs. Eddy satisfied with anything she wrote. The publication of each edition of *Science and Health* was simply a new challenge to make the next edition better. Between the table of contents of that first edition of 1875, and the latest of 1910,[96] there is not merely a wide difference but also a complete reordering. The first reads:

Natural Science; Imposition and Demonstration; Spirit and Matter; Creation; Prayer and Atonement; Marriage; Physiology; and Healing the Sick.

The latest edition runs as follows:

Prayer; Atonement and Eucharist; Marriage; Christian Science versus Spiritualism; Animal Magnetism Unmasked; Science, Theology, Medicine; Physiology; Footsteps of Truth; Creation; Science of Being; Some Objections Answered; Christian Science Practice; Teaching Christian Science; Recapitulation; Genesis; The Apocalypse; Glossary; and Fruitage.

All the way through the thirty-five years which elapsed between the first edition and the last, she was consumed with a desire to make her book more accurately express her meaning, more perfectly disclose the revelation she never doubted God had given her. Never could she be too busy — and no busier woman ever lived — to find time every day to work upon the book. The story in detail of her revisions would make a volume in itself. Before the author, as he writes, are the very copies in which her own corrections and additions are penciled on many a page in almost bewildering abundance.

Even in 1907, when she was eighty-six years old and the attacks upon her, culminating in the "Next Friends' Suit," were suggesting to her and to her friends that:

> When sorrows come, they come not single spies,
> But in battalions,

she was revising, and revising. Her pencilings crowd the margins, interline the text crosswise, and all but wear the flyleaves threadbare. Every problem then confronting her church, and as time was to prove almost every problem that could come, is reflected in her pencilings.

There were times, as in this 1907 period, when the copy which she then used of *Science and Health* evidently served somewhat as a diary in which she wrote down her inmost feeling. Did persecution strike her a new blow? She pencils the appropriate sentence, "It is our ignorance of God, the divine Principle, which produces apparent discord." [97]

Was there misunderstanding of her use of the quotation:

> I, I, I, I itself, I
> The inside and outside, the what and the why,
> The when and the where, the low and the high,
> All I, I, I, I itself, I?

She substitutes for it in pencil:

> O! Thou hast heard my prayer;
> And I am blest!
> This is Thy high behest: —
> Thou here, and *everywhere*. [98]

Were the "Next Friends" [99] pressing over much? In a burst of righteous wrath, supremely justified, she cuts out from page four hundred thirty of the following edition, the expression, ordinarily colorless, "next friends."

At midnight of September 25, 1907, she was reading about death on page one hundred sixty-four, when, as though anew to defy death, this woman, in her eighty-seventh year, changed the subjunctive to the indicative mood and declared that death "does not in the least disprove Christian Science." And then recalling St. Paul, she joyously exclaimed, "Death is swallowed up in victory."

Early in the 1880s Mrs. Eddy entered into those business arrangements which were to continue for many a year with John Wilson, [100] head of the University Press, the artistic craftsmanship of whose books has in all the years been matched by their intrinsic worth. With the entire firm her relations remained until the end both friendly and agreeable.

Indeed, the story of the successive editions of *Science and Health* can be traced in detail from the letters and the memoranda of such representatives of the University Press as John Wilson, William Dana Orcutt, and William B. Reid.[101] They are used here the more lavishly because they dismiss much idle speculation — including Mark Twain's — about the originality and the orderly development of Mrs. Eddy's thinking, as revealed from year to year in *Science and Health*.

From the first, Mrs. Eddy made on these substantial men a profound impression, which they saw no reason to change in a business and personal relationship lasting through an entire generation. To them she seemed a high-bred gentlewoman, to the manor born, sure of herself and her ideas, yet considerate and courteous to all. Upon every detail they indicate Mary Baker Eddy lavished care constant and untiring. She moved in a large orbit. She saw things whole. She saw things in their true harmony. To all, she was an object lesson, not merely in her penetrating insight but also in her habit of doing more than her share of the hard work necessary for its practical expression.[102]

From the head of the firm down to the youngest office boy, she knew them all. Her frequent visits were awaited with pleasurable anticipation. She earned the respect they freely gave her; and increasingly their personal affection. As late as February 11, 1897, John Wilson, head of the firm, after many years of business intercourse with Mrs. Eddy spoke of her "gentleness and sweetness." [103]

When she inquired where she could obtain the services of a trained editor, she found that the Reverend James Henry Wiggin, staff reader for the University Press, was "detailed to the work" (punctuation, capitalization and general

MASSACHUSETTS HISTORICAL SOCIETY,
30 TREMONT STREET, BOSTON.

Feb. 11, 1897.

Dear Mrs. Eddy.

How feeble, at times, are words to express the innermost feelings of the human heart! How true it is that acts speak louder than words! Your many words of kindness have, more than once, been put into a tangible form that verberate your gentleness and sweetness of Soul! May the good God continue to bless You and make You happy!

Your generous gift on Tuesday last of $500.00 sent a thrill of surprise and of delight through my heart that will never cease to thank You through Him the Giver of all.

Truly Yours,
John Wilson.

smoothing out as to construction of sentences); and, as he did this on his own time, Mrs. Eddy paid him for these services. "This was well known to those in our office," says Mr. Reid, "as well as in our proof reading department, and caused many a smile among us when we read, from time to time, the repeated assertion that Mr. Wiggin had written the book, and it tickled him, more than perhaps anyone else, to read that he was the *author* (instead of corrector)." In later years, Mr. Wiggin once remarked to Mr. Wilson: "Wouldn't it have been fine if I had?" [104]

Now and then some writer, unacquainted with such convincing documentary evidence as this in the files of The Mother Church, circulates again the overestimates of the very helpful service which Mr. Wiggin rendered Mrs. Eddy. It may, therefore, be worthwhile to quote another representative of the University Press, a man of no less standing than William Dana Orcutt, friend of William James and Theodore Roosevelt, Bernard Shaw and Sir Sidney Lee, who testifies:

> Mr. Wiggin was still proofreader when I entered the Press, and he always manifested great pride in having been associated with Mrs. Eddy in the revision of this famous book. I often heard the matter referred to, both by him and by John Wilson, but there never was the slightest intimation that Mr. Wiggin's services passed beyond those of an experienced editor. I have no doubt that many of his suggestions, in his editorial capacity, were of value and possibly accepted by the author, — in fact, unless they had been, he would not have exercised his proper function; but had he contributed to the new edition what some have claimed, he would certainly have given intimations of it in his conversations with me.[105]

There is finally another witness whose testimony may be of greater value because she always held her highly esteemed editorial assistant "in loving, grateful memory." [106] That is why these few extracts from Mrs. Eddy's letters to Mr. Wiggin[107] may seem timely:

July 30, 1885: Never *change* my meaning, only *bring it out*.

June 14, 1886: They (your corrections) are all right in grammar and I understood you should do no more for the proofs than to attend to that.

July, 1886: Please send both copy and proof to me and have no alterations made after I return the proof to press.

June 14, 1890: I shall request Mr. Wilson to send the proofs to you and then you to me and I to him.

Years later (in 1906) recalling again Mr. Wiggin's editorial service, Mrs. Eddy said, "In almost every case where Mr. Wiggin added words, I have erased them in my revisions." [108]

— 5 —

Founder

ON 1882, Mrs. Eddy
WENT TO LIVE IN BOS-
ton. The golden age had already dawned on the "Athens of
America."[1] The comforts of everyday existence were now
matching the charm ineffable which was gathering round
the city. More and more, rich memories were accumulating
as conditions changed. Dignified amenities were becoming
social customs which Bostonians observed, and practiced,
without boasting. To the political equality first flowering
out in the Town Meeting was now added a certain "quality," still suggested in the humorous verse of Samuel C.
Bushnell:

> Cabots speak only to Lowells
> And the Lowells speak only to God.

Though years had passed since grand dames milked their
cows on the public street and a little boy, named Ralph
Waldo Emerson, was doing his bit to add to the meager
family income by minding his mother's cow on the Common, Boston had retained its earlier simplicity, and had also
added to it a quality of thinking and of writing which then
made the city the undisputed literary center of the land.

By this time Boston had produced such a crop of native writers as no other city in the New World ever dreamed could anywhere be raised this side of the Atlantic. It was neither conceit nor affectation that occasioned the casual inquiry, when friends met in Cambridge, Concord, or on Park Street: "How is your new book coming on?"

And already from states south and west, where Holmes, Emerson, and Alcott had been lecturing, as far even as the Mississippi Valley, pilgrims with eyes wide open for "whole shelves of their library walking about in coats and gowns," were reverently wending their several ways to Boston. Some were still talking of Brook Farm with its coterie of cultural celebrities. As in his last years Hezekiah Butterworth showed the author over the site of that social experiment, he told him how Margaret Fuller came here to gaze at the stars and to her disgust discovered that she had to "milk a kicking cow." [2]

In 1882, Longfellow was just passing on, but Holmes and Whittier were not yet "nearing the snow line"; and, in addition, Lowell, Emerson, Aldrich, Whipple, Agassiz, Francis Parkman, and Charles Eliot Norton might be found, almost any Saturday morning, looking over the new books at the Old Corner Book Store, and at least once a month meeting for luncheon and high talk at the Saturday Club.

Marion Crawford was serving his literary apprenticeship before going to Italy.[3] Theodore Roosevelt was graduating from Harvard, where William James was then getting his start as a brilliant teacher. Henry James had already published his brief critical study of Hawthorne, shot through with penetrating criticism and over-punctuated with irritating condescension. Thus early, premonitory symptoms were showing of his exclusive interest later in things English; and it was about this time that Julia Ward Howe, on one occasion feeling that he "professed" too much, sharply remarked to him, "Don't lie to me, Henry."

The *Globe* was prospering under General Charles H. Taylor. The *Herald, Post,* and *Traveler,* too, were flourishing. With Louis Elson and Henry Austin Clapp on the *Advertiser,* music and the stage were adequately reported and interpreted. *The Evening Transcript* was almost a family oracle, and in its field *The Atlantic* had come to a preeminence which none disputed.

The cornerstone of the new Public Library on Copley Square was laid in 1888. Those were the days when Major Henry L. Higginson was founding the Boston Symphony Orchestra, and the audiences were all appreciation as William Gericke interpreted the great masters. Though Boston's literary lights had not been hasty to shine on aspiring art, the School of Drawing and Painting under the leadership of Otto Grundmann, who was called in 1877 to be its director, was growing apace; and William Morris Hunt was introducing Boston connoisseurs to the Barbizon school.

Past Hawthorne Hall, where in the eighties Mrs. Eddy won her first reputation as a preacher, Charles Sumner had strolled with his friend Thackeray; and James T. Fields had taken Dickens for the daily constitutional needed to keep him "fit" for his evening "appearance." The author, still a Fellow at the University of Pennsylvania, recalls walking in the nineties here with youthful pride between James Whitcomb Riley and the aged Edward Everett Hale, down whose bearded cheek a tear trickled as, retelling a story related to him in his boyhood by an aged veteran of the American Revolution, Dr. Hale would have his young friend know, "That was just three days before the British hanged my great-uncle, Nathan Hale."

In those years Boston had arresting preachers. The Reverends Joseph Cook and Adoniram Judson Gordon were in fighting trim; and Phillips Brooks, rated by Edwin D. Mead[4] as "the greatest preacher in the world," was at his best.

Mrs. Eddy was outgrowing Lynn. Then — as now — Lynn had people of importance. But small-town curiosity cabined her spirit and cramped her individuality. Back-door gossip always annoyed this woman of the stars. Through her long life, wherever she might be, Mrs. Eddy was "news"; her every accidental utterance town talk or "copy" for the papers. Eavesdroppers usually kept within earshot, keen to twist any casual word to her discredit. Sometimes she broke under the strain of keeping constantly on guard. Not even Red Rock,[5] with its outlook seaward, invariably brought the quiet and the isolation which her soul craved.

Long in need of someone more congenial than Barry, Spofford, Kennedy, and Arens,[6] in 1877, while still living in Lynn, she married Asa Gilbert Eddy. No easy role awaited him. His unassuming manner some mistook for weakness. His business, as he was well aware before his marriage, was to be helpmate to a wife indissolubly wedded to a public purpose already well defined. Amid these difficult conditions, he did himself credit. Wise in counsel, increasingly he won the recognition to which his sound judgment entitled him. A man of solid parts, he wore well. To her service he brought tact conjoined to tried efficiency at a time when his wife was harassed by the pretentiousness, the irresponsibility, the inefficiency, and the general inconsequence of those around her.

Miss Julia S. Bartlett's estimate of Asa Gilbert Eddy is

Mrs. Eddy in the early days at Boston

This picture was made at the request of Mrs. Eddy and hangs
on the wall of her Lynn home.

(From a crayon by Elizabeth S. Eaton.)

reliable. Grateful for the healing which he brought her, she was a frequent visitor in the Lynn house. As a friend and student, who often saw him, she writes:

> They kept no servant at that time, but Dr. Eddy did much to help in every way for the Cause that would otherwise take her time, and attended to business outside. He was always the kind husband and friend and ready helper in all things.[7]

Though his capacity for initiative was not extraordinary, he employed it when he could, and Mr. Frye, on June 27, 1895, wrote that Mr. Eddy was "the first organizer of a Christian Science Sunday School . . . also the first individual who put onto a sign the words Christian Scientist." [8]

In a letter dated June 27, 1882, to Colonel E. J. Smith, Mrs. Eddy said her husband had "the sweetest disposition" [9] she had ever known. To Judge Hanna she wrote, March 25, 1896, that he was gentle but firm. Two years later in another heartfelt letter to him she added, "You have said *all* When you touched on the tenderest chord of my human heart in your allusion to my late husband."[10]

During their first months in Boston, Mr. and Mrs. Eddy stayed with the Choates at 551 Shawmut Avenue. In her recollections, Mrs. Choate describes Mr. Eddy as incessantly busy with the publishers, arranging for the Christian Science services, the multiplying lectures, and also the Association meetings. Mrs. Choate characterizes him "a very gentle man, but firm & quiet." [11]

The man's unapologetic understanding of his position, his frank admission that his wife was the prime mover and he the helper, combined with freedom from all signs of false modesty and self-depreciation, are indicated in the following summation of the common enterprise in which they were all engaged: "Mrs. Eddy is the rightful head and we have never yet succeeded unless she filled that place and we abided by her direction." [12] Again:

> We have just been listening to the reading and explanation of the Scriptures by Mrs. Eddy as is our wont to do on the Sabbath and from which we are refreshed; though the hour seems dark and the exertion of the wicked great, yet in mercy and goodness will we abide.[13]

If to some Mrs. Eddy's final tribute to her husband, "Mark the perfect *man*," [14] seems overstrained, perhaps even they will admit that any man who adapts himself perfectly to the situation in which life places him and gets the best results attainable in the circumstances is no failure.[15] In a period when many others were making life almost unbearable for this woman with a vision, Asa Gilbert Eddy moved with discretion among the contradictory forces that crisscrossed her plans, acting with decision when there was need of action, and bringing to a woman often hard pressed the peace and understanding of which she often stood in need. When after their five years together, he passed on, by those who knew him best he was accredited the place Lowell allows to the modestly efficient:

> That loved heaven's silence more than fame.

The church Christ Jesus founded began, we are told, with a membership of no more than twelve. Only eight rallied to Mrs. Eddy's standard when, in the summer of 1875, she held her first church services in accordance with her revelation of 1866.

The program made provision for Sunday services in a hired hall, with Mrs. Eddy as preacher and director, on a

budget of ten dollars a week, to be paid by amounts
pledged by the charter members as follows:[16]

Elizabeth M. Newhall	$1.50
Dan'l H. Spofford	2.00
George H. Allen	2.00
Dorcas B. Rawson	1.00
Asa T. N. MacDonald	.50
George W. Barry	2.00
S. P. Bancroft	.50
Miranda R. Rice	.50

On July 4, 1876, Mrs. Eddy organized the larger Christian Scientist Association, and three years later, August 23, 1879, came the legal incorporation under the title "Church of Christ, Scientist," with a mandatory provision that the church be established in Boston.

While Mrs. Eddy gave the credit for the official organization of the Sunday School to her husband, she declared that Warren Choate, the pet of the household, was the little child who led to the genesis of the idea in her mind.[17]

As the year 1883 drew to a close, the Sunday services were held in Hawthorne Hall, at No. 2 Park Street, which, with its seating capacity of two hundred and thirty-two, seemed too big at first for that group of twenty-six. After two brief years the services had, in fact, to be moved to Chickering Hall, which was larger still. Mrs. Eddy was at last "arriving," and Boston was furnishing the platform from which her message was to cross the continent. Men and women still recall those Sundays in Hawthorne Hall. While the attendants were, in general, of a higher type perhaps than those at Lynn, not all, however, who came to Hawthorne Hall remained to pray.

At these meetings Mrs. Eddy always appeared well

dressed. She knew by instinct how to dress becomingly. Like many another wife who is a good manager, she could make a good impression on a small outlay. She wore her clothes well. She bore herself with an air of distinction, which made everything she wore count for more than it cost. In the hour set aside for questions from the audience rather impertinent inquiries were sometimes made. One Sunday she was asked:

> "Do you think it Christian to wear purple velvet and diamonds?" I'll never forget the sweet expression on her face while answering. She said as near as I can remember, "There are ladies here I presume with much more expensive dresses on, as this is velveteen, thirty-six inches wide, and only one dollar per yard. The cross and ring were given me by those who had been healed in Christian Science with the request that I wear them." [18]

Those Sunday services in Hawthorne Hall soon began to attract public attention. In their planning and conduct Mrs. Eddy devoted that tireless attention to detail which today gives Christian Science services an appeal different from others. She began, and closed, on time. Usually she opened with a familiar hymn like "Nearer, my God, to Thee." Then there was silent prayer ending with the Lord's Prayer. Another hymn was sung, and next the sermon was delivered.

Mrs. Eddy compelled interest in herself and her subject from the start. Sometimes even when scheduled, she would not begin because when the time came she did not feel the inspirational surcharge on which she counted to command her audience. She had pulpit personality. Her dainty and engaging figure, eyes "large, deep and soulful," waving brown hair,[19] her hands half outstretched in irresistible appeal, all aided her voice, which none ever forgot who heard it from the pulpit or the platform, to carry home her message. With or without notes, she spoke rapidly, and that Iowa woman, who found in Mrs. Eddy's sermon "never a trivial thought," was not alone in her findings. No matter what her text, her sermons all revolved around the central thought that God is Spirit, God is All-in-all, matter is insubstantial, and sin, sickness, and death can be vanquished by Spirit. But no one can today read back across her printed sermons without seeing the Way-shower in them all.

As to the content of her preaching, listeners might differ. But in the eighties — like John Wesley — she was still desiring "to have a league, offensive and defensive, with every soldier of Christ." Once she preached for three months in a Baptist Church,[20] without compromising her own message. That her attitude toward others of all types should be well understood and proper precedent be set her followers, she placed among the By-Laws of The Mother Church the specific admonition: "A member of this Church shall not publish, nor cause to be published, an article that is uncharitable or impertinent towards religion, medicine, the courts, or the laws of our land." [21]

As truly as William James, Mrs. Eddy was fitted to teach and her talents were already trained to a fine point by long practice when she arrived in Boston. Miss C. Lulu Blackman, who came in 1885 all the way from Nebraska, to join Mrs. Eddy's autumn class, wrote:

When she entered the classroom, I saw her for the first time. Intuitively, the members of the class rose at her entrance, and remained standing until she was seated. She made her way to a slightly raised platform, turned and faced us. She wore an imported black satin dress heavily beaded with tiny black jet beads, black satin slippers, beaded, and had on her rarely beautiful diamonds. These she spoke of in one of the later sessions. She stood before us, seemingly slight, graceful of carriage and exquisitely beautiful even to critical eyes. Then, still standing, she faced her class as one who knew herself to be a teacher by divine right. She was every inch the teacher. She turned to the student at the end of the first row of seats and took direct mental cognizance of this one, plainly knocked at the door of this individual consciousness. It was as if a question had been asked and answered and a benediction given. Then her eyes rested on the next in order and the same recognition was made. This continued until each member of the class had received the same mental cognizance. No audible word voiced the purely mental contact. Experience has been the lightning flash, that has revealed to me something of the mass mentality she confronted.[22]

The session began with so impressive a repetition of the Lord's Prayer that the same student reported:

It was not as though she had gone to the Father in prayer, but rather as though, because she was with the Father, she prayed. . . . After this audible repetition of the Lord's prayer, Mrs. Eddy took her seat and the students resumed theirs. As she began to speak, many of the students opened notebooks, and began to write. Instantly and peremptorily she said, "Put up your notebooks." I had written but one sentence and no other was ever added. There were others who refused to consider the command as final and, almost at once, covertly began again to make notes. With eagle eyes she detected the overt act, and again, repeated the words, "Put up your notebooks." All complied, some willingly and some with silent but resentful protest; there she resumed her teaching. A little later, one student began again surreptitiously to make notations. Stopping her discourse, Mrs. Eddy for the third time repeated the words emphatically and clearly and never again was there an effort on the part of any to write down a thought or word that came from this great Teacher. She at no time, made any explanation of this arbitrary requirement, but all my days I have blessed her for this ruling, because it compelled us to let the form go so that limited finite statements of Truth might not circumscribe the pinions of her thought. Her impartations transcended the medium of words. Words served only to convey her revelations. She gave both the letter and the spirit, but she took away the letter, lest any should substitute it for the wine of the Spirit.[23]

In such teaching no incidental interruption was tolerated. Even that bane of every classroom, noisy coughing, once received this firm rebuke from her: "Anyone with the least understanding of God does not cough." [24] Even today physical distractions like coughing and sneezing, so much a matter of course in other assemblies, are heard less often in Christian Science meetings.

Questions, however personal, Mrs. Eddy welcomed, and answered them without evasion. She encouraged comments out of a conviction that they might open the door to truth which otherwise, perhaps, could not come through at all. When some overzealous students in the class of 1889 volunteered the statement that they had tried in vain to bring back some who had strayed away and were no longer loyal to their teacher, Mrs. Eddy advised:

"Do not try any more. The love that is going out to the world through Christian Science is the greatest power there

is and the only thing that will change that thought" —
adding, "I have often felt these hard unloving thoughts of
others come about me like dark clouds, and seem to sur-
round me, but they never touched me, and why? Because
my thoughts were going out to them all the time in love
and with a desire to help them." [25]

It was perhaps in her presentation of God, as "incorpo-
real, divine, supreme, infinite Mind, Spirit, Soul, Principle,
Life, Truth, Love," [26] that Mrs. Eddy towered in her teaching. Sometimes, when she opened her soul concerning
prayer, her students were swept up to a perception of the
way to become a "new creature in Christ Jesus." Referring
last winter to the chapter on Prayer in the Christian Science textbook Dr. William L. Stidger[27] is reported by the
press to have said from a Boston pulpit, "I wish for my
own life, and my own home that I might have in it the
beauty and power and the spirit of prayer that is in that
chapter."

In every class there were Marthas cumbered with much
care and serving, and not infrequently weighted down with
the imponderable burden of fear. Some were small of mind,
some small of soul. Mrs. Eddy understood all. Of each she
sought to make something. She gave to all solicitude. But
she kept her mental balance. First things were put first in
all her teaching; and, say what one will about her terminol-
ogy, error never deceived her into regarding it as other than
the nothingness which she proclaimed it to be.

"What would you do," she once inquired, "if you knew
that some one was trying to kill you through mental argu-
ments?" With me this question created a great sense of fear
and I believe it was the same with other members of the
class. After waiting a few moments for an answer Mrs.

Eddy said, "Cast it in the waste basket." This light remark concerning the error, and her realization of the powerlessness and nothingness of the highest form of error, destroyed my sense of fear and left with me a great sense of peace and fearlessness of the claim of error to harm.[28]

She had a way of bringing students down out of the clouds of vain aspiring and idle sentimentalizing. Says Mrs. Foye:

One day a friend of mine, who was also a student of Mrs. Eddy's, called to see her on business. As she was about to leave, Mrs. Eddy invited her to stay for lunch, and just then the housekeeper came in, and, hearing my friend declining, said to her, "You had better take off your wraps and stay, I've just made a strawberry shortcake that will melt in your mouth." Whereupon Mrs. Eddy said, "There's a Scientist that isn't soaring o'er the church steeples." [29]

Bliss Knapp recalls that on another occasion, to a too dreamy student, she observed, "Come down. Your head is way up there in the stars, while the enemy is filling your body with bullets." [30]

Back of all the give and take of class contacts, back of every word she spoke and also of every gleam in her eyes, glowed a faith in her message, which she never failed to impress upon her students nor allowed them to supplant by any other interest. The correctness of her thinking might be challenged, never her sincerity. She was true to her conviction when she pronounced Jesus in nothing "more divine than in his faith in the immortality of his words." [31]

But it was not interest in sheer metaphysics which brought those students to Mrs. Eddy's classroom. It was eagerness to learn her method of healing. To theorizing about healing she habitually brought the sharp test of practice. The swift growth of Christian Science in Boston during the eighties was due to its effective healing. Critics might explain it as they would. There were by that time enough well people in evidence who once were sick, to bring of their own accord the sick of body and soul in ever growing numbers to Christian Scientists for treatment and then, automatically, to enlarge the group of prospective healers trained in Mrs. Eddy's classes.

Her understanding of the great need of the sick and sorrowing for healing is shown in a letter she wrote to Calvin C. Hill at the time he was leaving business in order to devote himself wholly to the practice of Christian Science:

> There are the sick the halt the blind to be healed. Is not this enough to be able to accomplish? Were I to name that which is most needed to be done of all else on earth — I should say heal the sick, cleanse the spotted despoiled mortal; and then you are being made whole and happy, and this is thine. "Well done good and faithful" enter thou into all worldly worth and the joy of thy Lord, the recompense of rightness.[32]

By 1883 not merely were Mr. and Mrs. Dresser in California hurrying East to have a hand in mental healing, which they were hearing that Mrs. Eddy was conducting with success, but pulpits also were unlimbering their big guns on something few as yet understood. Yet before the tumult and the shouting ceased, Mrs. Eddy was writing tenderly of her girlhood pastor, Dr. Bouton of Concord: "The religion that he taught and lived, I love and honor. It was the vestibule of Christian Science"[33]

No Boston preacher was more outspoken in censure than the Reverend Dr. L. T. Townsend. Nevertheless in the book which he wrote in 1887, to express his mature judgment, he freely admitted "that this woman . . . is successful in healing disease." Looking back today upon those same years one critic says, "There is a central core which is true." [34]

All the while hundreds, whose health had been improved by Mrs. Eddy's prayers, when subjected to cross-examination were quoting, to describe their experience, the man whose sight Jesus restored, "Whether he be a sinner or no, I know not: one thing I know, that, whereas I was blind, now I see." [35]

Out of many cases, a few of the more significant, because of the high reputation of the parties concerned, will now be cited to serve as types of healing in the period we are considering. Miss Julia S. Bartlett, later one of the early church officers, had for seven years been bedridden. Physicians who had done their utmost for her, would hold out no hope of recovery. In April, 1880, Miss Bartlett turned as a last resort to Mrs. Eddy. Under Asa Gilbert Eddy's care, "I began," says Miss Bartlett, "to improve immediately. I felt like one let out of prison. . . . The world was another world to me. All things were seen from a different viewpoint and there was a halo of beauty over all." [36]

A son of Ira O. Knapp, Director of The Mother Church from 1892 until 1910, relates in his privately printed recollections this family history:

> Mrs. Knapp, after thirteen years of ill health, had become a helpless invalid; the son had developed a supposedly incurable trouble, while Mr. Knapp had a slight indisposition. The skill of the physicians . . . had been exhausted. Her sister . . . advised Mrs. Knapp to try Christian Science. Mr. Knapp remarked laconically, "Well, we will try one more humbug." [37]

Mrs. Eddy assigned one of her students to the Knapp family; and, after absent treatment had been given, the student was asked to visit the Knapp home. On getting off the train, she inquired of the station agent if Mrs. Knapp had come to meet her. Overcoming his surprise that such a question should be asked about a woman crippled for so many years, the agent answered gently: "Mrs. Knapp will never come to this station again." Later, however, when the Christian Scientist was leaving her hotel, "a handsome, fresh-faced young woman came up the steps," inquiring for the guest. It was Mrs. Knapp herself.

"The first time," says one of her sons, "she walked to the home of her nearest neighbor, about a quarter of a mile away, the children all went too, dancing around her in the joy of seeing her able to walk again." [38] The practitioner remained only four days with the Knapps. She healed one of the sons and also the father. The Bible promises then became in the light of Christian Science so engrossing to the father that, as the son writes, he literally wore out the big family Bible.

Another Director of The Mother Church (1888–1909), William B. Johnson, became interested in Christian Science after exhausting all surgical, medical, and dietetic treatment for rupture and also for a legacy of diseases brought on by bad food and insanitary conditions during his three years of service in the Civil War. The expert who, one day in 1882, was making him a special truss, felt regretfully compelled to tell him that he could promise him no permanent relief, except possibly in Christian Science. In sheer despair, Mr. Johnson called in a student of Mrs. Eddy. When she came, she found her patient writhing on the floor in agony. His response, however, to treatment was immediate. His wife also was cured of tumor and catarrh.

Captain Joseph Eastaman, later a Director of The Mother Church (1892–93), brought his wife to Christian Science in a last effort to save her life. Boston doctors had declined longer to give encouragement. In a desperate "nothing to lose and everything to gain" spirit, he turned, in his discouragement, to Mrs. Eddy, who put the unexpected and astounding question to him: "Captain, why don't you heal your wife yourself?" Spellbound with amazement, he entered Mrs. Eddy's class, proved an apt student, and soon, he said, "as I understood the rudiments, I began to treat her [his wife]; and, so quickly did she respond to the treatment, that she was able to avail herself of the kind invitation of the teacher to accompany me to the final session." [39]

In a recent talk with Mr. Joseph G. Mann, for several years at Pleasant View, the author's attention was called to the remarkable story of his first experience with Christian Science. He had been accidentally shot, and the diagnosis of the four physicians, called to his bedside, revealed the ball from the thirty-two caliber revolver lodged in the inner layer of the pericardium of the heart. After a final consultation, the doctors agreed that the case was hopeless. Turning to Christian Science, he found his restoration to health was almost instantaneous.[40] This testimony would seem the more convincing because it is credibly reported that the community then believed the healing genuine.

But Christian Science healing, contrary to general opinion, includes the spiritual and mental as well as physical, and Mr. Albert F. Gilmore writes:

I joyously recall a testimony given in The Mother Church one evening which appealed to me so greatly that I have since remembered it. . . . He told of having been ill, in poverty, friendless, and hopeless, in the very depths of misery and despair. Someone told him of Christian Science. The appeal was immediate and he took up the study and sought the aid of a practitioner, with the result that he was soon healed of disease, was restored to an active business, and his friends returned. In the intervening years he had experienced a fullness and joy of life which he had never known before; and said he, "On more than one occasion so plentiful has been God's bounty, I have been tempted to say, 'Not quite so fast, O Lord; You are giving me more than I can take care of.' " To him the regenerating truth had been revealed; he had seen the perfect man with the result that, in goodly measure, he had come into his own; that is, he was laying hold and making use of the blessings which God has bestowed upon all His beloved sons.

Almost as soon as Mrs. Eddy could get settled in her Boston home the wisdom of her decision to locate in the larger city was amply justified by events. To her Sunday preaching and her Thursday lecturing, was added a correspondence which grew so rapidly as to become almost unmanageable. The classes in attendance were soon overtaxing 571 Columbus Avenue, and there was continued growth even after Mrs. Eddy moved, in 1887, to 385 Commonwealth Avenue.

As references to her in the newspapers became more frequent people came her way more and more to see what she was like. Casual contacts occurred with Frances Hodgson Burnett, Louisa M. Alcott, and Rose Cleveland.[41] Many unacquainted or ill acquainted with her teachings felt constrained to attack her in print; but, she was ever ready at a moment's notice to back up the faith to which she had given all allegiance, and it was not her wont to delegate the business to others.

Even when she was busiest, she made time to meet her critics face to face. A few still living recall how she looked and acted when she appeared in person one March Monday morning after pulpit attacks by the Reverends A. J. Gordon, Joseph Cook, and L. T. Townsend, to speak for herself in Tremont Temple where one of the then famous Monday lectures of the Reverend Joseph Cook was in progress. To Dr. Townsend she replied in *The Christian Science Journal* of April, 1885:

> Because of the great demand upon my time, consisting in part in dictating answers through my secretary, or answering personally the numerous inquiries from all quarters, having charge of a church, editing a magazine, teaching the principles of Christian Science, receiving calls, etc., I find it inconvenient to accept your invitation to answer you through the media of a newspaper; but for information as to what I believe and teach, would refer you to the Holy Scriptures, my various publications, and my Christian students.

Already with that prescience which gives her high place among constructive organizers of all time she was reaching out from Boston, through *The Christian Science Journal,* the first issue of which appeared on April 14, 1883,[42] to the victims of failure and frustration and low vitality on the isolated farms and in obscure communities from coast to coast. It was plain to her that neither the austere theology nor the periodic revivals then popular had substantial significance to those in greatest need of vital and inspiring faith.

In the opening editorial of the first issue of the *Journal,* she broadcast her proclamation of comfort and release to the drab legions for whom the *Journal* had a cheering message: "The purpose of our paper is the desire of our heart, namely, to bring to many a household hearth health, happiness and increased power to be good, and to do good."

Having recently studied the early issues of the *Journal,* the author is convinced that but little reason exists to doubt the strength of its appeal to the handicapped. Hosts of those in trouble of soul or mind or body were evidently helped by reading the healing testimonies straight from the heart and also by the successful union of Mrs. Eddy's monthly contribution of the didactic and the practical. Her editorials are sometimes sermons, oftener "leaders," comparable in their power to get their message across to those which made the fame of Charles A. Dana in the *New York Sun* and Horace Greeley in the *New York Tribune,* Lyman Abbott in the *Christian Union,* and John Fulton in the *Church Standard.*

Both as to substance and style, Mrs. Eddy is thoroughly at home in the good company of those who write as freely as they talk and with the same effectiveness. Her style has coloring too, which is rarely found elsewhere and which makes a spiritual appeal to those outside her circle as well as in. This extract from her fifteen hundred word "leader" in the *Journal* of September, 1886, is illustrative and representative:

> He alone ascends the hill of Christian Science who follows Christ, the spiritual idea who is the Way, the Truth, and the Life. Whatever obstructs this way, causing mortals to stumble, fall, or faint, Divine Love will remove, and uplift the fallen and strengthen the weak, if only they will forsake their earthweights, and "leave behind those things

The portrait of Mrs. Eddy painted in her latest years
(From painting by Alice H. Barbour.)

that are behind, and reach forward to those that are before."
Then, loving God supremely, and their neighbor as them-
selves, they will safely bear the cross up the hill of
Science.[43]

When "Dear Gilbert," as Mrs. Eddy fondly called her
husband, passed away in 1882, like Lee when Jackson fell
at Chancellorsville, Mrs. Eddy thought she had lost her
right arm. If she had needed Asa Gilbert Eddy in Lynn,
there was more need of him than ever with the increase of
responsibilities in Boston. To a student of this period, she
once said, "I could be happy with him in a hut, but God
means that I shall rely on Him alone." [44]

There had to be a helper at hand whom she could trust
in little things as well as great, to relieve her of details as
well as large responsibilities, to stand between her and those
who, with good intentions, would yet use up her increasingly valuable time, and to assure her the conditions necessary to carry on at all.

When Calvin A. Frye came in 1882 to remain — as it
proved — with Mrs. Eddy until the end, he was still under
forty. Reticent, retiring, devoted to what became his life
work, he went his tirelessly methodical way for almost thirty
years. Asking nothing and receiving only modest compensation, his loyal service was beyond all valuation to Mrs.
Eddy. No one did more to ensure her the proper conditions
for successful leadership, even protecting her from physical
discomfort. He was perhaps as nearly indispensable to Mrs.
Eddy as any one could be. No task was too large, or too
small, for him to undertake as she directed. He made her
appointments for her when she could see people, and her

regrets for her when she could not. He assisted in looking after her finances and her mail, and also copied her priceless manuscripts.

He lived to see responsibilities overtake her beyond his foreseeing when he joined her staff; but he never spared himself in helping all the while. As others came into her group, Mr. Frye maintained his habitual single-mindedness, always doing his utmost and his best, always illustrating the memorable words of the third Gospel: "He that is faithful in that which is least, is faithful also in much."

The maternal instinct was always strong in Mrs. Eddy. When definite word came of her son, a man well on in the thirties and with a growing family in the Northwest, she brought him East by telegram in 1879. Again in 1887, he came East with his family to see his mother. Both tried, at that late date, to forget those years of almost total severance and to make vital the blood relationship. But it was too late. With some of the essential characteristics of his mother, he was, however, too rough and too undisciplined after so long a break, to fit into her complex life. A mining prospector, with the prospector's instinct to venture overmuch, he was always wanting money, not so much for his family as to sink another shaft in search of silver and of gold.[45] Against her will, Mrs. Eddy had at last, in 1888, to recognize that much as she desired him by her side, she could not make a place for him in her menage and her widening plans, without wrecking all she had built up. He simply did not fit, and knew not how intelligently to try to fit.

Yet she needed a son's comradeship, a son's cooperation.[46] A certain Dr. Ebenezer J. Foster, who came her way about this time, was different from her son, different also from Mr. Frye. Turned forty, he was a slight man with a gentle disposition and kindly manners. He rarely offered counsel when it was not asked. He never interfered with what she thought or planned. Years later for the life of him he could not remember ever having crossed "Mother" in anything.[47] Graduated some years before, from the Hahnemann Medical College in Philadelphia, Dr. Foster represented much that she desired. He never forgot the tenderness with which she greeted him. Her love for him — a true mother love — led her to desire that he become a son according to the law. No longer young and strong, she needed such a staff on which to lean. Those near her were not adequate to meet her deeper needs. From that moment his heart instinctively went out to her, and he remained with Mrs. Eddy until 1896.

On November 5, 1888, by legal adoption, he became Ebenezer J. Foster-Eddy; and in her petition to the court Mrs. Eddy touchingly divulged her maternal yearning in the avowal that he "is now associated with your Petitioner in business, home life, and life work and she needs such interested care and relationship." [48]

Now sixty-seven years of age Mrs. Eddy depended on her son-by-law, since her son-by-blood had not turned out dependable. Dr. E. J. Foster-Eddy called her "Mother." He did much for her. He taught in her college. He succeeded William G. Nixon in looking after certain of her publishing interests. He was given various responsibilities. On many he made a pleasing impression. But in a few years he disappeared from the picture to reappear for a moment as a valuable witness for The Mother Church, in the litigation against the Board of Directors which ended in 1922. Now in his old age living, like many whom Mrs. Eddy loved, on a generous remembrance, he tenderly recalls that "no one ever heard me say one word against her." [49]

As the eighties drew on towards the nineties, this industrious woman was more industrious than ever. She kept her hand on everything from the incessant revision of her book, *Science and Health*, to the production in those years of such books as *The People's Idea of God, Christian Healing, Retrospection and Introspection, Unity of Good, Rudimental Divine Science*, and *No and Yes*.

Mrs. Eddy was always starting something new. Scarcely was she settled at 569 Columbus Avenue, when she placed on the front door a large silver plate, bearing the words, "Massachusetts Metaphysical College." During the nine years of its existence, it succeeded on a big scale, training hundreds of students to heal the sick, and bringing in large returns.

In those days, busy as she was, her labors on revisions of her book were unremitting. By 1891 *Science and Health* had reached its fiftieth edition. Few books ever written reach their fiftieth printing and fewer still, perhaps none, have produced a tithe of such results in so short a time. From the small beginnings in 1882 when she made the decisive move to Boston, the movement grew till at the end of this period it numbered two hundred and fifty trained practitioners at work throughout the land, twenty incorporated churches, ninety societies not yet incorporated as churches, and thirty-three academies and institutes.

Even before Mrs. Eddy's removal to 385 Commonwealth Avenue, Christian Science was rapidly pushing its frontier line to the Pacific. Strong centers were developing in various cities, particularly in Chicago, to which she paid her first visit in 1884.[50]

In 1888, came a pressing call to revisit Chicago, which

already, as Lyman J. Gage a few years later wrote, "ambitious to excel in everything," [51] was becoming a favorite convention city. Thus the National Christian Scientist Association had shown wisdom in planning for its third nation-wide convention in Chicago. Delegates from every state were sure to be present, for Mrs. Eddy had so worded her appeal as to make it irresistible. "Let no consideration," she said, "bend or outweigh your purpose to be in Chicago on June 13." [52] It was a virtual summons to meet her there.

Thousands, who in one way or another had felt the widening outreach of her thinking, longed inexpressibly to go to the convention that they might look upon the face, touch the hand, hear the voice of the one woman in all the world whose prayer, thought, and published words — especially in *Science and Health* and at that time also in the *Journal* — had been used of God to restore to sound health of body as well as mind many long regarded by themselves, and often also by others, as incurable.

As delegates began to arrive by every train headlines in the Chicago papers greeted them with the assurance that their "prophetess" would appear. When, on the second day, the doors of Central Music Hall opened, eight hundred delegates and many more were there, packed so closely that every inch of room was taken. Impatient to set eyes upon the woman of their dreams, many were all but ready to greet her with such lines as Auslander's:

> Balboa of your fate, you stared
> On a Pacific none had dared.

When Mrs. Eddy stepped upon the platform, the audience rose to its feet as one man. Not expecting to speak, not specially prepared — as was Bryan[53] when his hour struck in the Democratic Convention of 1896 — Mrs. Eddy hesitated for a moment. Those nearest detected the instinctive recoil of head and hand. Then, Mrs. Eddy walked down to the front of the stage, at her best as always when the unexpected challenged. A hush fell on the crowd as, confident, serene, and smiling, she delivered an extemporaneous address, which was later edited and printed with the title "Science and the Senses."

Without a note to aid her, without an abstract even in her mind, a pentecostal flow of golden eloquence began to pour from her lips. The substance of that sermon is in print.[54] Though superior to the published report of Bryan's Cross of Gold speech, the report we have is of small assistance in accounting for the effect of the sermon on that congregation. Some still alive who heard it become inarticulate when they attempt to describe the occasion. *The Boston Traveler's* account is this:

> The scenes that followed when she had ceased speaking will long be remembered by those who witnessed them. The people were in the presence of the woman whose book had healed them, and they knew it. Up they came in crowds to her side, begging for one handclasp, one look, one memorial from her whose name was a power and a sacred thing in their homes. Those whom she had never seen before — invalids raised up by her book, *Science and Health* — attempted hurriedly to tell the wonderful story.
>
> A mother, who failed to get near, held high her babe to look on their helper. Others touched the dress of their benefactor, not so much as asking for more.
>
> An aged woman, trembling with palsy, lifted her shaking hands at Mrs. Eddy's feet, crying, "Help, help!" and the cry was answered. Many such people were known to go away

healed. Strong men turned aside to hide their tears, as the people thronged about Mrs. Eddy with blessings and thanks.

Meekly, and almost silently, she received all this homage from the multitude, until she was led away from the place, the throng blocking her passage from the door to the carriage.[55]

Back to the Palmer House Mrs. Eddy was taken for a little rest and quiet. But for once she was not to have her way. Rich and poor had preceded her and were waiting there, bent on seeing her again. They would not be denied. To touch that healing hand, to hear again that captivating voice, the people hemmed her in on every side. Crushing the flowers with which the Palmer House had in her honor hurriedly been decorated, they sought to press in closer to her. Heedless of torn silk sleeves and mussed lace collars, unmindful even of the precious jewelry they trampled under foot, the crowd grew importunate to the point of inconsiderateness.

As usual, Mrs. Eddy was gracious. She yielded to this astounding claim of personality. The rich wine of recognition of her teachings was warm and welcome after all those arid years in Tilton and in Lynn, and the earlier years in Boston. She was deeply gratified to have the truth which she represented receive recognition. But, as always in her notable career, looking ahead she feared that in the afterglow, preoccupation with her personality would prove to have been a disservice to the truth.[56] She foresaw — some friends outside believe — that the tide of popular favor, now surging full and free, would as likely as not a little later ebb as fast away. The situation was not to her liking. In fact, in the Palmer House, she was overheard to say: "Christian Science is not forwarded by these methods." [57]

On her return to Boston, Mrs. Eddy found her worst fears justified. Dissension long growing within had at last turned into revolution. Outside, the Dressers, after their return to Boston in 1883, had been developing a mental science movement of their own, shading off into New Thought.[58] The books of the Reverend Warren F. Evans, more and more were being read. Arens's feeble and impertinent attempts to build up a personal business by displaying, as his own, goods which were really Mrs. Eddy's, were feeding a discontent now ready to break out. Almost under her eyes, Mrs. Sarah Crosse, whom she had trusted, was turning to other interests. Mrs. Gestefeld in Chicago, Mrs. Plunkett and Mrs. Hopkins were starting something in several western cities which they could not finish.

Before Mrs. Eddy could get back from Chicago, the "boring in" tactics of malcontents, endeavoring to dilute the larger faith of Christian Science and divest it of its wider implications, had turned into open rebellion already delivering its master stroke. A little group of thirty-six had obtained possession of the Association's books to facilitate the break they planned with Mrs. Eddy, without the danger and the degradation of expulsion. The Association's loyal Secretary, Mr. William B. Johnson, who had Mrs. Eddy's entire confidence, endeavored to induce the thirty-six conspirators to desist, reasoning with them that "now is the only time for us to meet in Christian love and adjust this great wrong done to one who has given all the best of her years to heal and bless." Some of the thirty-six returned. Nevertheless, most of them stood out a whole year, won at last their letters of dismissal, and went their way to oblivion.

But, those long and anxious months were for Mrs. Eddy

months of close thinking. She was meditating on the implication of events. She was testing various inferences which might be drawn from such occurrences. If it were possible for a revolution of such dimensions to break out within the camp at the moment when her movement, far from having a setback, was becoming national in scope, changes — at least in the machinery — seemed to be indicated. The stabilizing influence of her book, published in 1875, had saved the Cause shortly before. More now was needed, Mrs. Eddy was convinced, to conserve her Boston work by gearing it in irreversibly to the developments appearing in the West. The hour had struck to rally the far to support the near, and thus to give the Leader the larger status obtainable only from a Christian Science becoming nationalized, and on its way to being internationalized.[59]

Mrs. Eddy perceived the logic of the situation. She fearlessly accepted the facts observable at their face value. With a courage perhaps unsurpassed in history, with an indestructible confidence correspondingly unique in her central conviction, this woman, sixty-eight years old, dismantled the machinery which, out of tears as well as hopes, she had for years been building up. She closed her college. She gave up her active teaching. She retired from the editorial supervision of the *Journal*. She disorganized the Christian Scientist Association formally, though the members continued to meet for some years.[60] Most significant of all, Mrs. Eddy definitely, even sharply, ordered those who followed in her train to stop their at times sentimental and often unwise adulation of her personality. She charged them peremptorily to turn their eyes away from her, and to fix them on the truth. Then, to end the possibility of her becoming a storm center, in the future more dangerous to the Cause than to herself, she ordered published in *The Christian Science Journal* these Seven Fixed Rules.

1. I shall not be consulted verbally, or through letters, as to whose advertisement shall or shall not appear in the *Christian Science* Journal.

2. I shall not be consulted verbally, or through letters, as to the matter that should be published in the JOURNAL and *C. S. Series.*

3. I shall not be consulted verbally, or through letters, on marriage, divorce, or family affairs of any kind.

4. I shall not be consulted verbally, or through letters, on the choice of pastors for churches.

5. I shall not be consulted verbally, or through letters, on disaffections, if there should be any between the students of Christian Science.

6. I shall not be consulted verbally, or through letters, on who shall be admitted as members, or dropped from the membership of the Christian Science Churches or Associations.

7. I am not to be consulted verbally, or through letters, on disease and the treatment of the sick; but I shall love all mankind — and work for their welfare.[61]

Many years had passed since that evening on the streets of Lynn when, as though inspired, she said to young George Clark, "I shall have a church of my own some day." [62]

Now starting life anew as she neared seventy, Mrs. Eddy set her feet firmly on the path that led to the organization of The Mother Church, one day to include members from all parts of the world as well as Boston.

— 6 —

At Pleasant View

IT WAS DURING THE SIX-TEEN YEARS BETWEEN 1892 and 1908 that Mrs. Eddy, in retirement at Pleasant View, came to the fullness of her powers and the widening of her influence. Freer there than in Boston from ceaseless demands upon her time and her vitality, Mrs. Eddy could at last, by careful planning, obtain a larger measure of the ordered life which she had become convinced must be hers to discharge her rapidly expanding responsibilities.

To two of her friends, who were holding positions of importance in the Publishing Society, she indicated in July, 1898, that what she now was doing they too could do if they seriously set themselves to the task, even under less favorable conditions in Boston, of commanding the time which real thinking requires, and also of developing the ability to say "No" to unwarranted encroachments on their busy lives:

> You can take my method, bar your doors, and then hold
> your solitude with moral dignity by meeting the merciless
> selfishness of callers with a *fixed rule* and the divine imper-
> ative Principle to be alone with God and never break this

rule till you have your interval of study and prayer. I am an exception to all peace on earth — but not to "good will." The mail and the male and female claim undisputed powers to break my peace and rob me of all individual exemption from labor. But you have no need of thus surrendering your rights for others. I have written this in bed in the still hours while others sleep, — after 3 o. c. in the morning.[1]

No other woman so far along in life — and only a few men like Thomas A. Edison and Mr. Justice Holmes — are on record as having paid such a price for an opportunity to serve the public, as Mrs. Eddy had to pay even after she withdrew to Pleasant View on the edge of Concord, New Hampshire.[2]

Her day was laid out with precision. At six in summer and by seven in winter, Mrs. Eddy was accustomed to arise. Her hour for reading and for meditation she habitually observed. Of this one of her household tells us:

> Often she would preface some morning Scripture-reading with the confiding invitation: "Come and hear what God said to me this morning," and then she would read as God's ambassador, or as the good God speaking indeed. There was nothing of the assumed or artificial in all her reading; she read with the unaffected grace of a heart overflowing with humility and understanding, even as she spoke from demonstration, — as one who had suffered and who had a right to speak.[3]

Another says, who was with her those ripe years:

> It was Mrs. Eddy's custom when she came into her study in the morning to open her Bible and *Science and Health* and read the verse or paragraph on which her eyes first rested. Sometimes after she had read aloud the selections to

those in the room with her she would call the other students and give them a little lesson from what she had read or instruct them as to what it was necessary to handle at that particular time. During the first days I made a few notes of the lessons she gave which I will copy here. They may not be her exact words as they were written after the lesson.

July 15, 1907. Opened to Romans 14:22, "Hast thou faith? Have it to thyself before God. Happy is he that condemneth not himself in that thing which he alloweth."

Mrs. Eddy said, "We should allow nothing which we cannot justify. He who sees sin and condemns it not will suffer for it. Can we work out a problem correctly if one figure is not in accord with the principle of mathematics? Can I enter the kingdom of heaven if I allow one sin? Will not that destroy the whole problem?"[4]

Meals were served on the minute, and any member of her household who was late was invariably regretful. Practical and artistic, Mrs. Eddy set a table well furnished and attractive. Her standpoint in this regard is clearly indicated in her remarks: "To stop eating, drinking, or being clothed materially before the spiritual facts of existence are gained step by step, is not legitimate. When we wait patiently on God and seek Truth righteously, He directs our path."[5]

Her attention to the kitchen[6] was as minute as that she gave her study. On occasion she herself could cook.[7] An expert housekeeper of the best New England type, even in her difficult days at Lynn, she was once found by a noted visitor in dust cap and apron, doing her housework and without apology even scrubbing down the steps. Today the Chestnut Hill house, kept as she left it, is a model which any housewife would approve.

Because her life was lived according to a fixed routine,

often there was time for little extras. Every morning as she walked through her home, she had a cheery word for everyone, for cook and laundress, maid and friends. Sometimes she stopped a moment to rearrange some trifle on the whatnot or the mantel. Almost till the last, Mrs. Eddy could trip lightly down the stairs; or, as Mr. Joseph G. Mann has told the author, "come floating through the corridors like a young girl." In the pitch and toss of wit and humor, she was always quick on the catch and the return; both in hearty commendation of good works, and in the sharp reproof of slackness, she never failed.

In fair weather after an outdoor walk, sometimes around the artificial pond which her students had caused to be built for her, Mrs. Eddy would receive her secretary with the morning's mail. As the years went by, larger discretion was given him in sorting it over, with the help of others, to decide on what, in the light of his experience, he felt Mrs. Eddy would wish to see. Many of her letters she wrote with her own pen; and those dealing with the church or publishing concerns were likely to be sent by special messenger to Boston.

Dinner was at twelve o'clock, ending invariably with ice cream which she specially liked. One at least of her household recalls the welcome sound of the grinding of the freezer at eleven o'clock each morning.[8]

The daily drive immediately followed and the coachman reported many evidences of Concord's friendly interest in its most distinguished citizen. For everyone, Mrs. Eddy had a friendly greeting or a smile. They might be friends or strangers, adults or children. In every case, she measured up to the cultural test which John Cowper Powys sets in the memorable phrase: "No one can be regarded as cultured who does not treat every human being, without a single exception, as of deep and startling interest." [9]

Though she had left Boston, she had not forgotten the city where she saw her work expand, and she would have visited it more frequently had her busy life permitted.[10] On the visit unannounced of April 1, 1895, she spent the night in the room designed for her in the new church. It was on this first visit to her church that:

> She asked to have the lights turned on in the auditorium; she first walked down the center aisle and stood a little while nearly under the dome. Then she came back and went down on the right aisle to the platform and knelt on the first step for a few moments as if in silent prayer. She arose and went to the steps at the left and up to the first desk, where she repeated audibly the Ninety-First Psalm, then over to the next desk and repeated:

> Guide me, O Thou great Jehovah!
> Pilgrim through this barren land:
> I am weak, but Thou art mighty,
> Hold me with Thy powerful hand.
> Bread of heaven! Feed me till I want no more.

> Open is the crystal fountain,
> Whence the healing waters flow:
> And the fiery, cloudy pillar
> Leads me all my journey through.
> Strong Deliverer! Still Thou art my strength and shield.[11]

Although before she left Boston to make her home at Concord, New Hampshire, Mrs. Eddy had given the land for the new church, she was as always more concerned to win her followers to the spiritual life. Most of the organizations formed in early years were by this time broken up, to encourage concentration on things more lasting than material forms.[12]

The teacher, regarding with concern the growing tendency to give her adulation, had removed herself from the center of activity that her teaching might be taken at its own intrinsic value. To a student in a position of responsibility she minced no words in indicating her position:

First. Let my works, and not my words, praise me if I am worthy of praise.

Second. I always detested flattery.

Third. What is being said and written in such profusion of reference to, and praise of, me is not Christian Science and I hereby forbid its publication in the *Journal*.

Practically Christian Science is manifested by moderation, meekness, and love. "He shall not strive, nor cry; neither shall any man hear his voice in the streets. A bruised reed shall he not break, and smoking flax shall he not quench, till he send forth judgment unto victory. And in his name shall the Gentiles trust." [13]

Never did Mrs. Eddy lose her business sagacity. The "Optimist" [14] of Philadelphia, who interviewed her in 1907, was impressed with it. Anyone who tried to outwit her in business was not unlikely to regret his zeal. The following incident is one which Mrs. Eddy had delight in telling; it recounts an instance of her effective dealing with an avaricious neighbor.

With the improvement of Pleasant View in mind, Mrs. Eddy wished to purchase a little strip of land on which stood an unsightly barn. The old man who owned the

Mrs. Eddy speaking, June, 1903, from the balcony of
Pleasant View, to 10,000 Christian Scientists

objectionable adjoining half-acre seemed willing to accept
Mrs. Eddy's tempting offer, but for some unknown reason
raised his price as often as Mrs. Eddy agreed to meet his
advancements.

At last Mrs. Eddy divined that a crafty neighbor, for his
own benefit, was secretly manipulating the old gentleman.

She at once sent for this intriguing neighbor and, enlist-
ing him in her behalf, engaged him to buy the property for
her. She invited him to set his valuation on the barn in
question which he cunningly placed at two or three hundred dollars. He then named the price for which he thought
Mrs. Eddy might buy both lot and barn.

An agreement was made whereby he was to deliver to her
the deed for the property after which she was to make him
a valuable present in lieu of commission.

The transaction went through smoothly; the deed, accurate and safe in her hands, Mrs. Eddy said to her neighbor
agent, "Now I will make you a present of the barn, and
you may move it off as soon as you can."

The barn, really, was comparatively worthless, and Mrs.
Eddy's would-be deceiver had deceived himself.

Mrs. Eddy laughed heartily when she told of teaching this
schemer the lesson of his life, in letting him fall into the
pit which he had dug for her.[15]

While still worshiping in Hawthorne Hall, some of her
students tried to raise a fund for the building of a church.
Always alert, Mrs. Eddy was as often warning them, "let
there first be a Church of Christ in *reality* — and in the
hearts of men before one is organized." [16] As though to justify her warning, that first small fund was lost; but later
another nucleus was raised, and a site was chosen. Even yet
the money was not adequate and a mortgage had in consequence to be placed on the lot. When the mortgage fell

due and Mrs. Eddy found her students could not pay it off, she bought the lot herself and had it conveyed to the Board of Trustees to hold for the church to be.[17]

In spite of their good intentions those associated with her in the enterprise again fell into financial difficulty, and again she took the lot over to save the project. In September, 1892, it was reconveyed to four of her students, "thereby constituting them the Christian Science Board of Directors." This Board was bound by the deed of transfer to hold the land in trust for the whole body of Christian Scientists in accordance with a law which had been discovered that permitted property to be held in this way.

By the end of 1894, the way was open, without the aid of church suppers or church fairs, to secure with dignity and dispatch funds ample for the completion of the church. Built of gray Concord granite the church seated eleven hundred people, and the first service was held on December 30, 1894. In the next month's issue of *The Christian Science Journal* (January, 1895) after thanking all who had helped to bring the enterprise to success, the treasurer requested that, after January, 1895, since the fund was sure to be completed and the books closed that month, no further contributions be sent.

In developing her great idea and adapting it to widening opportunities, Mrs. Eddy more and more became a jealous guardian of her time. Too easily accessible to every chance inquirer while she was in Boston, at Pleasant View, with Mount Monadnock offering in the southwest a dim but lovely background, she found it easier, although an honored citizen of Concord,[18] to command the hours which she required to dream her dreams, to see her visions, and to express them all in print, in organization, and in stone.

To have written all she wrote between 1892 and 1907

would have taxed any genius. Few newspapers could match her record. In addition she started, in 1898, The Christian Science Publishing Society, perhaps the most successful organization of its kind in the world today; in 1898 the *Christian Science Sentinel,*[19] which every week continues to carry its message to many thousands; and somewhat earlier the *Christian Science Quarterly* containing the Lesson-Sermons which every Christian Scientist studies daily. To this period also belongs her *Miscellaneous Writings,* which for a year took the place of class teaching; and, in addition to being a graphic guide-book, contains the substance of such addresses as that made by her in Chicago in 1888. As early as 1895 followed the *Church Manual,* to all Christian Scientists the most vitally useful book, next to *Science and Health,* which this woman of "The Vision Splendid" ever wrote:

> To lift to-day above the past,
> To nail God's colors to the mast.[20]

At Pleasant View, Mrs. Eddy also found the detachment she required to think ahead. As her teaching increasingly touched the hearts of her followers everywhere, her vision splendid included a larger building as cosmic as her teaching. But she would not be hurried. She would have her people "strong enough in God to stand." [21] Ten years she had been living at Pleasant View before she suggested to the Church in Boston the need of a larger building. At the Annual Meeting in June, 1902, on motion of Edward A. Kimball, the Church was formally committed to the enterprise.[22]

In 1895, the first lot adjacent to the earlier building had been acquired. All land purchases were completed during 1903. The next year the corner-stone was laid. Then, in June, 1906, thirty thousand Christian Scientists from many lands came to share in the dedication of a church seating over five thousand, costing two million dollars, paid in advance — a church not unworthy to be compared with the cathedrals of the Old World.

The Christian Scientists who had come to Boston to see The Mother Church dedicated remained to attend the Wednesday evening meeting at which testimonies of Christian Science healing were given. The great temple was crowded from floor to dome, and overflow meetings were held in the original Mother Church and in four public halls. Many who were not Christian Scientists were amazed listeners to the outpouring of testimonies from every part of the great auditorium. Men and women arose in their places on the floor of the church and in the first and second balconies. As each arose he called the name of his city and waited his turn to tell of the miracle of health and virtue wrought in his life as a result of the study of Christian Science. The names of the cities called up the near and the far of the civilized world — Liverpool, Galveston, St. Petersburg, San Francisco, Paris, New York, Atlanta, and Portland. There were negroes as well as white men in that audience; there were French, German, and Scandinavian; there were army officers from Great Britain, and members of the British nobility, Americans of great wealth, jurists, former doctors and clergymen, teachers, clerks, day laborers. It was like a jubilation of an army with banners. And not only of the vanquishment of cancers, consumption, broken limbs, malignant diseases, and paralysis did these votaries of Christian Science testify, but of poverty overcome, victory gained over drunkenness, morphine, and immoral lives. It was a triumphant assertion of the health and power of spiritual living.[23]

Home from Cuba, with his Rough Riders, Theodore Roosevelt had just been elected to the Governorship of New York State and an honorable peace was being made in Paris, after our little unpleasantness with Spain, when Mrs. Eddy, on November 20, 1898, began to teach the last of all her classes.[24] Its membership was of her own choosing. Only those were admitted who were specially invited by letter or by telegram. Before the sixty-seven arrived, none knew who else was included — each invitation having evidently been marked "confidential." Her pride in them she expressed later by saying she was "glad to give to the world such men and women to demonstrate Christian Science." [25]

The recollections, written or oral, of several members of the class[26] are now before the author. George H. Moses, later a United States Senator (and not a Christian Scientist), says of the Leader, "She was exactly the sort of woman I should have liked my grandmother to have been." [27] None have been found to differ from Mr. George Wendell Adams that, though well on toward eighty years of age, Mrs. Eddy appeared much younger — "a mature woman," vigorous, vivid, and so highly spiritual that one member will "never forget the heavenly look upon our beloved Leader's face." [28]

"Escorted by Mr. Frye," Mrs. Eddy "came into the Hall that Sunday afternoon with her quick, graceful, gliding step, and took her place on the platform. She looked from one to another over the whole class . . . with the most sweet, tender and happy expression." [29] Out of the richness of her spiritual experience, now at its maturity, Mrs. Eddy gave the Class of '98, already well grounded in Christian Science, perhaps the best instruction which any class received during her many years of teaching. She increased their confidence in their power to heal. She showed them how to improve their technique. She convinced them that the Sermon on the Mount can be demonstrated in our everyday concerns. She bade them "run and not be weary," no matter how hard the way might seem, how baffling some of the cases which they wished to help. She emphasized the necessity of living the life they would have others live. The value of humility in all their relationships, she indicated by a personal experience which she once had at the bedside of a sick child. "In my anguish I bowed my head until it touched the floor, and when the assurance came again of the loving presence and healing power of God, the child responded instantaneously." [30]

Asked by one member of this last class:

> "Should we ever permit ourselves to speak harshly?"
> "Oh" she replied, "there is a tight place. We *must* separate Truth and error." Then slowly and sadly she said: "That has cost me more suffering than anything else. I have had to see error when I most wanted not to see it." [31]

Their minds were every instant concentrated on her words. Their emotions were deeply stirred. But she was an expert. She knew how to ease the strain, as in reference to that day, when, a tiny girl, amid the laughter of the other school-children, she said she meant to write a book. She knew how to use the timely story; as, at the expense of the more austere literalists, one day she said:

> Some men were employed on a farm to hoe. After working some time one of the men laid down his hoe and started toward the house. Another asked him why he was leaving his work, and the reply was that the man was thirsty and was going for a drink. "But," argued the second man, "that is not according to the Bible." "How so?" asked

the thirsty man. "Why, the Bible says, 'Ho, every man that thirsteth.' " [32]

She took a humorous fling at conventional philosophy in the story:

A tanner of hides bored a hole through his front door and put a fox's tail through it, letting the bushy part hang outside. People looked and wondered what it meant. One man passed the house many times, and finally the tanner asked him: "Are you a minister?" "No, I am not that." "Are you a lawyer?" "No, I am not that." "Well, may I ask what you are?" "I am a philosopher; and I have been wondering how that fox ever went through that hole." [33]

Aware of their unusual privilege, the Class of '98 learned that, first and last:

there was but one God, and consequently, there could be but one full reflection, which of course was the compound idea, man. She dwelt at length on the point that there could be but one full or complete reflection of one God, and that fact must be the basis for all scientific deduction. She indicated that only as her students grasped the fundamental fact that one God could have but one full reflection did they have the right basic sense of Christian Science, and know that there is no other starting point.[34]

Every religion with "bite" in it reckons with the devil. As Goethe pointed out, man's way to heaven leads through hell, and in hell he meets the devil.[35] Men may try to ignore the devil or to cut his acquaintance after they have met him; but, as Faust discovered, this is a large assignment. "The backward pull" is strong on all of us. Honesty compels agreement with St. Paul that "when I would do good, evil is present with me." [36] More than once, Jesus indicated that his business here was to beat the devil, and to transmit to his disciples the power to do the same.[37] St. Paul's "thorn in the flesh" he once described as "the messenger of Satan."[38] The Church Fathers debited the devil with all their erroneous doctrines as well as evil practices. In the Castle of Wartburg the stain on the wall, from the ink bottle which Luther is reported to have flung at the devil, still awes an occasional pilgrim.

Some of the substantial pious in the Valley of the Connecticut were disquieted when, in 1741, in the most telling sermon which he ever preached, Jonathan Edwards multiplied the minions of the devil to his heart's content, and adjured his shivering people to believe that "the devils watch them; they are ever by them, at their right hand; they stand watching for them like greedy, hungry lions that see their prey and expect to have it." [39]

Mrs. Eddy was not the first defiantly to face the devil, or to doubt his power over souls. Nor is it surprising that, with the term "animal magnetism" so loosely used by many a tongue on both sides of the Atlantic that Disraeli said London was "mad" with it, Mrs. Eddy, when she was developing her teaching, should have coined the special name of "malicious animal magnetism," and in her correspondence abbreviated it to "M.A.M."

It was natural for Mrs. Eddy, with her insight into things spiritual, to understand the apparent attractiveness of evil which she, like others, was thought at times to personalize. There was nothing unnatural in her solicitude in season and out, to keep those around her on their guard against the subtlety and insidiousness of evil. Miss Shannon says:

Mother explained to us what that was, and her explanation of evil indulged in was indeed terrifying. She showed us that, if we neglected to do our duty and did what was wrong without detecting, correcting and overcoming error, but continued repeating the same mistakes and justifying ourselves, the suffering which would result would be simple interest, which we would have to pay; then, if Christian Scientists refused to see the error when it was shown, and wilfully or maliciously continued to repeat it, allowing their thoughts to be governed by hate, malice, jealousy, or any of these subtle conspirators, this would result in moral idiocy, and would bring compound interest. Then the experience of hell would ensue.[40]

Miss Lucia C. Warren wrote in *The Christian Science Journal,* June, 1930:

Hers was the tender sensitive consciousness of the mother who must discipline and counsel her young, must feel responsible for their welfare and future attainments, must guard them from outward and contrary influences, must fit them to encounter alone, and without her, the billows of mortal experience, and to encounter them triumphantly.

Jesus set the precedent. He bade his disciples avoid the very appearance of evil. In the prayer Jesus offered as a model for us all to use, occurs the counsel: "Lead us not into temptation, but deliver us from evil." Jesus realized that most of those with whom he had to deal were apt to go to sleep when there was the greatest need that they should keep awake. It was, unhappily, the three closest to him who all but missed his transfiguration on the Mount because they were sleepy-headed; and in Gethsemane — in spite of his pathetic plea — they could not keep awake one hour when:

Into the woods my Master went,
Clean forspent, forspent.
Into the woods my Master came,
Forspent with love and shame.
But the olives, they were not blind to Him,
The little gray leaves were kind to Him,
The thorn-tree had a mind to Him,
When into the woods He came.[41]

Slow of comprehension, many associated with Mrs. Eddy had to be treated like irresponsible children inclined to make something out of nothing. Even that Class of '98 had the arresting question put to them by a teacher who left nothing unsettled: "Why make so much ado about nothing? Error is no more than a row of ciphers added from one wall to another, unless you place a unit with it and make something out of it." [42]

But she paid them the distinctive compliment of saying nothing about M.A.M. Years later she herself wrote that she had not referred to it in teaching them.[43] Valuing beyond price what they had learned at Concord, the Class of '98, from none of whom Mrs. Eddy would accept any compensation, went their way to promote harmony among Christian Scientists and also to teach with more authority.

At Pleasant View the days for all passed quickly. Everyone was busy. By her own devotion to the duties which each day brought, Mrs. Eddy furnished an example which her household were keen to follow. Save for the daily drive, she allowed herself no recreation. Always engrossed in her work, she was never too engrossed to be kind. Painters working outside in the winter might feel the cold. Though Mrs. Eddy herself never drank coffee, she saw to it that her workingmen had coffee in abundance, steaming hot.[44] She expressed the tolerant views which she illustrated with the painters in a letter to General Charles H. Grosvenor: "Upheld by divine Love man can make himself perfect but he must not attempt this too rapidly with his neighbor." [45]

With many still living among those employed at Pleasant View and later at Chestnut Hill, the author has talked. All tell the same story of a woman unlike anyone else whom they ever knew and indescribably attractive. Their heartful recollections bring tears to the eyes and a sob to the throat. Several eminent citizens of Concord — not all of her faith — have put themselves on record. A former Mayor expressed the well-considered conviction that Mrs. Eddy was "keen of intellect and strong in memory." [46] "Reserved, deliberate, just," an editor[47] observes. And a lawyer was impressed by her "physical activity not ordinarily to be found in persons many years younger." [48]

Even from the small details of the lives around her she did not hold aloof. She spoke the word that helped, whether in admiration or in admonition. Never was she above the sharing with them of her intimate experiences, the entering fully into theirs. Says Mrs. Grace A. Greene:

She would often say to me, "I make *my* pumpkin pies thus and so," or "I make puddings like this." One day I said, "Mother, can you really make pies and puddings?" She replied, "Of course I can." And then she told me of making herself a bonnet and dress when she was too poor to hire them done, although she had never done such a thing in her life before. She finished by saying, "If you are an ordinary cook, dressmaker, or milliner, Christian Science will make you *perfect* in any of these lines, and everyone should seek to perfect himself *wherever* he is, or *whatever* his calling." [49]

As for her enemies, she was quick to detect and resourceful to checkmate any move to hurt her Cause. But the evidence abounds that her settled policy was, "Love your enemies, bless them that curse you, do good to them that hate
you, and pray for them which despitefully use you, and persecute you." [50]

Even those who had once been close to her, and then
went away and sometimes "willfully or mistakenly perverted
her teaching," [51] she kept on loving. But she always drew
the line between sin and the sinner, and once with gravity
and regret she indicated what might in some cases prove
the natural result of sinning: "Nothing except sin, in the
students themselves, can separate them from me. Therefore
we should guard thought and action, keeping them in
accord with Christ, and our friendship will surely
continue." [52] Because she did love humanity, she was quick
to reprove the errors which she saw in individuals, obscur-
ing the perfection of the real man. No matter how she
made others suffer, she suffered more herself. Hers was that
vicarious suffering, more terrible to bear than that of persons on whom, for their good, she felt obliged to inflict
pain.

Never did this woman of much loving speak more from
the heart than when she said:

> There is a flower whose language is "I wound to heal."
> There is a physician who loves those whom He chastens.
> There is a woman who chastens most those whom she
> loves. Why? Because like a surgeon she makes her incisions
> on the tender spot to remove the cold lead that is danger-
> ous there. [53]

Even a small part of her letter writing at Pleasant View would have taxed the time of the modern woman. The collected masses of letters, mounting up into the thousands, which she wrote with her own hand, are bewildering to examine. Her secretaries helped her all they could in correspondence routine; but there were many burdens which she alone could carry, and these she carried with dignity. As back in her girlhood, when she was writing to Augusta Holmes about the thousand and one things that interest young people, so in the days at Pleasant View, her mind now teeming with projects for the benefit of millions, Mrs. Eddy became a great as well as a voluminous letter-writer, unsurpassed in the range of topics covered, in the widening sweep of her vision.

Says Miss M. Louise Baum, sometime on the editorial staff of *The Christian Science Monitor:*

> Even as the English Bible stands as the great monument of English style for the centuries until now, and even as Dante made Italian speech by epitomizing it in his fervent poem, even so the writings of Mrs. Eddy are certain to stand as models of twentieth century style, of direct actual saying the thing itself, with every ornament inherent in the thinking, never a piece of verbal trickery or tracery added from without, with every sweeping passage of eloquence borne on the actual high tide of spiritual revelation. Mrs. Eddy's word is yea, yea, and nay, nay. She is herself what she says. She has lived it out, and so it is that her words live and kindle life in others.

All through her letters runs that Victorian disposition to lend to duty an inexorableness for which present-day behaviorism is a poor substitute in the conservation of the higher things of life. Friendship-love, based on a faith in God as well as man, which every age requires, appears in her letter of March, 1896, to Judge Hanna:

> Words fail to tell how much comfort your letter gives me. It sometimes almost overcomes the sense of being to breast the storms of mortal mind. Then to hear such a bird note, then to see such a ray divine of light and love coming from human pen — O, is it not comforting? I thank you, God loves you, that is enough. He will finish and furnish all that remains to be felt and known by us and all poor sinners. Yours and Camilla's photos are in my album side by side; but on my mantle your face and Gen. Baker's are face to face. That is the way you are in my heart. For I know you to be two of the most genuine characters I have ever known, and I have known grand and glorious ones.[54]

Though Mrs. Eddy did direct The Mother Church, she was habitually wise in training others to bear responsibility. February 12, 1895, she writes:

> My beloved Students:
>
> I cannot conscientiously lend my counsel to direct your action on receiving or dismissing candidates. To do this, I should need to be with you. I cannot accept hearsay, and would need to know the circumstances and facts regarding both sides of the subject to form a proper judgement. This is not my present province, hence I have hitherto declined to be consulted on these matters, and still maintain this position.
>
> These are matters of grave import, and you cannot be indifferent to this, but will give them immediate attention and be governed therein by the spirit and the letter of this scripture: "Whatsoever ye would that men should do unto you, do ye even so to them."

I cannot be the conscience for this Church. But if I were I would gather every reformed sinner that desired to come, into its fold, and counsel and help them to walk in the footsteps of His flock. I feel sure that as Christian Scientists you will act relative to this matter up to your highest understanding of justice and mercy.[55]

Businesslike, forethought for the Church is also shown in her constant regard for the observance of all legal requirements. July 28, 1892, she wrote the clerk:

Remember dear student, that this Church must be properly chartered, and its Constitution and Bylaws correctly made, and accepted, and the whole proceeding be strictly legal. Then, we have complied with civil law (and I always recommend this being done, wisely done) and then, every Church of Christ, Scientist, will have a precedent to follow whereby to establish the Gospel of Christian Science.[56]

In an emergency she took the helm, and issued commands too plain to be misunderstood. On September 29, 1893, with plans well along for the original edifice of The Mother Church but one detail after another delaying the beginning of the work, she wrote the Directors:

My dear Students,

Do not delay one other day to lay the foundation of our Church, the season will shut in upon you perhaps, and the *frost* hinder the work. God is with you, thrust in the spade, Oct. *1st* 1893 and advertise in next No. of Journal that you have begun to build His temple a temple for the worship and service of Divine Love the living God.

With great love Mother
M.B.G.E.[57]

Man as he was, St. Paul tried to mother each little group of converts which he left behind in town and city on his missionary tours. When visiting in those pre-airplane days was not practicable, he wrote them letters aglow with mothering counsel for their nurture in the Christian Faith.

In the Founder of Christian Science, also, that mother instinct was strong. It included those near, those far, and those to follow in her train in all the years to come. There is nothing, perhaps, in all the history of womankind quite like Mrs. Eddy's loving forethought, flowing out toward all her spiritual children. As she looked back even to the sixties when she was building up her book, she realized that it had always been the invasion of wrong ideas, mortal mind,[58] into the circle around her that disturbed, unsettled, detached, sometimes took from her those who needed most the guidance which she gave. It was specially for them that she wrote in *Science and Health:*

> The lame, the deaf, the dumb, the blind, the sick, the sensual, the sinner, I wished to save from the slavery of their own beliefs.[59]

It was for them she began in 1883 to publish *The Christian Science Journal,* in 1898 the *Christian Science Sentinel,* and in 1908 *The Christian Science Monitor.* Monthly, weekly, daily, she would have the members of her church read what she was convinced would make them immune to error. But, besides all her many books and papers, from *Science and Health* in 1875 to *The Christian Science Monitor* in 1908, something was needed for the complete mothering of her people, for the binding of them up so closely to the church that nothing could steal from them her revelation of 1866,

Mrs. Eddy leaving Pleasant View for her daily drive
Taken in June, 1900.

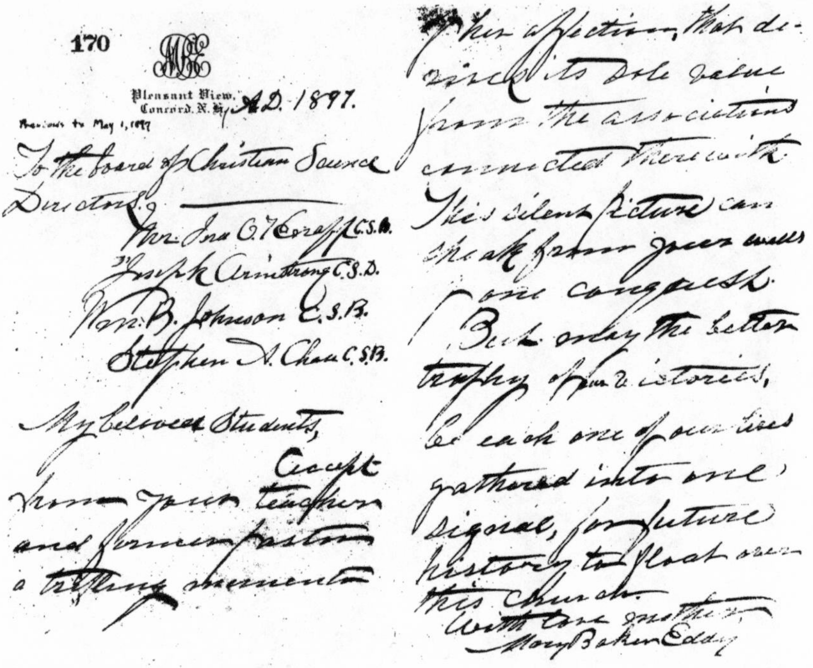

170

Pleasant View,
Concord, N.H., A.D. 1897.

Previous to May 1, 1897

[handwritten letter:]

To the board of Christian Science
Directors:
    Mr. Jno C. Cross C.S.A.
    Joseph Armstrong C.S.D.
    Wm. B. Johnson C.S.B.
    Stephen A. Chase C.S.B.

My beloved Students,
    Accept
from your teacher
and former pastor
a trifling moment . . .

. . . her affection, that derives its sole value from the associations connected therewith. This silent picture can speak from your walls more than words. But only the better trophy of your victories, be each one of our lines gathered into one signal, for future history to float over this Church.

With love mother,
Mary Baker Eddy

— which for forty years and more she had been emphasizing, interpreting, enlarging, and widening as new problems came and pressed for a solution.

That is the reason why, among Christian Scientists, the *Manual* of The Mother Church today ranks next to *Science and Health*. They see in it the Discoverer and Founder of Christian Science, mothering her flock long after she had passed on, protecting them from ills when she had gone from sight, forestalling temptation and misunderstanding, and earnestly endeavoring to continue in the spirit — through the *Manual* — to protect them from their own mistakes and from the hurts which others might inflict.

To Miss Susie M. Lang she said on August 2, 1896, "I

was compelled by a sense of responsibility to put up the bars for my flock." [60] Miss Shannon loves to recall that:

> The first time that Mrs. Eddy saw the need of a manual for The Mother Church was in connection with teaching, and she told me to write to Mrs. Adams and Mrs. Webster of Chicago, whom she used to call "the twins." She wanted to see them to explain to them the need that she saw to preserve the teaching of Christian Science pure and unadulterated for future generations, and the wisest way she could see at that time was to have a Manual on teaching Christian Science. They came, and she showed them the right thing to do was to have a Committee of her old loyal students, with themselves, and for them to compile a set of by-laws in connection with teaching. This was done. Afterwards, God showed Mother that it was wise to make by-laws to govern all church members as well as teachers, which ultimately developed into the present Manual of The Mother Church, which includes articles and by-laws for teachers and teaching, as well as for Church discipline.[61]

In *The First Church of Christ, Scientist, and Miscellany* (p. 230), we read, "Notwithstanding the sacrilegious moth of time, eternity awaits our Church Manual, which will maintain its rank as in the past, amid ministries aggressive and active, and will stand when those have passed to rest."

Rising to a more official relationship, Mrs. Eddy, on February 27, 1903, addressed the Directors:

> Beloved Students: I am not a lawyer, and do not sufficiently comprehend the legal trend of the copy you enclosed to me to suggest any changes therein. Upon one point however I feel competent to advise namely: Never abandon the By-laws nor the denominational government of the Mother Church. If I am not personally with you, the Word of God,

and my instructions in the By-laws have led you hitherto and will remain to guide you safely on, and the teachings of St. Paul are as useful to-day as when they were first written.

The present and future prosperity of the cause of Christian Science is largely due to the By-laws and government of "The First Church of Christ, Scientist" in Boston. None but myself can know, as I know, the importance of the combined sentiment of this Church remaining steadfast in supporting its present By-laws. Each of these many By-laws has met and mastered, or forestalled some contingency, some imminent peril, and will continue to do so. Its By-laws have preserved the sweet unity of this large church, that has perhaps the most members and combined influence of any other church in our country. Many times a single By-law has cost me long nights of prayer and struggle, but it has won the victory over some sin and saved the walls of Zion from being torn down by disloyal students. We have proven that "in unity there is strength."

With love as ever

MARY BAKER G. EDDY

N. B. I request that you put this letter upon our church records.

M. B. E.[62]

The *Manual* was issued during the first full year that her flock began to worship in the new building of The Mother Church. When Mrs. Eddy was no longer visible, the *Manual* was her representative. Through its By-Laws she still speaks in preservation unadulterated of her teaching, in the government through the Board of Directors of her Church, and in the regulation of its services. Over her own signature the six Tenets of The Mother Church appear as follows:

WORKS ON CHRISTIAN SCIENCE
BY
REV. MARY BAKER G. EDDY.

325

Address all inquiries to JOSEPH ARMSTRONG, C. S. D.,
95 FALMOUTH STREET, BOSTON, MASS

Pleasant View,
N. H.

Dictated.   Feb. 27, 1903

Christian Science Board of Directors.

Beloved Students:

I am not a lawyer, and do not suffic-
iently comprehend the legal trend of the copy you enclosed to me to suggest any
changes therein. Upon one point however I feel competent to advise namely: Never
change the By-laws nor the denominational government of the Mother Church. If I
am not personally with you, the Word of God, and my instructions in the By-laws
have led you hitherto and will remain to guide you safely on, and the teachings
of St. Paul are as useful to-day as when they were first written.

                    prosperity
The present and future of the cause of Christian Science is largely due
to the By-laws and government of "The First Church of Christ, Scientist" in Boston. None but myself can know, as I know, the importance of the combined senti-
            Church
ment of this remaining steadfast in supporting its present By-laws. Each of
these many By-laws has met and mastered, or forestalled some contingency, some
imminent peril, and will continue to do so. Its By-laws have preserved the sweet
unity of this large church, that has perhaps the most members and combined influence of any other church in our country. Many times a single By-law has cost me
long nights of prayer and struggle, but it has won the victory over some sin and

(over)

WORKS ON CHRISTIAN SCIENCE
BY
REV. MARY BAKER G. EDDY.

325

Address all inquiries to JOSEPH ARMSTRONG, C. S. D.,
95 FALMOUTH STREET, BOSTON, MASS

Pleasant View,
CONCORD, N. H.

(2)

saved the walls of Zion from being torn down by disloyal students. We have
proven that "in unity there is strength."

With love as ever

Mary Baker G. Eddy

*N. B. I request that you
print this letter upon
our Church records*

M.B.E.

*Entered on page 85 of Church Record
Book Vol. 3*

1. As adherents of Truth, we take the inspired Word of the Bible as our sufficient guide to eternal Life.

2. We acknowledge and adore one supreme and infinite God. We acknowledge His Son, one Christ; the Holy Ghost or divine Comforter; and man in God's image and likeness.

3. We acknowledge God's forgiveness of sin in the destruction of sin and the spiritual understanding that casts out evil as unreal. But the belief in sin is punished so long as the belief lasts.

4. We acknowledge Jesus' atonement as the evidence of divine, efficacious Love, unfolding man's unity with God through Christ Jesus the Way-shower; and we acknowledge that man is saved through Christ, through Truth, Life, and Love as demonstrated by the Galilean Prophet in healing the sick and overcoming sin and death.

5. We acknowledge that the crucifixion of Jesus and his resurrection served to uplift faith to understand eternal Life, even the allness of Soul, Spirit, and the nothingness of matter.

6. And we solemnly promise to watch, and pray for that Mind to be in us which was also in Christ Jesus; to do unto others as we would have them do unto us; and to be merciful, just, and pure.

MARY BAKER EDDY.[63]

Before ever big business or nations, in peace or war, had learned how to mold public opinion through the press, Mrs. Eddy provided in her *Manual* for a Committee on Publication, now found in every state and every land where Christian Science has organization, "to correct in a Christian manner impositions on the public in regard to Christian Science, injustices done Mrs. Eddy or members of this church by the daily press, by periodicals or circulated literature of any sort."[64]

As recently as last year [1929], the Board of Directors,

with the *Manual* before them, broadcast the announcement,[65] "We assert the right to defend and protect our religion and persons connected with it from public misrepre-
sentation;" and, as usual, they based their right on the specific words of Mrs. Eddy, "A lie left to itself is not so soon
destroyed as it is with the help of truth-telling." [66] But they
also counseled discretion, using their Leader's very language,
"Meekness and temperance are the jewels of love set in wisdom. Restrain untempered zeal." [67]

It was the multitudinous contacts with the public through
the press in carrying out her mothering program, which
made Mrs. Eddy a mystery woman to many outside her
fold and at last drew upon her the light of pitiless publicity. Democracy is impulsive. Democracy resents privacy.
Democracy wants to know it all. Regardless of the Declaration of Independence, which declares for all "Life, Liberty,
and the pursuit of Happiness" — by reason of which the
United States Constitution promised for all time to secure
to us the right to worship God in our own way — democracy worked itself up into an unseemly and even passionate
curiosity to learn what Mrs. Eddy really was like. To learn
by what means she had amassed a competence reported to
be large, and how she had built up a church which was
thrusting its searchlight, as the Marquis of Lothian has
lately said, "past what all the greatest teachers have recognized to be the transient and unsubstantial phenomena of
mortal existence into the eternal reality which is the kingdom of God." [68]

With the opening of the twentieth century, the big stick
was in full swing and the muckrake was plied busily, seeking the unsavory in public life. "Tainted" money became a
slogan with professional reformers, and upon many of them

Mr. Dooley's humorous suggestion that the final proof of
tainted money with some is " 'taint mine" was lost.

Any man with sufficient brains and purpose to lift his
head above the mass ran the risk of being listed with the
"scamps." Although there was much public indignation at
the inhuman treatment which French procedure meted out
to Dreyfus, a growing disposition was in evidence to substitute for the Anglo-Saxon habit of assuming innocence until
guilt was proved, the French habit of taking guilt for
granted and requiring the accused to prove his innocence.

Great things were already on record to Mrs. Eddy's
credit. Her book was long since built. Her church, too, was
built and was becoming news to the whole world. Men of
consequence, here and there, were observing that Christian
Scientists did seem to be bearing the fruits of the spirit.
Mark Twain dropped his jesting for a moment to predict
that "Christian Science is destined to make the most formi-
dable show that any new religion has made since the birth
and spread of Mohammedanism."

But Mrs. Eddy's withdrawal from publicity to the privacy
of Pleasant View, her success in so ordering her life as to
secure the freedom needed to carry on her work and the
quiet in which to hear the voice of God, tended to make
her practically unknown, not only to America at large, but
also to many of her followers whom she was constantly
urging to put Principle before personality, her teaching
before her visible self. Nor did the few pilgrimages, made at
her invitation to Pleasant View, alter the case, no matter
how much pleasure they brought the pilgrims. On the occasion in 1903, when ten thousand went by special trains to
Concord, Mrs. Eddy spoke to them from the balcony
outside her window. However, rumors continued to gain
credence that the head of the Christian Science Church,

overcome by physical infirmity, had "fall'n into the sere, the yellow leaf"; that she was at last in the power of a little selfish coterie who were managing her vast interests as they chose and concealing her not only from the public but even from her son, her adopted son, and her former intimates.

Big city newspapers were beginning to wonder whether, after all, Mrs. Eddy was still alive, whether she had not actually passed away, and whether a substitute, her face hidden behind a parasol, was not now in Mrs. Eddy's stead driving out every afternoon to deceive the world.

In May, 1905, departing from her custom, Mrs. Eddy granted an interview to a representative of the *Boston Herald,* whose write-up of the interview seemed so satisfying that Mrs. Eddy wrote the editor a message of appreciation. The next year, however, America gave an exhibition of that national inquisitiveness which Owen Wister[69] characterizes as "peculiarly disagreeable" and "a perfectly unwarrantable invasion of one's privacy."

With the opening of October, reporters of a New York daily came prepared to spend some time in Concord, commissioned by their paper to find out whether Mrs. Eddy was alive or not. A few weeks later, on Tuesday, October 30, 1906, representatives of the Associated Press, the Publishers Press, and all the larger daily papers of Boston and New York — numbering fifteen — arrived at Pleasant View to interview her again. The report read that, though not conspicuously strong, Mrs. Eddy was very much alive and evidently capable of attending to her work.

Individual journalists, also, of the type of Arthur Brisbane and William E. Curtis visited her soon after, and a critical reading today of their impressions gives them even a more convincing finality than when they were first published.

Arthur Brisbane almost naïvely said, "Nobody could see this beautiful and venerable woman and ever again speak of her except in terms of affectionate reverence and sympathy." [70] William E. Curtis, as skillful in his day in interviewing world celebrities as was Isaac Marcosson later, had just returned from China. Accompanied by Michael Meehan, a local Concord editor, he was received by Mrs. Eddy, to whom he explained in some detail the then recent Boxer Rebellion.

Mr. Meehan records:

In the course of preliminary remarks, he made a statement about affairs in China, touching which Mrs. Eddy asked for more detailed and definite information, and quite unconsciously, seemingly, she took the topic entirely out of his grasp, and for more than an hour, dwelt on the detail of the Chinese situation, with such wonderful insight and with such intimate knowledge of its social, political and economic conditions, as to quite confound the man.

When she had closed her quiet talk, she rose, and after answering briefly some conventional questions, the audience was ended.

As we were leaving the room, Mrs. Eddy halted us and said facetiously,

"I hear I am not the person who goes for a short drive each day. If you wish to remain outside for a few minutes, you will see me enter my carriage and drive away."

We did as directed. In a short while, Mrs. Eddy stepped through the doorway and into her carriage, smiling recognition at us as she passed.

As we drove from Pleasant View, Mr. Curtis marveled how a woman who so completely excluded the world could possibly know so much about the world's affairs, and particularly how she could have acquired such accurate and comprehensive acquaintance with the history and national habits of the Chinese, a people so little known, and with the court customs and the unpublished intrigues of its rulers. As we parted, he said, "Just one more surprise, one more instance of where we came to preach and remained to pray."[71]

Through 1907 and well into 1908, magazine articles which attracted much attention were exploiting her life story, based on such information as could then be unearthed and written with much journalistic skill. But at last the most incredulous were having to admit that Mrs. Eddy was at least alive.

However, a new flock of rumors was let loose — that she might as well be dead, that she had fallen into unfriendly hands, and was no longer altogether capable of caring for herself and her friends. With an adroit change of tactics the suggestion was put forward that it would be only kind, in the distressing circumstances, to invoke the law in Mrs. Eddy's best interest, to bring her legally into court that all the world might learn her real condition and join the law in saving her from her "household," and in turning her over to responsible guardians, described in law as "Next Friends." Although without large business experience the "Next Friends" seemed quite willing to assume responsibilities, vast and complex, for the management of the millions which they appeared to hope Mrs. Eddy possessed.

Her nearest heir was her son George, who was still in South Dakota, hoping prospector-like to strike pay-dirt in his paternity, and thus break into the ranks indicated in Madison Julius Cawein's line:

Some shall reap that never sow.

Without undue prodding, George's memory recalled a letter
Mrs. Eddy once wrote him in which, motherlike, she confided, "I am as lone as a solitary star." To his mining
enterprises he had added risky building projects; and,
because of them, he more easily remembered that her
replies to some of his requests for money with which to
experiment had not been precisely what he could have
wished. He was not the first son to attempt to cajole a
mother into being too indulgent for his good, nor the last
son to turn against a mother who denied him for his good.
George W. Glover required but little coaxing to become the
flying wedge in the "Next Friends" game, the success of
which would give him, he hoped, some opportunity to share
in the handling of his mother's fortune, including obviously
valuable copyrights.

Among the increasing number of requests which came to
Mrs. Eddy for financial aid, there were letters written by a
nephew, whom she could personally have known but little.
Only son of George Sullivan Baker and his wife, "Mathy,"
of whom Mrs. Eddy in her Tilton days had been fond,
George W. Baker, also, developed a grievance. His letter,
offering to sell some family heirloom to his aunt, had been
answered by a secretary at a time when the task of personally attending to her vast correspondence was out of the
question. A small-town mind possibly could not be expected
to understand how one could be so busy; nor was it surprising that George W. Baker was willing, at any inconven-
ience, to come down from Maine and do what he could, in
his small way, to save his rich aunt from those she knew
and trusted, but who were scarcely even names to him.

With an array of notable lawyers, led by ex–United States
Senator William E. Chandler, "The petition of Mary Baker

Glover Eddy who sues by her next friends George W.
Glover, Mary Baker Glover and George W. Baker *against*
Calvin A. Frye, Alfred Farlow, Irving C. Tomlinson, Ira O.
Knapp, William B. Johnson, Stephen A. Chase, Joseph
Armstrong, Edward A. Kimball, Hermann S. Hering, and
Lewis C. Strang" [72] was presented on March 1, 1907, to the
Superior Court at Concord, for the appointment of a
receiver for Mrs. Eddy's business interests.

The petition alleged that Mrs. Eddy was incompetent to
care for her property, and questioned the loyalty of the
"men and women near her." [73] The distinguished chief
counsel appeared to expect little difficulty in winning the
suit. To court he brought his considerable legal ability, wide
experience, and more than local prestige. Nevertheless, in
his very opening statement, in which he endeavored to draw
a distinction between medical and legal insanity, he fell
promptly into the old pitfall of trying to prove too much;
for if in following his line of argument he established the
insanity of Mrs. Eddy, he would inferentially establish the
insanity of countless thousands sharing her views. Since no
court, State or Federal, has ever yet regarded seriously any
effort to draw an indiscriminate indictment against any large
body of people in good standing, the Honorable Frank S.
Streeter, leader of the opposing counsel, had little difficulty
in persuading the court to dismiss that part of the case during the first day's session.

Next, an effort was made to bring into court by summons Mrs. Eddy in person possibly with the expectation
that her age might place her at a disadvantage. But this
scheme also failed, and the court took advantage of the
opportunity promptly to raise the level of the proceedings by
appointing three Masters to take her testimony — Dr.

George F. Jelly (the noted alienist), Judge Edgar Aldrich of the United States District Court, and Hosea W. Parker of Claremont. By appointment, on August 14, the Masters, with the senior counsel on each side, came to call on Mrs. Eddy in her study at Pleasant View.

A woman past eighty-six, her restless fingers indicating awareness of the object of their visit and perhaps of a situation unparalleled in American Court procedure, received with grace and dignity her odd visitors, the strangest, perhaps, who ever crossed her threshold. Throughout the proceedings, the Masters were considerate. Lifting his kindly face a bit, Judge Aldrich at the outset requested Mrs. Eddy to give notice if, at any moment, she began to feel fatigued. At her best, as usual, in a crisis, Mrs. Eddy answered, "I can work hours at my work, day and night, without the slightest fatigue when it is in the line of spiritual labor."[74]

The purpose of the visit was disclosed in the question — which needed no explanation — next courteously put by Judge Aldrich: "What would be a sound investment of money that comes from life insurance or anything else?" Her answer, and the succeeding questions and answers which it called forth, made it evident to all that Mrs. Eddy was qualified, out of court as well as in, to make sound investments, and even to give instruction to others in their handling. Questions and answers are therefore given in full as contained in a volume, withdrawn without general circulation, to which the author has had access:

Replied Mrs. Eddy:

> Well, I should invest it in the hands, at my age, of trustees that I could vouch for from my own knowledge. And why? Because, when I found my church was gaining over 40,000 members, and the field demanding me all over the

world, I could not carry on the letters, make answers to inquiries that were made of me. Then I said, "Which shall I do, carry on this business that belongs to property, or shall I serve God?" And I said — and it came to me from the Bible — "Choose ye this day whom ye will serve. Ye cannot serve God and Mammon." Then I chose, and I said, "So help me God," and I launched out, and I gave my property — I gave $913,000 to the trusteeship, to others for the benefit of my son — no, not for the benefit of my son, but — $913,000 into the trusteeship for myself. For my son I gave $125,000 into trusteeship for himself and for his family.

Q. (By Judge Aldrich.) Where did that idea of putting your property into the hands of trustees originate, with yourself or somebody else?

A. Utterly with myself. It came to me in an hour in this room, and I think the first one that I named it to was Laura Sargent, and I said to her, "Do not speak of it, but I feel impressed that it is my duty."

Q. When was that?

A. That was in February, 1907.

Q. Last winter, you mean?

A. I do.

Q. Now this is all interesting and useful, but still I have not quite made myself understood. For instance, without regard to your trusteeship now, if you had a hundred thousand dollars to invest today, and we will lay aside for the purposes of this question the matter of trusteeship, what kind of investments would you consider sound, municipal bonds, or government bonds, or bank stock, or what?

A. I prefer government bonds. I have invested largely in government bonds, and I prefer bonds to stocks. I have not entered into stocks.

Q. Why?

A. Because I did not think it was safe for me. I did not want the trouble of it, that was all. Perhaps I was mistaken, but that is my business sense of it, and the only time I took the advice of a student and went contrary, I lost ten thousand dollars by it.

Q. What was that?

A. That was an investment that was made in property in the West, where the land, they said, was coming up and going to be a great advancement in value, and I lost it, and I never got caught again. I always selected my own investments.

Q. How do you select them now?

A. Now?

Q. Yes.

A. I leave them to my trustees.

Q. Before that?

A. I will tell you. I have books that give definitely the population of the states, and their money values, and I consult those, and when I see they are large enough in population and valuation to warrant an investment I make it.

Q. Well, now, upon what philosophy do you base your calculations upon population? Why do you take population as the standard?

A. Because I think they can sustain their debts and pay them.

Q. Well, I should think that was pretty sound. Would you go West for municipal investments, or would you rather trust yourself in the East, in New England we will say?

A. I would rather trust my trustees now. I do not take those things into consideration.

Q. Dr. Jelly desires that I should ask you, laying aside for the present the matter of trusteeship, what would be your idea, whether there was greater security of investment in Eastern municipalities or Western?

Returning to Pleasant View. Mr. Frye on the box.

A. The East I should say.[75]

After this, by request, Mrs. Eddy began to tell the story of the rise and development, and to explain the teachings of Christian Science. But something had happened. The atmosphere had changed. Never altogether at their ease, during an hour over long for them, though Mrs. Eddy was, as usual, courteous and kindly, the visitors were ready to go home. Her answers to the questions put the "Next Friends' Suit" into a parlous state. As Senator Chandler and a friend hurried down the stairway to the front door, the Senator was overheard, half to himself, to say, "That woman is smarter than a steel trap."

Through an ordeal, which perhaps few women in their prime could undergo, Mrs. Eddy had borne herself with engaging simplicity and sincerity. As always, she had dressed specially for the occasion. "She wore," says Miss Still, "a black grenadine dress with white chiffon and lace vestee and collar, and white ruching in the neck and wrists."[76] As she was waiting for her visitors, she was serene, and even merry. Looking out toward Mount Monadnock, more visible than ever on that bright August day, Mrs. Eddy casually observed, "The 'Nexters' have fine weather for their trial." Miss Still, who was near her at the very moment Masters, attorneys and others came into the library, has lately told the author that "as one looked at her that hot afternoon there was no sign of fear expressed, but her face was calm, clear, and confident, and the moment that the opposing lawyer saw her sitting there in her study, he knew that he hadn't a ghost of a chance of winning his case."

But the experience hurt to the heart a noted woman,

whom Theodore Roosevelt[77] once compared with other religious leaders decidedly not to her discredit.

To one of her household she confided, "If I were a man they would not treat me so."[78] Never was her good sense more evident than when she said: "During forty years I have had many trials and when this came up I was not disturbed. If the world calls me a fool, that does not make me so."[79]

While the suit was still on Mrs. Hulin — she tells the author — once found Mrs. Eddy looking depressed, and heard her sadly say as if thinking aloud, "I don't know, perhaps they will have their way." Mrs. Hulin replied, "Mother, they will not. We love you. You will win." Then Mrs. Eddy brightened up, and was herself again. She was not a woman to take chances which she could avoid, or to fail to take precautions against further annoyances. Of one of her associates she inquired:

> If you let this case remain as it now is could the "next friends" take possession of my person? If they could not then is it not better to let this suit stand *as it is?* I fear if you press it they will get Judge . . . to decide it against me and give my person to my enemies (called "next friends") and they will take me away from my real friends, students, and thus *get rid* of me by such means, then fight over my last will.[80]

But not even this bitterest of all experiences that ever came into that many-sided life could distract her from her daily study and habitual revision of the book, from her habit of meditation and persistent praying, and also from her loving thought for others. In the midst of this strange invasion of her busy life, she gladdened one worker, just home from the field, by expressing the pleasure it gave her to learn of the proposed building of his little church. She added, "I like those small beginnings. First, the right thought, then right words, and words proved by the hands." [81]

Michael Meehan, the capable and cultivated editor of Concord, was, from the beginning, closely identified with the litigation of 1907. The participants on both sides, he personally knew. At the request, afterwards, both of Mrs. Eddy and of Boston friends, Mr. Meehan prepared a book for publication intended to preserve for all time the salient facts of a case which might one day become as famous in legal history as that other New Hampshire suit, the Dartmouth College case, which, some years ago, Alfred Russell stated had been cited more frequently in judicial decisions than any other case in American law reports.

Of *Mrs. Eddy and the Late Suit in Equity* — a costly book to publish — five thousand copies were that next spring off the press. The first copy was promptly sent to Mrs. Eddy. Till far into the night she sat up reading it. Next day she wrote its author that she wished the book withheld from sale and circulation. Perceiving and accepting the moral obligation involved, she added:

> You will render me a statement of all expenses to which you have been put. Make liberal allowance for those who have aided you in the work. Put a value upon your own time and service while engaged on it, and when you have done this, double the value you have placed on your own work, and double it again, and then send me the bill.[82]

Mr. Meehan says:

> I did this, and as soon as a complete bill was rendered, she wrote out a check in full of account, amounting to many thousands of dollars.

At the moment when most of us would have wanted to put before the public a permanent vindication from such unworthy charges as lay in the "Next Friends Suit," Mrs. Eddy was thinking of larger and less personal interests. Years before, in 1896, she had written Mr. William P. McKenzie, "Love unselfed, love of one's enemies, humility, moderation, strength, are the cardinals of Christian Science." Again she was practicing what she preached.

This book which today appears to at least one privileged reader to be in many respects a model of successful refutation Mrs. Eddy feared would "keep alive a memory of bitterness and discord, where obedience to God's law of harmony should be the aim of all." [83]

And so, under God, the "Next Friends' Suit" collapsed. And under God, Mrs. Eddy, nearing the advanced age of eighty-seven, moved on unhindered to her next world-vision task, the establishment of *The Christian Science Monitor.*

— 7 —

"The Full Grain in the Ear"

*O*N SUNDAY AFTERNOON, JANUARY 26, 1908, AS bright a day as ever May could bring, Mrs. Eddy with the ease and grace of a much younger woman, walked across the platform and stepped aboard the special train scheduled to leave Concord at two o'clock to take her to her new home in Chestnut Hill, Massachusetts.[1]

To help a woman, even the youngest, into a railway coach is the courtesy which gentlemen are expected instinctively to volunteer. But Mrs. Eddy was in the car before anyone could efficiently give aid. There was good reason, too, why she did not desire assistance, even though she was in her eighty-seventh year. However, the "faithful John"[2] was allowed to walk beside her across the platform from the train shed. But that was all.

In defiance of the facts, rumors of infirmity and abnormality had long persisted; and always mentally alert, always looking ahead, Mrs. Eddy was not the woman to confirm erroneous accounts of her condition. What the merely curious and irresponsible might say to injure her, mattered less to her than the possibly evil effect of some carelessly spoken word upon the Cause she loved. Her concern, in consequence, was to insure that if anything were reported to the hurt of Christian Science, it should have no true basis, slight as it might be; that untruths, however studiously circulated, should without delay be known for what they were — sheer fabrications.

Besides, never, perhaps, in all history did another woman appear to understand as clearly as Mrs. Eddy the unreality of error, the transitory nature of untruth. Never, could there have been a woman who looked forward more steadily than did Mrs. Eddy past the individual erroneousness of the present to the general truthfulness of the ultimate.

Seldom could death have been in Mrs. Eddy's thought. When, on August 14, 1907, the "Next Friends' Suit" precipitated upon Pleasant View a group of unwelcome visitors as ill at ease as they were glad at last to bring their curious visit to a close, one of them referred to life insurance, Mrs. Eddy promptly answered, "God insures my life." [3]

Less than the robust Gladstone, passing at eighty-eight, did Mrs. Eddy almost as old either favor herself or ask those near to make allowances for her. At Chestnut Hill, she took an hour's rest each afternoon, sometimes dozing off a bit. But she was not unlikely to awake at three the next morning, to jot down a new idea or even to write a confidential letter.[4] With her rapidly increasing work, while she followed the routine approved at Pleasant View, she was more engaged than ever. She wasted no time on the unnecessary. She gave no thought to curious contemplation of the future. Her faith was reaching and outreaching, till at last — in Dante's phrase — it "eternalized" her life. No one more triumphantly than the joyous sage of Chestnut Hill agreed with St. Paul, "Death is swallowed up in victory." [5]

If, earlier, anyone had intimated that as 1908 opened she would be saying farewell to Concord, she would have given a retort characteristic and unmistakable. Not all Concord citizens were Christian Scientists, but almost all held in high esteem — many in deep affection — the woman who had made the capital of New Hampshire more widely and lastingly known than ever Emerson, Thoreau, and the Alcotts had made the Concord of Massachusetts. She identified herself with Concord by little nameless deeds of kindness, timely gifts of shoes to scores of poor children, thoughtful gifts of flowers and fruits to neighbors and to strangers, and by a large generosity in promoting matters of great moment to the city, and by a liberal support of all worthy Concord enterprises.[6]

An evening or two after Mrs. Eddy said goodby to Concord, a group of men at the Wonalancet Club — as reported in the *Manchester Mirror* of February 3, 1908 — made an effort to determine what Mrs. Eddy's stay of almost twenty years among them had brought financially to Concord. The most conservative figures the evening produced ran as follows:

The Christian Science church, — Mrs. Eddy's gift	$ 225,000.00
Charitable donations	25,000.00
For good roads	25,000.00
Miscellaneous gifts and contributions	25,000.00
Pleasant View estate	40,000.00
Household expenditures	100,000.00
Income from special privileges granted to Concord manufacturers and business men . . .	40,000.00

Granite contracts for Christian Science churches
  obtained because of Mrs. Eddy's residence
  and through her influence 1,000,000.00
Other known expenditures 90,000.00

Total $1,570,000.00

The City Council was prompt to pass resolutions of
unfeigned regret at her departure, and Mrs. Eddy wrote in
appreciation:

> To the Honorable Mayor and City Council, Concord, N.H.
>
> GENTLEMEN: — I have not only the pleasure, but the
> honor of replying to the City Council of Concord, in joint
> convention assembled, and to Alderman Cressy, for the
> kindly resolutions passed by your honorable body, and for
> which I thank you deeply. Lest I should acknowledge more
> than I deserve of praise, I leave their courteous opinions to
> their good judgment.
>
> My early days hold rich recollections of associations with
> your churches and institutions, and memory has a distinct
> model in granite of the good folk in Concord, which, like
> the granite of their State, steadfast and enduring, has hinted
> this quality to other states and nations all over the world.
>
> My home influence, early education, and church experi-
> ence, have unquestionably ripened into the fruits of my
> present religious experience, and for this I prize them. May
> I honor this origin and deserve the continued friendship and
> esteem of the people in my native State.
>
> Sincerely yours,
MARY BAKER G. EDDY[7]

But the hour to go had struck. Larger plans, requiring
that she be nearer Boston, engaged her interest. She was
also ill at ease about those "Next Friends," who might, she
suspected, let their chagrin lead them to make more trouble for her.[8] Slow in getting into court, the suit was also

slow in reaching final settlement. In fact, the final settlement with her son was not effected until November 10,
1909. Though she filed no complaint, she — with others
— felt that a grave defect had been laid bare in the laws
of her native and much loved state, or it could not have
been so easy for designing men to persecute a citizen — a
woman, at that — to feed avarice, to make "news," or to
satisfy a merely morbid curiosity. Her years alone should
have sufficed to protect her.[9] Massachusetts might furnish
conditions more auspicious for her expanding usefulness.
She could hope to have more peace of mind. Whatever the
reason, the hour to go had struck.

The trip[10] from Concord to Chestnut Hill was almost
uneventful. Save her own party, none were at the station in
time to see her off. Comfortably settled in her stateroom,
Mrs. Eddy was an interested traveler, appearing at the journey's end as fresh and animated as when her train pulled
out of Concord.

Dr. Alpheus B. Morrill traveled with her; but as the
nearest kin at hand, rather than as her physician. Mr. Frye
and Mrs. Sargent were on duty. Mr. McLellan was with her
and also Mr. Tomlinson, who recalls her cheeriness along
the way. Mr. John C. Lathrop was, as usual, ready to render such secretarial assistance as might be needed.

Arriving at Chestnut Hill Station, one of Mrs. Eddy's car-
riages, sent on ahead from Pleasant View, was awaiting the
train. As others of her party entered the "hacks" ranged
along the station platform, Mrs. Eddy walked quietly to her
carriage and at once started to drive the last mile to the
new home.

As her carriage drove into the grounds, Mrs. Eddy
detected in front of the house a group of newspaper men,
notified by telephone from Concord after she had left, that

she was on the way. In the last "hack," John Salchow also observed them, jumped down, ran up to Mrs. Eddy's carriage as she was ready to step out. She said, "John, can you get me into the house?" He answered, "I surely can."

Then, before the newspaper men could guess his intentions, John gathered Mrs. Eddy up into his stout arms, pressed through the bystanders, and carried her straight into the house. Up the stairs he bore her, set her down in a comfortable chair, and then her joyous laugh rang[11] through the hall. The only explanation of the episode which the papers of the next day had to give was that, "A huge Swede grabbed Mrs. Eddy and ran off with her."

The new house at Chestnut Hill had some time before been unobtrusively bought for her by the trustees, and remodeled to meet the needs of Mrs. Eddy and her expanding household. Mrs. Eddy's own suite, at her request, would shortly be made as like as possible to her familiar rooms at Pleasant View. Mount Monadnock and her birthplace, Bow, were no longer within sight; but from her sunny study window Old Orchard Road lined with well-kept estates was visible, and the hazy outline of Blue Hills.

At Chestnut Hill, the Pleasant View ménage was continued. If possible, however, more care than ever, under the *Manual*,[12] was exercised in selecting those fitted to give Mrs. Eddy the special aid she required to keep up with the multiplying calls upon her time and strength. By this time, it had become a highly prized distinction to be called to spend three years in Mrs. Eddy's household. Those summoned, eagerly, gladly, humbly complied, although the material compensation was a mere trifle. However, Mrs. Eddy sometimes reminded the friends near her that "trifles make perfection, but perfection is no trifle." There was, too, the Scriptural uplift: "Every one that hath forsaken houses, or brethren, or sisters, or father, or mother, or wife, or children, or lands, for my name's sake, shall receive an hundredfold, and shall inherit everlasting life." [13]

Mrs. Eddy required of those nearest her a literal interpretation of the command of Jesus, "Watch and pray." [14] On May 29, 1930, one of them says:

> With the penetrating spiritual luminosity which shone through her as from out the heart of God's allness, Mrs. Eddy untiringly reiterated to her household, and to a benighted world, the Master's warning; — "Watch." The Godliness of her ever alert being exemplified her own Godly watch — and she loved her household as she loved herself by her indefatigable call to them that they have oil in their lamps, and watch to keep them trimmed and burning, — so that evil's serpentine machinations be foreseen to the forestalling of its workings through their sleepiness, their unwariness, or their insufficiently spiritual aliveness.[15]

When, now and then, Mrs. Eddy gathered her "experts" for an intimate talk, she made short shrift of sluggards. All were made to understand that their watching and their praying were to be taken as seriously as Mrs. Eddy took her own. She knew no God *emeritus;* and those with her were permitted to know none. To her, as she wrote in her textbook, "God is infinite, therefore ever present, and there is no other power nor presence," [16] and in the name of such a God — the Only God — she bade them "Watch and pray."

"You can't alter meteorological forces by words," observes Dr. Shailer Mathews, Dean of the Divinity School of the University of Chicago. "I'm almost sure of that — almost. . . . If I were in a storm at sea, so severe it seemed we should sink, I'm pretty sure I'd pray. . . . If only to get peace, courage, inner unity." [17]

Mrs. Eddy set no limits to prayer. She prayed as Jesus bade us pray, with the same understanding assurance, which Jesus had, that with God all things are possible. She even sought through prayer, intelligently offered, to bring about more harmonious weather conditions. Hers was a deep confidence in the efficacy of prayer, God willing, to control the weather. Perhaps it is worth noting that prayers of the same type are still found in the Protestant Episcopal Prayer Book, twenty years after Mrs. Eddy has passed on.[18]

The faithful Mrs. Laura Sargent specially "attended to the weather." But Mrs. Eddy would have her entire household understand what "attending to the weather" involved. No nonsense would she tolerate with regard to praying. One day she called several of them into her sitting room, made them stand up before her like schoolchildren, and, going down the line she asked, pointing her finger at each in turn:[19] "Can a Christian Scientist control the weather?" Each answered, "Yes, Mother." Sharply, even scornfully, she said to each and all, "They can't and they don't. They can't, but God can and does. . . . A Christian Scientist has no business attempting to control or govern the weather any more than he has a right to attempt to control or govern sickness, but he does know, and must know, that God governs the weather and no other influence can be brought to bear upon it." Every Christian Scientist must pray in faith, and leave the rest to God.

Years never staled her sense of humor. Even her sharpest admonition was likely to be softened by a loving smile. A playful twitching of the lips would reveal "the funny side" of a situation, which sometimes suggested a schoolboy frightened in the presence of his teacher. Under severe correction, her students one day were promising that next time they would do better when, with a ripple of mirth, Mrs. Eddy said:

> I am afraid you are like the Irishman that used to work on my father's farm. He was so useless about the place that my father finally called him and said, "Mike, I shall have to let you go. You're not earning what I am paying you and it is not right for me to keep you under the circumstances." Rather than be discharged, the Irishman pleaded to be kept in my father's employ. He said, "If you'll only keep me, sir, I will work for my week's board." "But," replied Mr. Baker, "you don't earn your board in a week." "Well, sir," he said, "if I can't earn it in one week, I'll do it in two." That is what your promises sound like to me. You are not doing your work as you should, and you protest that if you haven't done it heretofore, you will hereafter.

Upon another occasion, seeking to illustrate the tendency of mortal mind to misrepresent, Mrs. Eddy spoke of a neighbor in New Hampshire who wanted to sell her father a horse. He represented the horse as perfectly sound, gentle in disposition, and having all the qualities of a family carriage horse.

> My father said, "I am afraid he is too skittish for me. My family needs a quiet animal that would not be frightened at anything." "Oh," replied the neighbor, "Mr. Baker, you couldn't scare this horse, no matter what you did." My father replied, "Why, that horse would jump if you were to say 'boo' at him." The man stoutly denied this and offered to put the case to a test. The arrangement was that while Mr. Baker crouched behind a large stump in the field, the owner was to ride the horse by the stump, and Mr. Baker

was to jump out, and shout "boo." All was ready. The horse loped past the stump. Mr. Baker jumped out, threw his arms up in the air and yelled a vigorous "boo." The horse made a sudden lunge, threw his rider, and dashed across the country. The Irishman got up, brushed the dirt from his clothes and said, "Well, Mr. Baker, that was too big a 'boo' for such a small horse."

Never was Mrs. Eddy more human than in the ordinary give and take of social contact. She affected nothing. She abhorred all stiltedness in conversation, all pretentiousness in bearing. She put everyone at ease, and knew how to bring out the best in those around her. With her lovely voice often, in those later years, she joined her household in singing such old favorite songs as "Auld Lang Syne," "Comin' Through the Rye," "Annie Laurie," and "The Old Oaken Bucket"; such familiar hymns as "Nearer, my God, to Thee," "Guide me, Oh Thou Great Jehovah," "Jesus, Lover of My Soul," and "I Love to Tell the Story." [20]

While she was still at Pleasant View Mr. John C. Lathrop[21] and his mother gave her that music box which she carried with her to Chestnut Hill, and often played. It was during the first winter there that the new Victrola came. The superior music, which it furnished, delighted Mrs. Eddy. Her joy was like a child's; it bubbled over. For a time she played her Victrola every day; and, when the new record — "Home, Sweet Home" — came, she had her household accompany the Victrola in singing it for her. As the last strain died away, playfully she addressed the Victrola, as though it were a human being, "Thank you, Mr. Singer Man, but I prefer my own choir to the choir invisible." Then turning serious, she meditated aloud to those present:

Home is not a place. It is a power. Going home is doing
right. If you cannot make home here, you cannot anywhere.
I am glad all of you, so many, are going with me. . . .
Blessing immortal, eternal, infinite, comes not through personality, but through understanding of Principle.[22]

Those were the days when in cities and at remote cross-
roads the big news was the discovery of the North Pole.
With his right to the discovery at last confirmed, Admiral
Peary was in demand by publishers and lecture bureaus.
One description, which he gave of his experiences in the far
North, was turned into a record. After listening, all intent
to it, Mrs. Eddy, in her inimitable way, quietly observed,
"Why, it is matter talking." [23]

William E. Curtis was not the only globe trotter to find
Mrs. Eddy, whose travels ordinarily extended no farther
than her library, unexpectedly well-informed about countries
distant as well as places near. Other guests at Chestnut Hill
departed full of the wonder which Mr. Curtis felt after contact with a stay-at-home mind as accurate as it proved well-
furnished. Lady Mildred Fitzgerald of England relates in
March, 1930, that on her several visits to Mrs. Eddy she
had been specially impressed with Mrs. Eddy's "grasp of
world affairs" and with her untiring efforts to bring England and America together by closer bonds. But those with
her every day had the most substantial reasons for respect-
ing her world-mindedness. When after a time at Chestnut
Hill, John Milton's birthday came on December 9, she
made Milton's line "They also serve who only stand and
wait," the subject of an extemporaneous talk on "Timeliness," which one today recalls for its vividness and impressiveness, closing, as it did, with the unforgettable sentence,

"The right thing done at the wrong time is no longer the right thing." [24]

The author, in the course of his researches, has met many of her Chestnut Hill entourage. All have added to the totality of the steadily accumulating impressions of Mrs. Eddy's genius for attaching the rightly disposed to her by her unfeigned interest in human beings.

One of them says, "I loved to hear her laugh, — a wonderful laugh when she had time to laugh." [25] He also recalls the physical agility of this extraordinary woman long after she could be called young. She loved sometimes even to slip nimbly up into her desk chair, curl her feet under her in tailor fashion like a college girl today, and go merrily to her work. He remembers her intimate familiarity with the details of the life around her, an insight into everyday existence which grew more penetrating with the passing years. "When she looked me in the eye," one says, "she seemed to look clear through me." [26] One of the faithful seemed one day a bit depressed, and he still carries in his heart the little note she wrote him after he had left her house:

Dear Student
   You looked sad to-day. Is anything not right that troubles you? If so what is it? I thought it might be something about Maggie's stay here. Perhaps I can help you.
                                        With love   Mother.[27]

Another tells how she scared him almost out of his wits when, in reply to her inquiry whether he was doing his work, he answered, "I am trying to do it"; and she came back at him with this quietus for his irresoluteness: "Let me see you do it now." Off he hurried to his room to attack more vigorously the work to which he had been assigned. Within the hour, he was summoned to her study, and was received with smiles and tenderness and praise. She knew, before he spoke a word, that he had pulled himself together and actually done his work.[28]

And how she missed her loved ones when any of them had to be away! Sometimes she felt the separation so poignantly that she could scarcely bear it. With her, all through her pilgrim journey, to say farewell was a great grief. Eyes would, indeed, be dry that could not shed a tear when told how their beloved Leader, finding one of her helpers would have for a time to be away, would hide her face in her hands, unable to say goodby. On one of these occasions Mrs. Eddy called the faithful round her and tenderly remarked, "We are all one family, and when my parents would go away we children used to get together and say to each other, 'Now you will be good to me while they are gone, won't you?' So we must all be good to each other while one of us is away." [29]

Her love for those who gave her help embraced all dear to them. It extended even to the pets — the cats and dogs of students. A little note, written shortly before to one of her faithful helpers, reads:

My Darling Son:
   Pull up the strawberries — they are not in the proper place. Give my love to Pauline and greetings to *kitty*.
                                                             Mother.[30]

Today "Sam" Shoemaker[31] is contributing much to the development of genuine personal religion. Perhaps no feature of his technique is more significant than the emphasis he places on self-disclosures in associating with those who

The Chestnut Hill Residence

are hungry for the riches of the inner life. Jesus loved to
talk his heart out to his comrades by the way. He wanted
them to realize that he, like them, was human, and had to
solve the same problems which came to them. No open-
minded reader of Mrs. Eddy's writings can misunderstand
either the general drift of her teaching or such forthright
and downright words as these: "To think or speak of me in
any manner as a Christ, is sacrilegious." [32] Already in 1901
she was counseling her people: "Follow your Leader, only
so far as she follows Christ." [33]

Feeling the responsibility to safeguard herself against
excesses of adulation, or any other disposition to set her
apart from her fellow human beings, she was ever on the
alert. Many-sided and ample as was her personality, there
was no room in it for spiritual conceit. St. Paul had no
exclusive copyright to the thought, decidedly hers as well as
his:

> Brethren, I count not myself to have apprehended: but
> this one thing I do, forgetting those things which are
> behind, and reaching forth unto those things which are
> before, I press toward the mark for the prize of the high
> calling of God in Christ Jesus.[34]

But her humility found its choicest expression in the outpouring of her heart to those who knew her best: "Oh
what a reward for the 'cup' it is to know that God has
made me, me, so poor, so nothing in my sight the means
of telling His power and grace and glory!" [35]

Christmas Day dawned clear and cold in 1909 in the
gray stone house on the hill. Always up by seven in the
morning, the Leader that day entered her study earlier than
usual. As, responding to her call, the happy household came

with a smile into the room, she greeted them with, "A cheery, Holy Christ Mass to you all."

Never in the years that followed could they recall a day when she seemed more alive mentally, more vigorous physically, more gracious in manner, or more tender in word. None needed to be told, although all were keen to hear:

I love to observe Christmas in quietude, humility, benevolence, charity, letting good will towards man, eloquent silence, prayer, and praise express my conception of Truth's appearing.

The splendor of this nativity of Christ reveals infinite meanings and gives manifold blessings. Material gifts and pastimes tend to obliterate the spiritual idea in consciousness, leaving one alone and without His glory.[36]

To turn Christmas Day into a riot of extravagant giving never made any appeal to Mrs. Eddy. She would keep the holy season true to its profounder meaning, and members of her household still recall the impressiveness with which, on that last Christmas Day, she said, "A holy, uplifting sense of Life, Truth, and Love is the true Christmas."

Though none foresaw that it was to be her last Christmas Day with them, her next word sounded grave: "By another Christmas there will be great changes. See that you make them for the better."

Before noon, again the faithful were called round her, and Mrs. Sargent read to them what the beloved Leader had just written on a sheet of letter paper lying on her desk:

My *Household*
Beloved:
A word to the wise is sufficient. Mother wishes you all a
happy Christmas, a feast of Soul, and a famine of sense.
Lovingly thine
MARY BAKER EDDY.

To this woman of the spirit, Easter brought a happier
opportunity than Christmas Day to speak her supreme message. The Easter couplet was of her own writing:

Joy — not of time, nor yet by nature sown,
But the celestial seed dropped from Love's throne.[37]

Her lifelong love of flowers reappears in her proclamation
to the children of her faith to gather "Easter lilies of love
with happy hearts and ripening goodness." Though she discouraged careless giving, she always took into account the
motive. One of the friendliest of her Easter messages was
written to Mr. Edward A. Merritt, who later became a
member of the Board of Directors of The Mother Church:

Your Easter memory expressed by this most *beautiful* and
unique design is prized by me quite beyond words to
express. Accept my heart's thanks for this priceless pin.
I will wear it in memory of you at the throat of my best
gown.[38]

To Mrs. Eddy, Easter had one overwhelming meaning,
and one only: "Mortality's thick gloom is pierced. The stone
is rolled away. Death has lost its sting, and the grave its
victory. Immortal courage fills the human breast and lights
the living way of Life." [39]

One of the faithful reports the substance of the little Easter sermon she preached to her household. The text has
slipped from memory, but the context would indicate it was
from Ephesians 4:22–24:

My. Household

Box G. Brookline, Mass Dec 25,
1909.

*Beloved; A curse
to the crise is soft
friend. Mother
wishes you all
a happy Christmas,
a feast of Soul,
and a Famine
of sense.
Lovingly thine
Mary Baker Eddy.*

That ye put off concerning the former conversation the old man, which is corrupt according to the deceitful lusts; And be renewed in the spirit of your mind; And that ye put on the new man, which after God is created in righteousness and true holiness.

As this member of her household noted at the time, Mrs. Eddy first gave the true meaning of Easter. Next she spoke of putting off, not keeping, "the old man." Then she said in substance:

We have but one Mind; and to abide in this perfect freedom of individuality is the resurrection, — is to have risen above material or lower demands. The resurrective sense is positive; it is "yea, yea and nay, nay." The resurrective sense does not listen compromisingly to error. It is *always* about its "Father's business," — reflecting Principle. Jesus' whole life was resurrective; that is, his life was a constant conscious rising spiritually above sin, sickness, death; and his resurrection from the grave was to sense a type of divine Love's final triumph over the human belief that matter is substance, or has power to impose limitations to Mind or man.[40]

Like the *Manual, The Christian Science Monitor* was a product of the Leader's mothering instinct. She would have the minds of those she loved immune every day, as well as every week and every month, to the evil influence which she believed newspapers exerted. Long had this peril been in her thoughts. When as early as 1883, she was establishing *The Christian Science Journal,* she wrote:

Looking over the newspapers of the day, one naturally reflects that it is dangerous to live, so loaded with disease seems the very air. These descriptions carry fears to many minds, to be depicted in some future time upon the body. A periodical of our own will counteract to some extent this public nuisance; for through our paper, at the price at which we shall issue it, we shall be able to reach many homes with healing, purifying thought.[41]

All through that first spring at Chestnut Hill, she was preparing to launch her daily paper. In July, she took the Board of Directors into her confidence. Businesslike as ever, she held back, however, until the last of the indebtedness on the Publishing House was cleared. But the very next month, on August 8, 1908, she wrote the Board of Trustees:

> It is my request that you start a daily newspaper at once, and call it the[42] *Christian Science Monitor.* Let there be no delay. The cause demands that it be issued now.
>
> You may consult with the Board of Directors, I have notified them of my intention.[43]

The reply of the Trustees, dated August 11, is one of the most important letters in the Archives. It runs:

> Beloved Leader:
>
> Your letter of August 8th was delivered to us yesterday. The announcement contained in your letter is good news. We are confident that this move is timely; that the Monitor will be a mighty instrument for the promotion of Christian Science; and that it will be a success from a business standpoint. We rejoice to have this additional opportunity of assisting you in your plans for the welfare of humanity.
>
> As soon as we received your letter we immediately began the work of starting the new Daily and we shall proceed with it without delay. To-day we consulted with the Board of Directors. To-morrow and next day we will confer with two practical newspaper men from Pittsburgh and Chicago whom Mr. McLellan has called here as advisers.

> Gratefully and lovingly yours,
> Wm. P. McKenzie
> Thomas W. Hatten
> Clifford P. Smith
> Trustees of the Christian
> Science Publishing Society.

The mere intimation that Mrs. Eddy was starting a news-paper at once brought in almost four hundred thousand dollars, which was enough to construct on land already in Church hands the addition to the Publishing House that was necessary. While the construction was still in progress and Boston reporters were working overtime to find out what actually was happening, the new presses were placed; and, on October 17, 1908, an editorial in the *Sentinel* announced that:

> With the approval of our Leader, Mrs. Eddy, The Christian Science Publishing Society will shortly issue a daily newspaper to be known as *The Christian Science Monitor*. In making this announcement we can say for the Trustees of the Society that they confidently hope and expect to make the *Monitor* a worthy addition to the list of publications issued by the Society. It is their intention to publish a strictly up-to-date newspaper, in which all the news of the day that should be printed will find a place, and whose service will not be restricted to any one locality or section, but will cover the daily activities of the entire world.
>
> It will be the mission of the *Monitor* to publish the real news of the world in a clean, wholesome manner, devoid of the sensational methods employed by so many newspapers. There will be no exploitation or illustration of vice and crime, but the aim of the editors will be to issue a paper which will be welcomed in every home where purity and refinement are cherished ideals.

For this new publication, Mrs. Eddy took the full initial responsibility. No one wished to snatch it from her, few to share it with her. No one envied her such brave initiative. There was no precedent to guide her. For her novel task, she had no special training. In her eighty-seven busy years there had been no spare time to learn to run a daily paper. No religious organization whatever had before that made a success of a daily paper. Most of the weekly denominational journals were then — and many still are — run at a deficit when they are not actual failures.

Some loyal Scientists, not the Trustees of the Publishing Society, hoped that the two words "Christian Science" would not be in the title of the new paper. Why add to the obvious difficulties? When before its first appearance she named the paper *The Christian Science Monitor* and even stressed the *The,* some had misgivings which proved too strong to conceal. She was earnestly solicited, at the very last, to recall her decision. When the first copy of the *Monitor* came off the press, it was taken out to Chestnut Hill for Mrs. Eddy to approve. With trepidation, Mr. Archibald McLellan,[44] who had definite convictions about the matter, went into the Leader's study to make one last appeal for the abbreviated title. Almost as soon as he disappeared, he reappeared, disappointment and dejection in his habitually cheerful face. "It is no use," he said, "the name will have to remain *The Christian Science Monitor.*"

In spite of the counsel of some friends, and the expectations of some enemies, she gave her paper the name it bears today, directed that the cover should be "illustrated with a pretty design," and placed on the editorial page the motto: "First the blade, then the ear, then the full corn in the ear." [45] Even the first style type font, best of its day for newspaper use, was of her selection. Later, at the request of the Board of Trustees, she expressed in print the desire that Christian Scientists should subscribe to the new paper. Every wish of Mrs. Eddy was, and is, a command to loyal Christian Scientists. In every detail, her interest was constructive and constant. One of the first editors a few years later wrote:

> No wonder Mrs. Eddy was an ever-inspiring Leader to work for, and no wonder there grew up around her a body of devoted assistants. No matter how hard they might work, she worked harder still; and for months and years, while they were receiving her constant and incisive instructions, they read with mingled amusement and amazement the stories of her mental incapacity and the failure of the movement which then, very much as now, constituted in the Press the news of Christian Science.[46]

The Christian Science Monitor made its bow on November 25, 1908, the day before Thanksgiving. The editorial leader was from Mrs. Eddy's pen. It struck the keynote of a policy unchanged in all the years: "The object of the *Monitor* is to injure no man, but to bless all mankind."

From that first issue, the author has made it his business to record impressions and collect opinions about the *Monitor,* in newspaper offices on either side of the ocean. He recalls his talks, during World War I, with editors of daily papers in London, Paris, New York, Chicago, Kansas City, Denver, San Francisco, Los Angeles, and other cities of the new world and the old, and the frequent tributes which he heard paid by eminent newspaper men to the *Monitor.* Of a certain substantial college in New England, a representative has observed that it is the second choice of more graduates of other colleges than any other institution in the land. It might be first choice were some starting new. No higher praise could be desired. Among newspapers, the *Monitor* would seem to occupy somewhat the same position as that college. Every editor is loyal first to his own paper. Practically all the many with whom the author has discussed the *Monitor* speak next for it. Last May the *Monitor* was singled out by Batten, Barton, Durstine, and Osborne for first place as a national advertising medium, with no other daily paper even a close second.

There is, perhaps, no field in which success is achieved with greater difficulty than in journalism. Certainly no service which the Christian churches could render is potentially superior to the establishment and the maintenance of high-grade newspapers, standing for the best things in public life. But the author is here but faintly echoing professional opinion of more importance than his own. An editorial in German in *The Christian Apologist* of December 25, 1929, published by A. J. Bucher, Methodist editor at Cincinnati, pays this impressive tribute to the *Monitor:*

> Regardless of what one may think of the health society which terms itself The Church of Christ, Scientist, we must at least concede them one thing, and that is they have brought forth what all the Christian churches in the United States combined have thus far failed to produce, namely, the publication of a daily newspaper edited in a thoroughly Christian spirit. Their *Christian Science Monitor* stands high above our American daily papers, both as to contents and form. It carries good and dependable information concerning the most important incidents of the day, both domestic and foreign. Each issue contains an excellent and dignified leading editorial on some question or topic which stands in the foreground of public interest. Christian Science doctrine is held entirely in the background. Shouting headlines, found

on the front pages of our daily papers, are entirely missing, as are also the sensational and the professional newspaper fiction. Each good reform movement is observed and is vigorously supported. The paper takes its place resolutely on the side of law and order, as for example, on the prohibition question. A good clean atmosphere pervades its sections of light literature. It serves the most varied needs and interests of an intelligent group of readers. With its handsome proportions, excellent paper and print, the *Monitor* presents a distinguished appearance.

If all those in the American Federation of Churches would lend a hand, there is no doubt but that we could publish a Christian daily newspaper — and that, too, with a large measure of success — which is one of the most crying needs of the present time. This would be a newspaper which would not consciously and deliberately lie, but would give out the truth, which would not serve sensation but information, which would not be in the pay of alcohol interests nor stand in political cross currents, and which would keep from its pages the immorality through which we must wade in the average daily paper. It would be a newspaper that we would not be afraid to have our children read. Here would be an opportunity to put on record the fact, which we stress so zealously, that we Protestants, with all our differences in minor points, are nevertheless one in essentials. It is high time that we had such a newspaper in America. When will it appear?[47]

Not even those days, crowded with details necessitated by the launching of the *Monitor,* were free from the characteristic annoyances which seemed ever at the heels of this woman of expanding interests. With opera glasses, the caretakers in the next house were spying much on her. In addition, a young girl would stand near the gate to stare at

Mrs. Eddy as she started for her drive.[48] To reprove outsiders was not Mrs. Eddy's habit. She reserved reproof as a compliment to those for whom she felt immediate responsibility.[49] But love, unclouded by resentment, almost always proved effective in her dealing with strangers. At last, when the intrusion had degenerated into rudeness, Mrs. Eddy sent her driver to the girl with an overflowing basket of delicious peaches and her card on which she wrote a brief word of kindly interest. Curiosity turned at once into respect, and the young woman is reported to have come to like Mrs. Eddy.

Never was any Christian Scientist more assiduous in the daily study of the Bible Lessons than was the Founder of the faith. Each of the many thousands devoted to the Cause has his own hour, or hours, for studying the Bible and his textbook. Business men and women are often up at five o'clock to devote two hours before breakfast to the study of their Bible Lessons. Some busy homekeepers take an hour in the morning or the afternoon for the same purpose. A few sit up late at night to do their work. Whatever hour they choose, they study their Bible Lessons every day. This is a spiritual phenomenon to which Christians everywhere may well give increasing heed, and by which there may be, as years go by, profit beyond all estimating to the Church of Christ.

Mrs. Eddy's reliance on the Bible was absolute. The well-thumbed and much-marked copy which she used at Chestnut Hill, the author has had the privilege of using in the preparation of this chapter. Out of the Old Testament, she drank deep of spiritual truth. Not morbid and yet not unmindful of the claims which advancing years were making, the author finds her one day in 1909 meditating on Isaiah 46:4: "And even to your old age I am he; and even to hoar hairs will I carry you: I have made, and I will bear; even I will carry, and will deliver you."

But her favorite in those days was Philippians 4:8–13:

> Finally, brethren, whatsoever things are true, whatsoever things are honest, whatsoever things are just, whatsoever things are pure, whatsoever things are lovely, whatsoever things are of good report; if there be any virtue, and if there be any praise, think on these things.
>
> Those things, which ye have both learned, and received, and heard, and seen in me, do: and the God of peace shall be with you.
>
> But I rejoiced in the Lord greatly, that now at the last your care of me hath flourished again; wherein ye were also careful, but ye lacked opportunity.
>
> Not that I speak in respect of want: for I have learned, in whatsoever state I am, therewith to be content.
>
> I know both how to be abased, and I know how to abound: every where and in all things I am instructed, both to be full and to be hungry, both to abound and to suffer need.
>
> I can do all things through Christ which strengtheneth me.

He would indeed be unresponsive who failed to feel the uplift which this woman of large faith received as she gave to the Scriptures such interpretations as the following words which I find marked, in 1909, from the last copy of *Science and Health* which she used:

1. God is All-in-all.
2. God is good. Good is Mind.
3. God, Spirit, being all, nothing is matter.
4. Life, God, omnipotent good, deny death, evil, sin, disease. — Disease, sin, evil, death, deny good, omnipotent God, Life.[50]

Even in the gathering twilight no joy was so great to Mrs. Eddy as studying her Bible Lessons. There were times, indeed, when, with all her heart and soul, she wished she could be a member of the Lesson Committee; and thus have a larger share in the spiritual education of the people of her heart, rather than in "settling impending difficulties, the effects of mortal sin." [51]

Until the very last, she was editing and re-editing her book. In each new edition she made minor changes, and occasional larger alterations, as she was convinced the Spirit led her more deeply into the truth. Her command of words grew. No changes except those authorized by Mrs. Eddy have been made in the book since Mrs. Eddy passed on. But her own copy employs a vocabulary of ten thousand vital words, which has been assayed thus:

> Every word means something. Not one is thrown in as a make-weight or as a padding. The weight and fluency of her style inheres in her thinking. There are no extra words to veil thought or to cover vacancy. She has achieved the great thing; her thinking stands forth in its naked sincerity as if she had done away with the medium of speech and had brought forth the Word itself which is one with thought and deed.[52]

At Chestnut Hill, while Mrs. Eddy had secretarial help, yet with her own pen she still wrote many a letter. Ruthless in planning the hours for those around her, Mrs. Eddy was yet more ruthless in planning her own program so as to insure an extra minute here and there for the work which, in no circumstances, could she bear to neglect. This quaint note in Mrs. Eddy's own handwriting speaks for itself: "Maid one half hour to dine at noon. Mrs. Eddy has twenty minutes." [53] She knew the secret of finding time for everything important, and once observed, "just a little duty performed each hour and each day, and at length a symmetrical unity." [54]

Some of her letters bear marks of the pressure under which they were written. But not one is recalled which is marred by indiscretions or retaliations. What John Hay[55] in his advancing years admitted, there was no need for Mrs. Eddy farther on in years to admit: "Every day I still write notes filled with indiscretions, and I can't help it." Mrs. Eddy could, and did help it.

Motherly in conversation with those around her, she was as much so in correspondence:

> Your sweet letter at hand. I am *sensible* of the zeal and good works of dear Mrs. . . . and you. But none can know *my necessity* to *reprove,* rebuke, exhort, but the loving Father and Mother of us all. You all are babes in Truth and Love and the older you are the more the Mother sees to *love,* and to *reprove.* Why? because you *attempt* more, and each endeavor is an experiment with a student; whereas it is an old and proven effort with me and I know just how it will come out. The danger to the student is popularity and power, selfseeking instead of self abasement I have washed their feet and continue to do thus, and they must wash one anothers feet instead of elbowing each other, or they never can follow the example of our Exemplar.[56]

How considerate she was! To the Board she wrote:

Mr. F.... is carrying too big a burden. His salary does not pay his rent and clerks! Please vote to amend the By-law to read instead of three thousand dollars annually for the Pub. Com. not less than three thousand dollars. Then vote to increase his salary to five thousand dollars annually.[57]

To sacrifice herself was an instinct:

After forty years in your service I need more of my time to watch individually. I have neglected myself for others; now help your Leader by helping yourself. This is all I ask of a student; and is it too much, and will you not grant my request?[58]

Mrs. Eddy was not arrogant or pretentious. When in 1907 she began to look about for another home, she wrote:

I give up the thought of the estate in ... for several reasons, one of which is I dislike *arrogant* wealth, a great show of it, and especially for one who *works* as well as preaches for and of the nothingness of matter.[59]

In business matters she was always strictly honest. To a student she said:

In doing business I am careful to account for all I take or appropriate, and I require this of my students. I may give them all I please, and they have that privilege with me, but I *demand honesty* of myself and of others — and strict accounts.[60]

Mrs. Eddy came even closer than that disciple who inquired if it was his business to forgive as much as seven times, to an understanding of the inexhaustibleness of the

Christ spirit of forgiveness. To one long dear to her, and then for a time estranged, at last Mrs. Eddy wrote:

> This lovely morning I wish I could see you and put my arms round your neck and tell you how much I love you. I never can feel so happy as when thinking of you in the old way and asking God to bless my child that so many years I have been accustomed to do, and must continue to do as long as memory lasts.
>
> I have forgiven you in years past, and can and do again, because I love you and I cannot hold any enmity against one who has done the good that you have done; or even if they had done much that was wrong I must love all, because I cannot help it. I *feel* it and cannot feel otherwise.[61]

She did at times grow weary. Once she wrote:

> Give oh give me peace — for one 24 hours in 30 years! You dear one, are fresh in the conflict I an old soldier weary of battle.[62]

But on she pressed until the very end, deserving Chesterton's inspiring lines:

> So, with the wan waste grasses on my spear,
> I ride forever, seeking after God;
> My hair grows whiter than my thistle plume,
> And all my limbs are loose, but in my eyes
> The star of an unconquerable praise;
> For in my soul one hope forever sings,
> That at the next white corner of a road
> My eyes may look on Him!

Her foreign correspondence brought Mrs. Eddy special joy. When The Mother Church Extension was dedicated three years before, in June, 1906, delegates had come from

Mrs. Eddy's study, Chestnut Hill

This room resembles in some detail the study she occupied for sixteen years at Pleasant View.

many countries, their very presence testifying that at last
Christian Science had put a girdle around the globe. Even
so, an eminent London surgeon was then predicting that in
another quarter century, the edifices of Christian Science in
London would be turned into music and lecture halls. But
he was one of many in that time who needed to meditate
upon the wisdom of the humble humorist who said, "Never
predict unless you know"; for in June, 1909, news came
that the First Church of Christ, Scientist, in London had
not only paid for, but also dedicated, on June 13, 1909, a
new building at a cost of four hundred thousand dollars. In
addition, it had sent a thank-offering of some seven thousand dollars to the Publishing House.

Scarcely had Mrs. Eddy's joyous letter of congratulation
gone overseas to her London followers when, in November,
Christian Scientists of Scotland announced that they were
ready to begin the building of the First Church of Christ,
Scientist, in Edinburgh. To them she wrote a letter ringing
with the peculiar satisfaction which such news as they had
sent her must have brought to one whose ancestors had
been Scotch:[63]

> Beloved Christian Scientists:
>
> Like the gentle dew of heaven and the refreshing breeze
> of morn, comes your dear letter to my waiting heart —
> waiting in due expectation of just such blessedness, crown-
> ing the hope and hour of divine Science, than which noth-
> ing can exceed its ministrations of God to man.
>
> I congratulate you on the prospect of erecting a church
> building, wherein to gather in praise and prayer for the
> whole human family.
>
> Lovingly yours,
> MARY BAKER EDDY.[64]

As she drew near her earthly end, the woman of the stars seemed to be living in two worlds at once. Day by day she drew closer to God. At times she seemed to think aloud to Him. She advised her maid to speak to God about her own personal problems.[65] To one of her secretaries she casually observed, "I'll tell you what God has told me today." Once, after making a remark which she wished at once to recall, she placed her finger to her lips and said, "That was Mary talking, now let God talk."[66] In emergencies, she gave her household special spiritual directions which they needed in their work.

Before any public appearance, however minor, she prayed to God to use her in His own good way. Once, at the end of a day filled with vexations, she prayed aloud, "Oh, Father, we turn like tired children to Thee; Thou wilt not leave us comfortless."

Mrs. Eddy accepted literally the account which Christ Jesus gave of himself: "I and my Father are one." But she said, "I cannot be a Christian Scientist except I leave all for Christ."[67] She never doubted that the familiar promise would be kept: "Lo, I am with you alway, even unto the end of the world." Jesus was her Way-shower.

Her eagerness to know what Jesus would do, if he were in her place, was sometimes very touching. Once, in approaching a problem, she remarked to a friend, "I wonder what Jesus would do." On another occasion it comforted her to observe, "Jesus would know what I am going through." Perhaps no leader of her time had better right to quote the lines attributed to St. Patrick:

Christ, as a light
Illumine and guide me!

Christ as a shield o'er-shadow and cover me!
Christ lie under me, Christ be over me!
Christ be beside me
  On left hand and right!
Christ be before me, behind me, about me,
Christ this day be within and without me!

Never had she been quite so naïve, so childlike, as in those final weeks. "One night," says one of her helpers, "she called me to her bedside. She talked about the work. At last she had me tuck her in. But somehow she was not comfortable. She tossed about. She 'fussed' a bit. Then quieting down, with the smile we loved to see, she looked at me and said: 'Forgive me, Dear. I always was such a Betty.' " 68

Happy Pilgrim of the Infinite, Mary Baker Eddy grew quieter as the days grew shorter. After supper, seated in her study, she would look down the driveway, watch the light come in the electric globes on either side of the gate; then tell out the stars as, one by one, they brightened up the sky. Thinking of the things invisible, she would often glance a moment at her blessed Bible or her own *Science and Health* lying open on the desk.

Until the end she took her daily drive. The frosty fingers of an early winter were, with the coming of December, reaching out to touch the window panes, the woods, the hills. As she stepped into her carriage on the first afternoon in December, a heavenly smile was shining from her face and eyes. Each happy band of children, waiting here and there along the road to greet their "dear old lady," waited not in vain. Returning home, she rested a few moments in her study. Then, at her request, a pencil and tablet were brought to her. Hesitating a moment, Mrs. Eddy stooped slightly forward, and on the tablet wrote these words:[69]

Next day she was up and about. Her household gathered in her study, and she talked with them. They realized that she was failing. They had, however, so often seen her rally from a weakness even greater that, though foreboding, they were not overanxious. All through the day, however, as they worked and prayed, they were ill at ease.

On the evening of December third, her faithful household group around her, Mrs. Eddy passed quietly away.[70]

The final services, on December eighth, were as she would have had them. Across the snow-clad lawn at Chestnut Hill came, on that Thursday morning, about fifty guests. At eleven o'clock Judge Clifford P. Smith[71] read the ninety-first Psalm, together with portions of the Gospel of St. John, chapters thirteen and fourteen. Mrs. Carol Hoyt Powers, Second Reader of The Mother Church, read Mrs. Eddy's poem "The Mother's Evening Prayer." [72] The Lord's Prayer was recited in unison. Then the casket was taken up on the shoulders of affection, borne through the open gateway, and carried to Mount Auburn near Boston; and over the last resting place of this woman of the stars, the stately oaks now keep watch in solemn dignity.

— 8 —

"By Their Fruits"

HROUGHOUT HER VIVID
LIFE, MARY BAKER EDDY
often figured in the news columns. She paid the price
which always must be paid for startling complacency or for
breaking with conservatism. There were long stretches when
room for some new depreciation or disparagement was
about the only space she was allotted in the daily papers.

Only after she was gone, did Mrs. Eddy "make" the editorial page — a steeper grade to make than the news page.
At last appreciation displaced the depreciation of earlier
years. The adulation, against which in her lifetime she
never ceased to warn her chosen, won readers from dark
disparagement. Now that she was beyond the touch of idle
gossip, not a few wondered why anything but praise could
have been spoken of a woman who had kindled in the
hearts of uncounted many a spiritual fire which showed no
sign of dying out.

In her beloved Boston, the editor of the *Globe* com-
mented on her passing that: "Present day testimony must be
one of respect for a woman of remarkable mind and of
unusual ability." The editorial reference to her in the *Post*

264 ——————————————————— *"By Their Fruits"*

was a tribute to her for reviving primitive Christianity and adapting it to present day conditions. The editor of the *Evening Transcript* put Mrs. Eddy in the company of Julia Ward Howe, who some weeks before had passed on after winning earlier in her distinguished career a well-deserved immortality by the writing of her famous patriotic poem. Mrs. Eddy's verse is sung each week by millions around the world; her books many read; and her newspaper no one from the first has grudged a place among the most substantial papers of the time. Hers was a "career," according to the editor of the conservative *Springfield Republican,* "from which everyone may draw immense inspiration . . . that must come from the spectacle of astonishing achievement. . . . One may search history from the beginning and have difficulty in matching Mrs. Eddy's performance, between the ages of fifty and eighty, in making a million people accept her at her own valuation."

Outside of New England, where praise or blame is more outspoken, tributes to the Leader of Christian Science developed into such panegyrics as few persons in all history have evoked. Editors in New York, Philadelphia, Baltimore, Washington, Atlanta, Chicago, St. Louis, Kansas City, Denver, San Francisco, Los Angeles, and many other cities with one voice placed Mrs. Eddy among those of whom it has been said that:

> Never to the mansions where the mighty rest
> Since their foundations, came a nobler guest.

If all such tributes to this woman who yearned more for the praise of God than for any praise of man be ruled out of reckoning, still no one seriously doubts that Mary Baker Eddy was born to leadership. Scarcely one of its essentials did she lack. When he coined his phrase "a prodigious example of insubmission, courage, perseverance, and ingenuity," Maeterlinck might have been painting Mrs. Eddy's portrait. Glimpsing in her girlhood the goal of her life work, she set her feet on a long trail which was to stretch across a century, and she followed on until the end. Her ineffable charm, which the years could never blight, brought many to her. By a process of careful selection and reselection, based on spiritual fitness, she was sometimes making those changes in her entourage which the higher interest of her Cause demanded. She let all count with her, but — as Kipling advises — "none too much." To counsel she listened, but she made her own decisions.

When criticism seemed to her in order, she preferred to criticize in private. To praise, when she honestly could, she gave publicity; and never could one call it "the praise of men's forgetting." True, there were times when some charged that she played favorites; but none was ever bold enough to charge that she set her own interests above the Cause she loved and those who tried to capitalize any distinction thus conferred upon them to the injury of the Cause might find waiting for them around the corner the demotion which their indiscretion merited. She always followed through, and any in her train who failed to follow after were one day likely to discover that they had been left far behind.

Patient, sometimes over many a year, with the shifty and even the disloyal, Mrs. Eddy always drew the line the moment the good of the Cause demanded it. Insubordination she never tolerated. To seek a quarrel was not her way; but, when a quarrel was thrust on her, the regret at the outcome was rarely hers. In the life of Mary Baker

Eddy, as of Ellen Terry,[1] opposition called out her highest fighting power. More than once, in order to win, with one stroke of her pen she demolished old machinery and constructed — it sometimes seemed — almost over night new machinery better fitted for the changed conditions.

Many a pitched battle she fought to gain breathing space in which to write, to discover, to build, to organize, to construct; and if now and then, in an almost continuous struggle against handicaps covering some fourscore years and ten, she was stricken, her spirit remained as unbroken as the Scotchman's in the ballad:

> Fight on, my men, Sir Andrew says,
> A little I'm hurt, but not yet slain;
> I'll but lie down and bleed awhile,
> And then I'll rise and fight again.

On the far-flung battle line of the faith she founded, Mrs. Eddy turned a page as new in modern religion as Einstein's page in modern science. Some doubted this while she was here. A few were certain that her work would not outlive her. But even fewer now worthwhile think in terms of death of her extraordinary movement. From Count Hermann Keyserling's announcement that "every spiritual American who can be considered representative, actually belongs, whether he knows it or not, to the wider circle of Christian Science,"[2] to the admission of Harry Emerson Fosdick, "Anything that floats must have some good timber in it, and Christian Science never could have floated as it has if there had not been sound wood there,"[3] agreement has become general that Christian Science lives and grows and must be reckoned with.

Between Mrs. Eddy's discovery and Einstein's, the likeness is amazing. Changes in men's thinking have taken place since two centuries ago Newton conferred on space definite physical reality. Faraday, a century later, developed the "ether" concept to explain the electromagnetic field. Within the memory of readers middle-aged, matter, once solid as a mountain in men's thoughts, has crumbled into molecules, the molecules into atoms, and at last the atoms into immaterial "particles" of radiation. Yesterday Einstein casually observed that space is "eating up matter,"[4] a concept not altogether inharmonious with Mrs. Eddy's concept of God as good since M. K. Wisehart on his return last season from Europe reported Professor Einstein as now convinced that "God is as valid as a scientific argument."[5]

It is, however, in the field of imparting religion, that Mrs. Eddy's leadership excels. She is a literalist, wherever the spiritual teachings of Christ Jesus are involved. Hers is a spiritual technique highly effective. She has set the feet of millions in the path that leads up to the mount where the Ten Commandments are thundered forth to be obeyed and the Beatitudes break in blessings to be lived. The religious services of the Christian Science churches are well attended, both on Sunday and on Wednesday evening. Weather matters little. The author has looked in on nights when it was pouring rain, and The Mother Church was well filled. He has made it his business to test attendance on a very hot night in early summer, and the people were there.

Reasons why Christian Scientists go to church as a matter of course are as evident as they are easy to set forth. For one thing, the details of their worship are so designed and perfected as to hold the close attention of the worshiper. The service is always brief. All present on Sunday share with the two Readers in prayer and join in the singing, which in Christian Science is as distinctive as it is truly congregational. Yet neither in the Sunday nor the Wednesday evening service is any stress laid upon the emotional. Nor is there any "long face" ever in sight.

A great teacher developed the Christian Science service to suit student worshipers. Not even Mark Hopkins on one end, with his student on the other, of that over-ridden log, deserves a higher place among the teachers of America than Mary Baker Eddy. She, too, first taught one at a time; and later, when increasing calls upon her hours obliged her to group her students into classes, she tried to keep the number down so as to give them the maximum possible of individual attention.[6] For all her teaching, she personally made careful preparation, and by the time her Church was going strong she had a Committee at work preparing the Bible Lessons far in advance for all student worshipers.

One can be a Christian Scientist and little heed the magazines and newspapers, but one cannot be a Christian Scientist and omit the daily study of the Bible Lessons. The world over the author knows Christian Scientists, and he has yet to find one in good standing who cannot quote his Bible with a readiness and an accuracy which few outside that faith, even preachers of our day, can match.

The study of the Lesson for the preceding six days acts as a feeder for the Sunday service in which the same Bible passages which have been studied through the week, are read from the platform accompanied by correlative sentences from the Christian Science textbook.

Every Sunday congregation, therefore, no matter where assembled, is both a company of worshipers and a group of students met together to receive more light on the studies they have made day by day, through the preceding week. Even in traveling, by land or sea, or in vacation time, wherever Christian Scientists are — however few — they read their Lessons. Though no Christian Science church may be within reach many when Sunday comes have their little service as though they were at home. With the same Lessons studied everywhere on week days, and on Sundays read in church throughout the world, there is constituted a democracy, both of study and of worship, going far to explain "the crowded churches" which outside of Christian Science are the fascination and despair of Christian leaders. Rarely, in fact, are they to be found elsewhere save in the case of the few congregations fortunate enough to have a brilliant preacher, and even he must not often take the risk of preaching long.[7]

Every religious fold has some excellence by which other folds may profit, but the approach to it from the outside must be with understanding and with sympathy. Perhaps Rufus Jones[8] has stressed the greatest of all Christian needs, in making the awareness of the presence of God the one essential. Standing for the same eternal principle, Mrs. Eddy worked out a technique which keeps her followers, every one, constantly aware of God. But to this boon, she added practical demonstration of the intrinsic value of the Bible Lessons used daily and their reading at the public services on Sunday and a literal acceptance of the healing promises of Jesus.

For a discussion of healing, no apology is made. The interest in the revival of apostolic healing is now widening. Many years ago the late Bishop Brent, while still in the Philippines, wrote the author in approval of Christian healing, and immediately after, he even wrote a book for the author's editing in explanation of what the life of God' in the soul of man can do for anyone. No later than last May,

Bishop Remington of Eastern Oregon is reported to have summoned the church to recover the lost art of healing. After twenty and more years of experimenting, started most intelligently by the Emmanuel Movement, the Protestant Episcopal Church has its Nazarene Society helping many; its Commission on Healing carefully studying with the church's approval the ways and means of restoring what should never have been lost; and its latest General Convention seriously agreeing that "Christian healing has passed beyond the stage of experiment and its value cannot be questioned."

Mr. Frederick Dixon wrote:

> People frequently talk of Christian Science as if it were nothing more than a mammoth dispensary; as a matter of fact, that is an almost ludicrous misconception of what its healing means. It means — the eradication from the human consciousness of all those mental causes which produce sin, disease, and death. It means that in order to be healthier every patient must become a better man. It aims not merely at the destruction of sickness and pain, but of sorrow and want, of misery and vice.[9]

The knowledge that the understanding mind does deeply influence for good the body pathological is not confined exclusively to the pages of *Science and Health*. Three hundred years before Mrs. Eddy announced that "Whatever is cherished in mortal mind as the physical condition is imaged forth on the body," [10] Spenser, in his *Faerie Queene,* was reminding a believing public:

> For of the soule, the bodie forme doth take,
> For soule is forme, and doth the bodie make.

Some twenty-three hundred years before Mrs. Eddy wrote, "Moral conditions will be found always harmonious and health-giving,"[11] Socrates said to Charmides, "First then and above all, the soul must be treated if the head and the rest of the body are ever to be made whole."[12]

In making the observation that "When spiritual being is understood in all its perfection, continuity, and might, then shall man be found in God's image,"[13] Mrs. Eddy was simply leading men back to the teachings of Him whom John Charles Earl thus describes:

> He pours the flood of light on darkened eyes,
> He chases tears, diseases, fiends away;
> His throne is raised upon those Orient skies,
> His footstool is the pave whereon we pray.
> Oh, tell me not of Christ in Paradise,
> For He is all around us here, to-day.[14]

While theologians were over-busy speculating about the personality of Christ Jesus, Mary Baker Eddy went to the heart of the practice of Christ Jesus and revived his healing ministry. She never claimed to have originated, but only to have discovered and restored, what had too long lain dormant since the passing of our Lord, and to have furnished a healing technique which all can learn to practice who will take the trouble in both faith and prayer. A study firsthand, with a mind unbiased, of her words and works usually substantiates her claims.

"The gods give thread for a web begun." In her long life on earth, Mrs. Eddy began a web, and in the twenty years which since have intervened, thread has been furnished in abundance to those she designated to carry on when she was gone. After the pattern she set, that web is still aweaving.

What the finished product is to be no one as yet foresees. No prevision is adequate. Those who understand the teachings of their Leader are content to make the best use they can of the thread given them. The ultimate they leave to God.

Meanwhile the world at large keeps an eye on Christian Science. Every year it expects more of this faith. "By their fruits" the world is judging Christian Scientists. Some of the fruits of this new faith it is, therefore, now in order to consider.

At first, not all the fruits of Christian Science ripened. Not all, as early as Mr. James A. Neal,[15] of revered memory, brought forth fruit abundantly. Many of the earlier Christian Scientists were plain folk. Many of the men worked in factories, or in the field. The women were housekeepers, often broken on the wheel of drudgery. But they came to Mrs. Eddy. They sat at her feet. Something told them she had a message for them; and in listening to her words a reorientation came to them of which through all their later years they never tired of speaking. To some — as several told and also wrote the author years ago — the days they spent in Mrs. Eddy's class opened to them a new heaven and a new earth. Not in all cases, however, did this entrancing experience last. The vision which she gave was sometimes allowed to fade out. Some of those earlier followers turned back to the trivial round and found it as trivial as it was before, to the common task and it seemed commoner than ever. But there were others who conserved their vision until the end, and until the end they testified that the healing touch which body and mind had felt lasted, and outlasted, time.

One of the earlier Scientists testified to healing of an illness before she ever met the woman wonderful. So deeply moved was she by her experience that she packed her bag, and hurried to Boston to see her benefactor. Not realizing that Mrs. Eddy had already become a very busy woman, the visitor was disappointed on ringing the door bell to learn that Mrs. Eddy was too engrossed to see anyone. Not to be entirely frustrated, the well-meaning visitor begged to be shown a portrait which she had heard hung in the parlor. Almost as soon as she was admitted to the room she discovered herself in the presence of the woman she had come to see and thank. With both hands outstretched, Mrs. Eddy stepped forward, put her arm around her visitor, and promptly said, "I was in my study writing as busily as ever I wrote in my life when suddenly I put down my pen and came to this room. I knew not why." Before leaving the house the visitor had become a member of Mrs. Eddy's class, and later proved a worthy student.

Even in these sophisticated days the primitive type of faith persists, naïve and blessed in proportion to its simplicity. Coming down the automatic elevator in a city office building, late one night when the street floor seemed deserted, the author stopped a moment at the hallway desk of the watchman who was not then in sight. But near a low reading light a chair was drawn, and on the chair a book lay open — a little much-worn copy of *Science and Health with Key to the Scriptures*. On solitary guard this faithful man, through the still watches of the night, was seeking intently for a clearer understanding of the truths he found in Christian Science. With a curiosity the author hopes is not beyond all pardon, he spied these words on the open page on which the watchman's eyes had rested and which he had marked:

Truth will be to us "the resurrection and the life" only as it destroys all error and the belief that Mind, the only immortality of man, can be fettered by the body, and Life be controlled by death. A sinful, sick, and dying mortal is not the likeness of God, the perfect and eternal.[16]

Dropping in one Wednesday evening at a service in a suburban church, the author heard a plain man tell his story. He was all humility, although for twenty years, as he explained, he had been a persistent student of Christian Science. During all that time he had never faltered, whether on the mountain top or in the valley far below. Some small success had come his way, sometimes also failure. Through the years, however, he had stood firm, and modestly he hoped he could with truth report some headway gained. For all that Christian Science had done for him he was grateful, and to the casual visitor his words rang true.

The testimony of the Christian Science lecturers is significant because, in lecturing to groups, sometimes numbering thousands and including many persons not of their own faith, they have to treat their subject in a generous spirit, of which such words as these are representative:

Christian Science is essentially Christian. It is calm, peaceful, serene, and divinely secure. It resorts to no emotionalism to excite an interest in itself. On the contrary, it appeals through pure reason and logic to the very best in one's nature. It repeats the saying of ancient times: "Ho, every one that thirsteth, come ye to the waters." [17]

The best practitioners have stories to tell from real life which, for spiritual insight, can scarcely be surpassed. Their work is not perfunctory. In emergencies, they remain in the sickroom day and night, denying discord and asserting

The Leader in her Chestnut Hill days
(From an oil painting by Margaret F. Richardson.)

God's presence and power until the hour strikes for the results to come. Back, therefore, of their calm and measured words, there is a wealth of hard facts to give weight to their words:

> Christian Science is vital to men and women, because it presents a scientific explanation by which all may work out their own salvation. It explains all cause and effect as mental; and that sin, disease, and death are overcome by the understanding of the same divine Principle which enabled Jesus to heal the sick and raise the dead. Contrary to popular opinion, this healing is achieved not by any use of the human will or suggestion, but by the understanding of that which is absolutely true in the sight of God. It is indeed the "Spirit of truth," the Comforter which Jesus promised.[18]

The testimony of both the business man and business woman is to the author all the more impressive because he has talked with many of this type, from the expert secretary to the big business man, although it must not be forgotten that in Christian Science there is no small and great. In its spiritual democracy, Kipling's millennial lines find immediate fulfillment:

> And no one shall work for money, and
> no one shall work for fame;
> But each for the joy of the working, and
> each, in his separate star.

Of nothing in this book is the author more certain than of business efficiency in Christian Science. Not once has he failed to find the loyal Christian Scientist living up to the high business ideal which insures success. That ideal has been happily expressed by Mr. Charles E. Heitman in the words: "Alertness, worthiness, and love of our work determine its productive value." The Christian Scientist's eye is never on the clock. He wastes no time in loud or idle talk. He is never overtaken by brainstorms. His vitality he does not waste in worry or in hurry. Undercutting and sidestepping the true Christian Scientist never practices. His single-mindedness and happiness of spirit carry over into business life and make his every effort count toward high success. How could it be otherwise, when an hour, often two hours, he sets aside each day — sometimes in the early morning — for the study of the Bible Lessons, which brings the quiet mind, the ordered energy, the poised personality?

Nor is the author without much good company in his opinion. Years ago Michael Meehan — not a Christian Scientist — confirmed it:

> Christian Scientists are successful. Why? They are in harmony with the law of the presence of God in all things, as forcibly demonstrated by the Founder of Christian Science; their complete acceptance of God's law makes them quickly responsive to the laws of their country and enhances their value as citizens; they do not gossip — they have neither the time nor inclination; their petitions over wrongs and grievances are not clogging court records; they are never found patronizing questionable resorts, nor are they engaged in questionable practices; they do not meddle in the affairs of their neighbors; they avoid even the appearances of evil.[19]

Mr. Clarence H. Howard, a business man of St. Louis, who long ago became convinced of the value of the tests which Christian Science sets up and which Mr. Meehan describes, successfully applied them in the development of the manifold activities of his Commonwealth Plan, until at last the Commonwealth Steel Company of Granite City, Illinois, of which Mr. Howard was President, has become one of the major industries of the Mississippi Valley.

Another outstanding example of business men who were Christian Scientists was Mr. William Delavan Baldwin, Chairman of the Board of the Otis Elevator Company, who testified:

> It is now about forty years since I first became interested in Christian Science, and during all of this time I have been and am a strong and devoted adherent of the teachings of Mary Baker Eddy. Each year brings to me an ever greater appreciation of her wonderful character and the tremendous influence for good her revelations and teachings have had, and are now having with ever increasing force. The world needs the higher spiritual understanding and knowledge of spiritual healing taught by Mrs. Eddy, to solve and heal its complex material problems. Christian Science rests on demonstration.

No field has been more productive of a type of Christian Scientist than the stage. Perhaps it is because stage folk have to pay a heavier price than most of us for any lowering of vitality. They must keep high their level of efficiency. Competition is so keen and public censure so immediate that if they do not give their best at every performance, they may have to say of the audience:

> They light me once,
> They hurry by,
> And never come again.

Twenty years ago *The Music Master* and *The Lion and the Mouse* were crowding theaters, and winning for their author,

Charles Klein, a deserved reputation and also a large income. He overworked. His health broke. Life lost its zest for him. His associates believed him through. Suddenly he snapped back into larger success than ever. Asked to account for such an unexpected resurgence of health and effectiveness, he replied that he turned to Christian Science. In the *Cosmopolitan* for February, 1907, he wrote:

> I gradually, indeed almost immediately, recovered my health, my peace of mind, professional and financial success, and happiness far beyond my wildest dream.

Since 1918, when as Vice President of the Association of American Colleges, the author was brought close to many an institution, he has wondered: "Does Christian Science touch the college mind?" More recently he has listened to many expressions of opinion, talked with representative students, and also read the files of letters from college students received by The Christian Science Board of Directors, while administering the late Ruggles Educational Fund, established in 1926 under the will of Dr. Georgia Sackett Ruggles of Los Angeles, California, to assist young men and women, not only in this country but also in Canada, England, Germany, Holland, France, Switzerland, and other lands, to complete their education.

Among the distinguished American institutions represented in these reactions to Christian Science are Harvard, Williams, Brown, University of Chicago, Northwestern, and University of Idaho. The author heard a young college man, at a Wednesday evening service, express gratitude for the help which Christian Science was bringing to him in his college life. Not merely had his faith equipped him, he said, to handle better the problems of his daily living; it had also helped him through examinations, by the elimination of fear and its replacement by such a spirit of confidence and serenity as made it possible for him to marshal all his resources, which else would have been scattered.

The author was so impressed with the thoughtfulness of a Christian Science student, senior in another college, in which he was well regarded, that finally there was procured from him this statement in writing:

> Of course, the average college man finds his religion up against a severe test when he first meets the cold lights of science and the paradoxes of philosophy, and the general attitude of skepticism which is so prevalent among undergraduates. I have seen many of my friends enormously disturbed as they watch the foundations of a none too objective religious background crumble out from under them. They often have to resort, in case belief in religion is not swept away, to retaining a nonrational and usually emotional faith, which is quite unsatisfactory to their reasoning intellect. For my part, having only just acquired a really workable knowledge of Science when I entered college, I have through college been most interested in putting it to the test under . . . conditions which ordinarily prove severe. I have even gone out of my way to do this as much as possible.
>
> I can truthfully say, Dr. Powell, that there has been no problem that I have found in any of the departments of the college work, which I have not been able to settle definitely by using Science. I am constantly amazed at the completeness of Mrs. Eddy's writing. Using the concordances carefully, the most detailed points in such a highly complex subject as philosophy will be explicitly decided in her writings, with the scientific logic which characterizes the entire

system. Or if there is not a direct answer to a given problem, the student can find statements which will enable him to decide for himself. I never have found a question which I could not solve in a way wholly consistent with Science, — to my complete satisfaction. I cannot tell you the value of having a firm and completely stable mental and spiritual system, which I have never known to fail. It means a mental vigor and decision which could come, I think, only from a consistently inclusive Science.

On another occasion, the author was fortunate to obtain from a Phi Beta Kappa man, ten years out of a great university, this thought-provoking opinion:

If I could speak to the college youth of today I would say this: the study and the practice of Christian Science will make you a better student with less effort; from my own experience in helping others I can say that there are no conditions of pain or suffering which Christian Science cannot eliminate, that there is no fear which it cannot cast out, no financial problem which it cannot solve; if my words have any weight it is only because they are backed up by proof, proof gained from such persistent evidence that it is impossible to draw any other conclusion except that neither luck nor human sagacity but the operation of a power above and beyond man is responsible for the multiplicity of harmonious results which have followed the application of the principle and rule set forth in the Christian Science textbook, *Science and Health with Key to the Scriptures* by Mary Baker Eddy.

Out of letters in the files of the late Ruggles Educational Fund from students at home and abroad, a few selected sentences are submitted:

As I walked to school each morning I kept saying Divine Mind works harmoniously. "All is infinite Mind and its infinite manifestation." [20] By declaring this I saw that I was not doing the work myself, but reflecting infinite Mind which neither works too fast nor too slow. Immediately my laboratory work speeded up and I caught up with the class and stayed with them to the end. For the first time in my life I have reached the point where I actually *love* to study and want to forge ahead and learn much more than is actually required in the courses. I am convinced now of the value of a college training if one really wants to get all the good possible out of it, and it seems to me that my understanding of Christian Science is being broadened rather than confused by it. The history either of a country or a literature is so much more explicable and meaningful in the light of Truth, and in studying it one gets rid of false prejudices at the same time that one sees the futility of all systems of thought or action resting on a material basis. Involuntarily I measure any theory or hypothesis with which I come in contact by the rule of Christian Science and value it according as it approaches or falls below that rule. I am all the more grateful for this *absolute standard* of judgment inasmuch as several of my friends have had their orthodox religious views completely upset in college and are now pretty much at sea.

Through holding fast to Truth and denying error I have overcome the difficulties which confronted me. (A German student in a German University.)

While in Berlin, I stood before an examination to last five hours . . . I made it clear to myself that the one infinite Mind alone filled me and that God governs us all: that nothing can be asked of me that I could not do. . . . To my great joy I began to see here too that my right thinking was victorious. (Another translation from a German student.)

There was a time when the attitude of Christian Science toward family life was not everywhere understood. Much ink was spilt in criticism. The simple fact is that Mrs. Eddy literally took her stand with Jesus, as she interpreted him. Jesus preached purity in all the relationships of life. Mrs. Eddy preached the same in somewhat the same language. But she was always practical. Once she observed:

> Be faithful over home relations; they lead to higher joys; obey the Golden Rule for human life, and it will spare you much bitterness. It is pleasanter to do right than wrong; it makes one ruler over one's self and hallows home — which is woman's world. Please your husband, and he will be apt to please you; preserve affection on both sides.[21]

Coming over on the *Olympic,* Zoe Beckley found Lady Astor with *Science and Health* always near her in her daily writing and "speech-preparing." Zoe Beckley's human interest story in the *Woman's Home Companion* (August, 1930) pictures Lady Astor as charming, vital, sensible, and adds: "She is religious, a Christian Scientist. Motherhood is a mania with Nancy Astor. 'I have only six children,' she says ruefully, 'I would like a full dozen.'" Nothing could better illustrate Mrs. Eddy's practicalness than in counseling the individual to live up to his own understanding of the truth before he interferes with the affairs of others. Mrs. Eddy says:

> Great mischief comes from attempts to steady other people's altars, venturing on valor without discretion, which is virtually meddlesomeness. Even your sincere and courageous convictions regarding what is best for others may be mistaken; you must be demonstratively right yourself, and work

out the greatest good to the greatest number, before you are sure of being a fit counsellor.[22]

Among the many letters received by the author in twenty-four years from men and women who had been with Mrs. Eddy in Lynn and Boston, is one indicative of the blending of the ideal and practical almost from the first in her experience. In reply to the author's inquiry for the exact truth concerning Mrs. Eddy's opinions on marriage when, in 1875, the writer often talked with her, the word came: "There was nothing at variance" with those lines in her chapter on Marriage in that first edition of *Science and Health* (1875): "Be not in haste to take the vow 'until death do us part' but consider well its obligations, responsibilities, and relations to all your future happiness; judge before friendship,[23] then confide till death." In the twenty years since Mrs. Eddy passed on, the practical bearing of her teaching has become apparent along with the lowering in the world at large of the high standard of purity set up by her. At a time when marriage seems menacingly unstable, and subject to easy dissolution, Christian Science is securing for it more stability. Christian Science calls the entire family to rally to the unifying standard of purity, unselfishness and recognition of the higher rights of every member. Writes the college-bred mother of one of the many attractive Christian Science families, whom the author has the happy privilege of knowing in their homes:

> There has been one sentence that has been like a beacon light to us in bringing up our three children. This was told to some of Mrs. Eddy's students who asked her how they were to protect their little children from aggressive propaganda of mortal mind. The sentence is as follows: "Give the children the truth at home, and then let them go." We

have found that in so far as we have lived up to this admonition, teaching them the moral principle found in the Ten Commandments and the Sermon on the Mount, that we could then send them forth into their school and college and social life, trusting them to God's care. We have tried to instill in them the desire for obedience to the spiritual import of the Bible, our textbook, *Science and Health with Key to the Scriptures,* by Mary Baker Eddy, and the *Manual* of the Mother Church, and to awaken in them the sense of the importance of daily study of the lesson-sermon. They have turned to the principle of Christian Science in working out all their problems and have found that, since each one of us must work out his own salvation, it is wise to attempt to solve a problem first through one's own understanding of the truth before turning to another for help.

We are learning through the teaching of Christian Science to treat the children as equals and to share all family problems and experiences with them as far as is practicable. We find that their response to this point of view is astonishing, and contributes to their confidence in themselves, and the progress, interest, and happiness of the home life. The children have been encouraged to have a special interest outside their prescribed school studies, such as athletic sports and music. Jesus prayed that his disciples should be kept not from the world, but from the evil in the world, and Mrs. Eddy gives us the practical application of this principle in her admonition: "... keep your minds so filled with Truth and Love, that sin, disease, and death cannot enter them." [24]

We have tried to arouse in the children the ideal of service to mankind in all they do. We discovered that one of them had adopted the plan of saying to himself mentally whenever he met a new friend: "What can I do for you?" A very important lesson for them is obedience to the laws of the land. This obedience to Caesar does not conflict with rendering what is due to God but unfolds the necessary quality of self-discipline in the individual. We have been learning as a family that happiness in the home life is due to the exercise of certain qualities, such as honesty, loyalty, purity, activity, charity and affection.[25]

"Wherefore by their fruits ye shall know them." [26]

Twenty Years After

ALMOST TWENTY YEARS HAVE PASSED SINCE Mrs. Eddy, on the little tablet which a member of the family brought her, wrote her last message to the flock she loved and was about to leave.

Since that December day in 1910, much has happened. Recently the author was one of a little group, a member of which, apropos of nothing, sagely observed: "Christian Science is now on its last legs."

Unless the author has altogether misunderstood and utterly misinterpreted the rich sources open to him first among all investigators, and on which this is the first book to be based, Christian Science, which has more than doubled its churches, societies, and membership in twenty years, far from being on "its last legs," is now going stronger than ever.

The very reserve concerning the publication of statistics by those responsible for the general policy of the movement has increased the author's respect for the management. Again and again, as he has come accidentally upon facts and figures not officially in evidence, he has discovered a systematic policy of understatement rather than of overstatement, and an appropriate spiritual modesty which Mrs. Eddy once called the "jewel" [1] of Christian Science.

While the author is aware that readers of this book will give only such credence to his opinions as they appear to deserve, he confidently believes that his general impression of the strong and steady development these twenty years past of Christian Science, will seem even to the incredulous to be amply justified.

Mrs. Eddy never claimed to have found something entirely new. On the other hand she said, "I have found nothing in ancient or in modern systems on which to found my own except the teachings and demonstrations of our great Master."[2] What Jesus brought to light, and then in the dark ages many lost, Mrs. Eddy brought to light again. No religious leader in all time has ever been more insistent than the Discoverer and Founder of Christian Science that Christ Jesus kept his promise: "Lo, I am with you alway."[3] No follower of Christ Jesus has ever testified more convincingly than Mrs. Eddy both to the naturalness and the effectiveness of his works.

> They are [she says] the sign of Immanuel, or "God with us," — a divine influence ever present in human consciousness and repeating itself, coming now as was promised aforetime,
>
>> To preach deliverance to the captives [of sense],
>> And recovering of sight to the blind,
>> To set at liberty them that are bruised.[4]

Objectionable comparisons never interested Mrs. Eddy. Hers was too busy a life to waste time on them. As she came to the fullness of her powers and her fame, not merely did she herself wish all Zion prosperity; but she also spoke thus for her followers: "A genuine Christian Scientist loves Protestant and Catholic, D.D. and M.D., — loves all who love God, good." [5] Incidentally, the author has had abundant evidence that at least once she indicated she would rather see a good Congregationalist than a poor Christian Scientist.

That was natural. Congregationalism had been her religious training from the cradle, and she never once denied the devoutness and democracy of the Congregational denomination.

If Mrs. Eddy did not specifically praise the "Disciples" (sometime called Campbellites) she illustrated the possibility of putting the Christian fellowship they preached above mere difference of definition.

The woman who wrote, "Divine Science derives its sanction from the Bible," [6] was not apt to be at odds with Lutherans, who from the first have kept the Bible at the center of their worship.

Making for itself a large place in history by the substitution of "conversion" for mere "respectability" at the very time that Mrs. Eddy was growing up, Methodism never emphasized "Ye must be born again" more positively than Mrs. Eddy emphasized the thought in such phrases as "The man born of Spirit is spiritual." [7]

The dignity and decorum which give distinction to Episcopal worship are matched in Christian Science through the explicit instructions worked out in the earlier days by its Founder.

If as Dr. J. Fort Newton believes, "something is missing in modern religion," it is not the fault of Mrs. Eddy, nor of those today who carry on not merely in her spirit but also in obedience to her definite and far-reaching instructions.

On February 27, 1903, Mrs. Eddy wrote The Christian Science Board of Directors:

> Never abandon the By-laws nor the denominational government of The Mother Church. If I am not personally with you, the Word of God and my instructions in the By-laws have led you hitherto and will remain to guide you safely on.[8]

Mrs. Eddy was still on earth when one of her critics who turned later to hearty appreciation said:

> The power, through loving mercifulness and compassion, to heal fleshly ills and pains and griefs — all — with a word, with a touch of the hand! This power was given by the Saviour to the Disciples, and to all the converted. All — every one. It was exercised for generations afterwards. Any Christian who is earnest and not a make-believe, not a policy-Christian, not a Christian for revenue only, had that healing power, and could cure with it any disease or any hurt or damage possible to human flesh and bone. These things are true, or they are not. If they were true seventeen and eighteen and nineteen centuries ago it would be difficult satisfactorily to explain why or how or by what argument that power should be non-existent in Christians now.[9]

Differ as men in 1930 may about Christian Science, all who have even scant knowledge of the organization agree that Christian Science under the conscientious conduct of a Board of Directors never unmindful of their spiritual responsibility to the Founder, has lifted the blight of poverty as well as sickness from many a life and many a home.

Under a technique of daily Bible study of their Leader's planning and with her still ever-present help through her writings, Christian Scientists have developed a habit of church attendance and of church financial support which in the minds of many other Christians is evolving out of doubt into aspiration.

Even more significant is the large percentage of Christian Scientists who indisputably — as even casual observers testify — bear those fruits of the spirit which St. Paul listed as "love, joy, peace, longsuffering, gentleness, goodness, faith, meekness, temperance."

Not a few outside of Christian Science who recognize its worth, now have little difficulty in agreeing with "Sonny's Father" in Ruth McEnery Stuart's story:

> I want to treat 'em white thet's all. Any sect thet dwells upon the beauty of holiness an' thet challenges every soul to find God in itself has got a great truth, an' there's so much health an' well-bein' in that one reelization thet we might forgive 'em ef their heads gits turned a little an' they become imbued with the idee thet they've cot a corner on the Grace of God.[10]

Most of us are quite willing that any group — if they can — shall get "a corner on the Grace of God"; for the only corner possible, in the nature of the case, on the Grace of God is a strategic place from which the Spirit drives us out to share the Grace of God with those who have it not.

If, these twenty years past, under the direction of the Board, Christian Science has actually gotten · "a corner on the Grace of God," none need be over-anxious. The best they have Christian Scientists were never keener than they are today to give away, without solicitation and also without proselytizing, "to them that are far off and to them that are nigh."

What the final judgment is to be on Christian Science, those who direct its course — though giving no evidence of concern — would be the last to venture to predict. They understand that their first responsibility — and that of all other Scientists — is to live the faith to which they bear witness. They know, too, that Clio, muse of history, still stands, as in pre-Christian days, with judicial pen suspended, always waiting — but never over-eager — to write the last word concerning men and movements.

With persecution passing, one peril still remains. It is the peril of prosperity. But even out of that peril, which has proved too much for many a worthy cause, there is a way for Christian Science. It is — as the incoming President of The Mother Church in 1924 clearly indicated — the way of gratitude

> . . . to the God of our fathers, who has carried us through this desert to the promised land; to Christ Jesus, "the author and finisher of our faith"; to our beloved Leader, Mary Baker Eddy, whose teachings have sustained our faith, and whose Church Manual has kept us in the right path; and to our Board of Directors, who, through stress and storm, have held our standard aloft without wavering.[11]

So long as Christian Scientists keep in this way, so long also as day by day they try to live up to the teachings of their Leader, so long will they take no thought for the morrow. "For the morrow shall take thought for the things of itself."[12]

Notes

Abbreviations Used in Notes

A. Archives and Library of The Mother Church
CSJ. The Christian Science Journal
CSM. The Christian Science Monitor
CSS. Christian Science Sentinel
LY. Longyear Museum and Historical Society

Published works of Mary Baker Eddy:

S&H. Science and Health with Key to the Scriptures
Man. Manual of The Mother Church
'00 Message to The Mother Church, Boston, June, 1900
'02 Message to The Mother Church, Boston, June 15, 1902
Mis. Miscellaneous Writings
My. The First Church of Christ, Scientist, and Miscellany
No. No and Yes
Pan. Christian Science versus Pantheism
Po. Poems
Pul. Pulpit and Press
Ret. Retrospection and Introspection
Rud. Rudimental Divine Science
Un. Unity of Good

Unpublished writings of Mary Baker Eddy:

A00000   article or poem
L000000   letter
V00000   photographic or other verified copy of a letter

Notes

Prologue

1. Alfred Farlow.

2. One of the staff at Christian Science headquarters, with some pathos, then explained to the author that in order to get through even ordinary routine, he was coming in from the suburbs every morning to be at his desk by seven and sometimes staying late.

3. Charles William Eliot (1834–1926): President of Harvard University from 1869 to 1909. Thomas Wentworth Higginson (1823–1911): American author who also as a Colonel in the Civil War commanded the first regiment of black soldiers. Higginson wrote biographies of Margaret Fuller, Longfellow, and Whittier, and edited Emily Dickinson's poems. Edward Everett Hale (1822–1909): American author and Unitarian minister. Hale was chaplain of the U.S. Senate from 1903 until his passing.

4. A. L01688.

5. *Cambridge History of American Literature,* Vol. III, p. 526. This passage was read at the annual meeting of The Mother Church in 1929, by Judge Clifford P. Smith, to an audience of five thousand.

6. *Cambridge History of American Literature,* p. 531.

7. Andrade's *An Hour of Physics,* p. 222. Robert Andrews Millikan (1868–1953): American physicist and educator. He won the Nobel Prize in 1923 for measuring the charge on the electron; Sir Arthur Eddington (1882–1944): British physicist and astronomer. He became an early exponent of the theory of relativity.

Many of his writings were concerned with the philosophical implications of modern scientific theory; John Scott Haldane (1860–1936): British scientist. This appears to be a reference to one of his later works, *The Sciences and Philosophy* (1929).

8. *Science and Health with Key to the Scriptures,* p. 468.

9. Otto's *The Idea of the Holy,* p. 158.

10. *Scribner's,* December, 1929; *Collier's,* April 19, 1930. In addition, Bishop Charles Fiske of Central New York is thus quoted in *The Living Church,* June 21, 1930: "Church attendance is not an infallible test of religious reality. It is, however, a fairly accurate thermometer by which to record the warmth of Christian loyalty. I have had a count made of the number of worshipers present at the principal Sunday service in some of our churches. The reports are amazing. In one city church having nearly 1,200 communicants, there was a Sunday morning congregation of 250. About the same number was present in a church reporting 1,300 members. In another, with close to a thousand communicants, the congregation numbered 225. In other churches with communicant lists ranging from 800 to 900 and upward, the proportion was about the same. Apparently the smaller churches showed a better record. City and town parishes with 400 to 600 communicants, and over, record an average attendance of about thirty-five percent. Village and small town churches of 200 total membership, or less, showed about forty percent. The count in several churches showed an appalling absence of men — about one-sixth of the congregations was all that could be mustered in several parishes, one-seventh in others. These are the facts. I can understand everything about them, save that clergy and laity who know the facts do not seem in the least anxious or concerned about them. The insoluble mystery is that so few of our leaders show serious dissatisfaction at such evident falling away.

"These figures do not reflect special discredit upon our own diocese. I was led to make the count here because of the publication of certain statistics of church attendance in New York City. Fifteen prosperous parishes, leading churches of the city, having a total reported communicant list of 23,196 had on a fair, cool day in summer an attendance of only 2,496 at the principal Sunday morning service. Of course summer attendance is hardly a true test, although even in New York everybody is not away for week-end holidays or enjoying an entire season's vacation for the heated term. A survey made on a fair Sunday at the peak of the winter season showed in the same churches 6,977 persons present, not counting the attendance at early communions, which in several of the churches must have been considerable. Attendance under favorable conditions, therefore, was less than one-third of the reported membership. Unfortunately, the figures do not tell the whole story, because five of the congregations counted were in famous metropolitan churches where there is usually a large proportion of visitors to swell the number of worshipers. Either parish communicant rolls are absurdly overpadded, or the religious habits of church members are tragically lax."

11. Everyone should read Channing Pollock's defense of the times in *The American Magazine,* July, 1930. In *Church Federation,* June, 1930, it is recorded that Charles P. Steinmetz, the world's foremost electrical engineer, in his last days, forecast the future in the following impressive words: "I think the greatest discovery will be made along spiritual lines. Here is a force which history clearly teaches has been the greatest power in the development of men and history. Yet we have merely been playing with it and have never seriously studied it as we have the physical forces. Some day people will learn that material things do not bring happiness and are of little use in making men and women creative and powerful. Then the scientists of the world will turn their laboratories over to the study of God and prayer and the spiritual forces which as yet have hardly been scratched. When this day comes, the world will see more advancement in one generation than it has seen in the last four."

As though to call Christians of all types to their cooperative responsibility the Right Reverend James De Wolf Perry, Bishop of Rhode Island and Presiding Bishop of the Protestant Episcopal

Church in the United States, said in Westminster Abbey August 10, 1930, in his farewell sermon to the Lambeth Conference as reported in the New York *Times,* August 11, 1930: "Hearts and minds everywhere are uniting in a demand for a way of life to guide them and light and truth to reassure them. Here is a singleness of need that will be satisfied only by the witness of a united voice."

12. *Renascence.*

13. *The Independent,* November, 1906.

14. *The Living Church,* October 13, 1928.

Chapter 1

1. Matt. 11:5.

2. The author was privileged in the summer of 1917 to share with the late Baron von Hügel the gracious hospitality of the Master's Lodge at Balliol College, Oxford, and to listen entranced to the Baron's now familiar interpretation of "Christianity as caring" — the very words the Baron uses in his letter to his niece.

3. John 9:25.

4. Luke 19:40.

5. William James, 1842–1910: philosopher and first major figure in American psychology. His *Principles of Psychology* (1890) is still a classic. James is also remembered for *The Varieties of Religious Experience,* a book version of his lectures delivered in Edinburgh in 1901.

6. Christian Science encircled the globe in Mrs. Eddy's time. Since she passed on, Christian Science has grown so rapidly that twenty-six countries besides the United States are now represented in the advertising columns of the *Monitor.* In London alone there are twelve churches instead of, as twenty years ago, only three, and in other European cities the cause is growing at a substantial rate every year.

7. Professor Hermann S. Hering: First Reader of The Mother Church, 1902–05; First Reader of First Church of Christ, Scientist, Concord, New Hampshire, 1906–09; member of The Christian Science Board of Lectureship for a total of 26 years between 1905 and 1939.

8. Quoted by Judge Clifford P. Smith, manager of Committees on Publication, at the annual meeting of The Mother Church in June, 1921.

9. *Religion and Medicine,* p. 10.

10. Albert Bigelow Paine, *Mark Twain: A Biography* (1912), Vol. III, p. 1271.

11. H. A. L. Fisher: British historian, as well as a member of Parliament from 1916 to 1926. He emphasized religious and political influences over economic ones in his writing, and is of interest here because of his book on Christian Science, *Our New Religion.*

12. The interest taken by Christian Scientists in other lands, other folds, and in all who need, is of the Scriptural type. They are averse to making the left hand acquainted with what the right hand does. Kipling's couplet describes them:

> Help me to need no help from men,
> That I may help such men as need.

At a time when individual Christian Scientists were very generous to the sufferers from the fire of 1906 in San Francisco, the church itself was criticized for holding aloof by some who did not understand the modesty of Christian Science giving. The criticism was soon silenced, however, by the relief action taken in accordance with their Leader's directions by The Mother Church.

All through the four years of World War I names of Christian Scientists stood high on the honor roll of war relief, not merely in the war zone lands, but also in countries only indirectly hurt by the world tragedy. Nor was their generosity confined to their own people. Beginning with the Red Cross, funds of their contributing were disbursed through the Y.M.C.A., the Boy Scouts, and other relief committees in many lands.

When the earthquake came in 1923 to Japan, The Mother Church was instant in relief, and the Japanese delegation which visited Boston last spring to thank the city for its generosity, on that occasion paid a special visit to the Directors of The Mother Church, bringing letters of appreciation from the Mayor of Tokyo and the bureau of reconstruction of the Japanese Government.

The author has seen letters from Episcopal, Methodist, and Baptist ministers expressing fervent gratitude for Christian Science gifts to them when they were overtaken by the floods, some in the Mississippi Valley, others in Vermont.

It has been said that Christian Science has no paid missionaries and does no systematic missionary work. Such critics, however, disregard the fact that every Christian Scientist is *ipso facto* a non-proselyting missionary: and among the most impressive data to which the author has had access are some — with illustrations — from the Philippine Islands, Brazil, Argentina, Southwest Africa, the Dutch East Indies, and other remote lands indicating that not merely are Christian Scientists doing works of mercy, wherever they may be, but that also in some lands — notably Africa and Oriental countries — Christian Science societies and churches are in consequence automatically resulting.

13. *The Literary Digest,* April 26, 1930. Joseph Wood Krutch was a writer, editor, and teacher. From 1937 to 1953 he was a professor at Columbia, and in his later years was known especially for his writing about nature. During the 1920s he was associate editor and a drama critic for the *Nation,* and it was probably in this capacity that Powell knew him.

14. Bunting's *The Radiant Life,* p. 11.

15. Phil. 2:12. The conception of the priesthood of democracy grew out of a discussion with Charles E. Heitman, member of the Board of Directors, and constructively helpful to the author.

16. *Mis.,* p. 154.

17. In the *Jewish Tribune,* July 26, 1929, Orwell Bradley Towne says: "Christian Scientists do not put on revivals or conduct campaigns openly or secretly to gain followers, or for funds with which to finance its activities. Christian Science as a religious organization seeks only to serve the cause of humanity as set forth in the Bible. Christian Science is not for any particular class of people, and its membership is not made up of any particular class of people."

18. In the report of the United States Bureau of Labor, dated October, 1929, on the "Care of Aged Persons in the United States," there appears (p. 129) a table showing a census of the aged in homes of various religious groups and also the average cost of caring for each resident. Christian Science heads the list with an average annual expenditure on each resident at Pleasant View of 1270 dollars, while the next nearest group is listed as expending only a little more than one-third as much, and some other groups below one-fifth as much.

19. J. Roscoe Drummond.

20. A suburb of Boston.

21. [Ed. Note: These benevolent associations are no longer under the control of The Mother Church, but along with several other sanatoriums run by Christian Scientists, are controlled by local boards of trustees.]

22. The Pleasant View home served this purpose admirably for several decades, until the property was sold in 1975. Those living in Pleasant View at that time were offered accommodations at the Chestnut Hill sanatorium.

23. *Po.,* p. 14.

Chapter 2

1. Mrs. Eddy wrote, December 28, 1899, to Rufus Baker that "affection craves legend and relics." (A. L12649.) From the collection of the Reverend Irving C. Tomlinson. For full discussion of Mrs. Eddy's pedigree, see Sibyl Wilbur's *The Life of Mary*

Baker Eddy, p. 6, long accepted by Christian Scientists as a standard biography. Hereafter when the author refers to this biography it will be designated as: Wilbur. Her closing words run thus: "It is therefore sufficient to state that Mary Baker Eddy's great-grandparents were akin to the McNeils." [Ed. Note: For a further discussion of Mrs. Eddy's forebears see Robert Peel, *Mary Baker Eddy: The Years of Discovery,* pp. 17–19.]

2. After her passing Reverend Richard S. Rust, D.D., close friend of the Baker family, wrote of Mrs. Eddy's mother: "The character of Mrs. Baker was distinguished for numerous excellences, and these were most happily blended. She possessed a strong intellect, a sympathising heart, and a placid spirit. Her presence, like the gentle dew and cheerful light, was felt by all around her. She gave an elevated character to the tone of the conversation in the circles in which she moved, and directed attention to themes at once pleasing and profitable. She appeared no less lovely in the sphere of domestic life. As a mother, she was untiring in her efforts to secure the happiness of her family. The oft-repeated impressions of that sainted spirit on the hearts of those especially entrusted to her can never be effaced, and can hardly fail to induce them to follow her to the brighter world. No sacrifice was esteemed too great, could it subserve their interests. She ever entertained a lively sense of the parental obligation in regard to the education of her children." (A. Mrs. Eddy's scrapbook.)

On February 28, 1890, Calvin A. Frye took down at the wish of Mrs. Eddy some of the early memories of her mother's bedtime visits with her little girl and how she tried to impress on her such maxims as: "Count that day lost whose setting sun finds no good done." Also such wise counsel as: "Now remember child that a word that's flown is in your hearer's power and not your own." (A. A11058.) Also this hymn the mother used with which to sing her little girl to sleep (A. A11061):

> How can I sleep while angels sing,
> And hover o'er my bed;

> And clap their wings in joy to Him
> Who is their glorious Head?

Also see the recollections of Miss Clara M. S. Shannon, companion to Mrs. Eddy for several years, for Mrs. Eddy's description of her mother's appearance. "Short and stout; she had golden hair, and beautiful blue eyes; she was a blonde" (p. 26).

3. A. Adam Dickey, reminiscence, p. 130; also Hermann S. Hering, notation, March 1919. According to the reminiscence of Clara Shannon, Mrs. Eddy stated that her mother, while pursuing household tasks, was suddenly "overwhelmed by the thought that she was filled with the Holy Ghost. . . . At that moment she felt the quickening of the babe, and then she thought, 'What a sin I am guilty of — the sin of presumption! in thinking that I could be filled with the Holy Ghost!' "

4. Mark Baker was a vigorous and inelastic personality. In later years Mrs. Eddy recalled to her household members, "Father kept the family in the tightest harness I have ever known" (Tomlinson, *Twelve Years with Mary Baker Eddy,* p. 17). Still he was known to friends and neighbors as "Uncle Mark" — there was a warmth and kindheartedness in his character. (See Peel, *Mary Baker Eddy: The Years of Discovery,* p. 5.)

5. *Ret.,* p. 31; also Miss Shannon and the written recollections of Miss Julia S. Bartlett, who lived with Mrs. Eddy at her Columbus Avenue home for several years, and William R. Rathvon, Mrs. Eddy's corresponding secretary and member of her household from November, 1908, until Mrs. Eddy's passing in December, 1910. [Ed. Note: Powell may have been referring in this note to the Shannon reminiscence, p. 33, the Bartlett reminiscence, p. 8, and the Rathvon addendum, p. 69.]

6. Rev. Irving C. Tomlinson, a member of her household at Concord and at Chestnut Hill, stresses Mrs. Eddy's unusual consciousness of God.

7. Professor Hering; Wilbur, p. 27.

8. *Saint Joan,* by Bernard Shaw, p. 60.

9. *Ret.,* p. 13.

10. A. Clara Shannon, reminiscence, p. 5.

11. Wilbur, pp. 26, 33.

12. The author recalls on several visits to the Chestnut Hill home, seeing the bed light Mrs. Eddy used until the last. Sometimes she woke — says Mr. Rathvon — at three in the morning to make notes on the pad she always kept on the little walnut table at the side of her bed, still there in her modest sleeping room, which is unchanged like her study in furnishings and appointments. (See also A. L05121.)

13. E. Mary Ramsay, *Christian Science and Its Discoverer,* p. 4. *Ret.,* p. 10.

14. G. Stanley Hall (1844–1924) was an American psychologist and educator. He helped organize the American Psychological Association in 1891 and was the first president of Clark University, from 1889 to 1920. Among Hall's books is *Jesus, the Christ, in the Light of Psychology* (1917).

S. Weir Mitchell (1829–1914) was an American physician and author. He was an early pioneer in the use of psychology in medicine, and also is remembered for his study of the nervous system.

15. That Mary Baker was already thus early in life, resourceful, enterprising, and gifted with a sense of humor, is indicated by the following incident she related to Mr. Rathvon in 1909: "Mark Baker was insistent that all of the family be present at morning devotions, which he conducted by reading from the Bible followed by extemporaneous prayer, with all present kneeling in silence. In his fervor he would sometimes extend his prayer beyond the limits of the little girl's endurance. On one occasion, after standing it as long as she could, she took a long shawl pin from the pin-cushion on the table, crawled along the floor until she got behind the chair where he was kneeling and vehemently exhorting, applied the pin at a point where it brought immediate results, and in the confusion that followed made her escape." Mr. Rathvon recalls that as she told him the

story eighty years after, the quiet smile, to which those near her were accustomed, lighted up her face.

16. *Ret.,* p. 7.

17. The business card of Albert, after his admission to the Bar, shows that he shared Mr. Pierce's office. Franklin L. Pierce was just graduating from the New Hampshire House of Representatives into Congress where he supported President Jackson. Six years later he joined Webster, Clay, and Calhoun in the United States Senate; later served in the Mexican War; and was elected President of the United States in 1852.

18. August 7, 1902, the Reverend Irving C. Tomlinson wrote Mrs. Eddy that he had learned the following fact "from your loving neighbor and loyal follower, Mrs. Mary D. Aiken. She was telling me of her mother, Mrs. Harriet P. Dodge, née Dunklee, who as a girl was well acquainted with your honored family.... Mrs. Dodge says, 'When I was quite a young girl I cut my finger and Albert Baker tried to persuade me that it did not hurt me any.' You and your dear brother were so close that these thoughts must have been your own." See also Mrs. Eddy's letter of April 17, 1837, in *Munsey's,* April, 1911, p. 10. (Original is in LY.)

19. Nominated for Congress in 1841 in a district in which a nomination insured election, Albert Baker died before the polling day at the age of thirty-one to the grief of relatives and friends.

20. Those inclined to think Mrs. Eddy was ever seriously influenced by Emerson may care to know that in her bold handwriting on the flyleaf of her copy of Emerson's *Nature,* published in 1836, the author finds the comment: "Emerson put so much reason into Mind and so much philosophy into Science that he lost the true sense of Spirit, God." [Ed. Note: While Mrs. Eddy may well have read Emerson earlier and formed her opinion then, she entered these words in a reprint of his *Nature,* dated 1905.]

21. That Mrs. Eddy was not altogether ignorant of English parliamentary speaking a while earlier would seem to appear

from a letter she wrote to her friend Judge Septimus J. Hanna, February 6, 1898: "You have shown yourself our American barrister for the legal rights of C. S. beyond the power of an English Fox that I as a child delighted to take in when reading his eloquent pleadings for equity." (A. L05209.)

22. On May 5, 1907, in a talk with George H. Kinter, one of her secretaries, she thus described her memory: "When I was a little girl I could remember whatever I read, never forgot anything, used to be the prompter for the entire family, my father and all of them. We had a chore boy, a good fellow, but one who had had no advantages of books, or schooling, so I used to read the Bible to him, a chapter at a time, and then repeat it to him. I wanted him to go to Sunday School, and my father did too, but he was bashful about it because he could not recite Bible verses as the others did. I adopted this plan, but he would forget it as soon as I had recited it to him, so I hit upon the plan of reading it aloud, and then closing the book, I would rehearse it to him, and then he could remember and did recite it himself in Sunday School."

23. Lindley Murray's *Introduction to the English Reader,* p. 100.

24. *Ibid.,* p. 102.

25. Plate and pictures of the Baker family shown the author March 21, 1930, by Mr. Arthur S. Brown in his home at Tilton, New Hampshire, give new evidence of the cultural influences playing round the early life of Mary Baker. Mrs. Brown's father, the late Mr. Selwin B. Peabody, was successor to Mrs. Abigail Tilton in her later years in the management of the large business interests of the Tilton family, and received from her many things of family value, which are now treasured by Mrs. Brown.

26. Many lively discussions on slavery appear in the newspapers of the day. In 1839, Albert Baker sat with a select committee, which adopted resolutions on non-interference of slave and non-slave states with each other, rebuked abolition propaganda methods, recommended that Congress should not interdict slave

trade between states and expressed the opinion that the abolition of slavery without expatriation of slaves, would prove disastrous.

27. A. Clara Shannon, reminiscence, p. 5.

28. Andrew Gault was the son of Sarah Gault, who as a close friend read and prayed with Abigail Ambrose Baker.

29. These verses of Mrs. Eddy now appear in print for the first time. (A. A11312.)

30. Paul Leicester Ford in *The True George Washington*, p. 38, says that Washington in writing to his London tailor for clothes in 1763 directed him to "take measure of a gentleman who wares well-made cloathes of the following size: to wit, 6 feet high and proportionably made — if anything rather slender than thick, for a person of that highth, with pretty long arms and thighs. You will take care to make the breeches longer than those you sent me last, and I would have you keep the measure of the cloaths you now make, by you, and if any alteration is required in my next it shall be pointed out."

Mr. Ford also says, p. 62: "To the end of his life, Washington spelt lie, lye; liar, lyar; ceiling, cieling; oil, oyl; and blue, blew, as in his boyhood he had learned to do. . . . It must be acknowledged that, aside from these errors which he had been taught, through his whole life, Washington was a non-conformist as regarded the King's English."

The reader will observe in this chapter the same improvement in Mrs. Eddy's spelling between her fourteenth and her eighteenth year as is usual with young people still at school. Like Theodore Roosevelt, she was a prodigious letter writer. Like him always hard pressed by her duties, she frequently added to, subtracted from, and interlined her letters. All through her life, she sometimes dropped her commas; sometimes she forgot her periods; and in many letters she did not cross her t's. Once she wrote her trusted friend, Judge Hanna: "I long to see you punctuate my matter just as you do your own; that is the modern way, but I know no rules for it and leave this to you. I have changed the poem a little in punctuation and composition which greatly improves it. I wrote it so quickly I had no time to choose words as is necessary." (A. L05154.)

31. Marcosson in *Munsey's Magazine,* April, 1911, describes the discovery of these letters in the former home of Mrs. George Sullivan Baker at Tilton, and writes an excellent critique of them. The letters are reproduced here through the courtesy of the Frank A. Munsey Company.

32. *Ibid.,* April, 1911, p. 7.

33. *Ibid.,* pp. 8, 9.

34. *Ibid.,* pp. 9, 10.

35. This appears to be the only reference in her correspondence to the Shakers, and it indicates no special interest then in them. But it is worth noting that it was in 1747 that a revival took place in England in the ranks of the Quakers, out of which emerged the sect of the Shakers. At first Jane and James Wardley were the leaders, then Ann Lee, daughter of a blacksmith. In response to a revelation, "Mother" Ann later removed with her followers to America where a settlement was established near Albany, New York. The first Shaker Society in the United States was organized at New Lebanon, New York, in 1787. As "Mother" Ann herself went about preaching and healing by faith, so her followers made converts with the result that sooner or later societies were established in Kentucky, Ohio, Indiana, and Florida as well as in New England. In 1874 there were fifty-eight Shaker communities, numbering 2,415 souls, but by 1905 the number had shrunk to one thousand. The Shakers were celibates, living apart in their own communities and holding property in common. According to the *Encyclopaedia Britannica,* they "held that God was both male and female. . . . In Mother Ann . . . the female principle in Christ was manifested, and in her the promise of the Second Coming was fulfilled." Their lives were of the simplest, without adornment in dress or surroundings. They were busy always with their good works and their

handicrafts, regarding physical disease as an offense against God.

36. *Munsey's Magazine,* April, 1911, pp. 10, 11.

37. A. L02676. In the home of Mr. and Mrs. Arthur S. Brown of Tilton now stands the imposing hall clock once in the Holmes' residence.

38. A. L02677.

39. [Ed. Note: Since the last printing of the Powell biography in 1966, it has been determined that a few of the letters previously attributed to Mary Baker were not in fact written by her, but by another "Mary B." With the omission of these letters, it has been necessary to add a few sentences of text in a few places in this chapter to bridge over these deletions. Such additions are indicated by the use of brackets in the text.]

[As a young woman, Mary Baker was interested in the popular literature of her day. However, her early interest in reading led to more serious literature in her adult years. Women in early nineteenth-century America who attained a high level of culture generally reached that stage only through self-education.]

Though in her adult years, Mrs. Eddy was given to reading Shakespeare — as the marked copy of her Shakespeare in the author's hands indicates and her allusions to him in her writings confirm — she could scarcely in her girlhood have done so much; for it was not then considered proper for girls to read his plays. Indeed, on this account, Charles and Mary Lamb, in 1807, published their interesting, but innocuous, *Tales from Shakespeare,* especially for girls. In the introduction occurs the paragraph:

> For young ladies too it has been my intention chiefly to write, because boys are generally permitted the use of their father's libraries at a much earlier age than girls are; they frequently have the best scenes of Shakespeare by heart, before their sisters are permitted to look into this manly book; and, therefore, instead of recommending these tales to the perusal of young gentlemen who can read them so much better in the originals, I must beg their kind assistance in explaining to their sisters such parts as are

hardest for them to understand; and when they have helped them
to get over the difficulties, then perhaps they will read to them
(carefully selecting what is proper for a young sister's ear) some
passage which has pleased them.

But family reading of Shakespeare at least was permitted; for
Mr. S. B. G. Corser, son of one of her early pastors, speaks of
dropping in sometimes "at the Baker homestead, where
Shakespeare perchance was the theme of conversation." Quoted
from personal letter dated July 17, 1902, to Mrs. Eddy (in
Archives).

Till her passing, Mrs. Eddy was an omnivorous reader. With
her little blue pencil in her hand to mark passages of special
interest, and not infrequently to insert in the margin her own
original comments, Mrs. Eddy read by day and sometimes after
she had gone to bed, with her droplight illuminating book and
pillow. Scores of her books, particularly of the last third of her
life, the author has handled, and most of them can be found in
many a minister's study. They include: Amiel, Arnold (Edwin),
Beecher (Henry Ward), Black (Hugh), Browning (Robert and
Elizabeth), Bunyan, Burns, Byron, Carlyle, Channing, Conybeare
& Howson's *Life of St. Paul,* Dickens, Drummond, Eliot
(George), Emerson, Farrar, Furness, Hillis, Hilty, Jordan
(William George), Keats, Kingsley (Charles), Longfellow, Mabie
(Hamilton W.), Maclaren (Ian), Markham (Edwin), Milton,
Munger, Parker (Joseph), Plato (Jowett's Translation), Pope,
Ruskin, Shakespeare, Talmage (T. DeWitt), Tennyson, Tolstoy,
Trench, Trine, Van Dyke, Whittier. As indicative of her wide-
ranging intellectual interests, Mrs. Eddy sent to Mr. William
Lyman Johnson on February 13, 1905, the newly published *Leg-
ends of Parsifal.*

Her guest room and the room for her maid were fittingly provided with devotional books; and to her own desk with regular-
ity came such magazines as *Century, Christian Herald, Contempo-
rary Review, Literary Digest, North American Review,* and *The
Outlook.* Many numbers are still preserved.

40. A. L02682. Mary Baker began her church going when as a little girl she was taken by her parents every Sunday to the First Congregational Church at Concord. She describes in *My.*, p. 147, how she spent the noon hour between the services under "the grand old elm." She joined the Tilton Congregational Church when she was seventeen years old.

41. A. Letter written by D. Russell Ambrose, April 9, 1876, to his cousin, Mary Baker Glover [Eddy].

42. *Munsey's Magazine* April, 1911, p. 11.

43. A. L02682.

44. A. L02678.

Chapter 3

1. Mrs. Sarah C. Turner, niece of the Cheneys, in a testimony embodied in a letter written May 5, 1907, by Albert E. Miller to Mrs. Eddy (in Archives), recalls that Mary Baker was fair to look upon. Her eyes were blue. Her cheeks were richly red. Soft chestnut hair fell in ringlets to her shoulders. Grace of manner and a becoming gown gave to these good looks a fascination all observed and few resisted.

The color of Mrs. Eddy's eyes (like her stature, which actually was five feet six inches) has often been the subject of discussion. The most informing note is furnished by Miss Emma McLauthlin, her friend and household companion at Pleasant View for several weeks late in the nineties. In her recollections Miss McLauthlin writes: "I asked her as to the much disputed color of her eyes; she put both her hands on my shoulders, and gently pushed me with my back to the window while she faced the light with her eyes looking smilingly into mine, and asked me what color I thought they were. I said 'They are hazel with such large pupils that they look very dark. I do not see a vestige of blue in them.' She laughingly said that reminded her of a disagreement between Judge and Mrs. Hanna over the same subject. The Judge was first called to meet her personally, and when he returned Mrs. Hanna asked him to describe her looks; in doing this he spoke of her eyes as sky-blue. When later Mrs. Hanna had had an interview with her, she asked her husband why he had told her Mrs. Eddy's eyes were blue, when there wasn't a vestige of blue in them. Many years later, during a stay with her of several weeks, one day as she sat gazing out of the window with a far-away look, seeing visions unknown to me, standing opposite, I noted with wonder that her eyes were blue as sapphires."

2. Report of Charleston Committee. *The Charleston Evening Post,* quoted in the *CSS.* 9:378, (January 26, 1907).

3. *Ret.,* (1st edition), p. 24.

4. In 1902 S. B. G. Corser, son of Corban Curtice's predecessor as pastor of the Bakers' church, recollected the following: "As Mrs. Eddy's pastor — and for a time teacher — my father held her in the highest esteem; in fact he considered her, even at an early age, superior both intellectually and spiritually to any other woman in Tilton, and greatly enjoyed talking with her. . . . I well remember her gift of expression which was very marked, as girls of that time were not usually possessed of so large a vocabulary. She and my father used to converse on deep subjects frequently (as I recall to mind, from remarks made by my father) too deep for me. She was always pure and good. . . . During my residence of some years, previous to the fall of 1843, in or near the present town of Tilton, I never heard a lisp against the good name of Miss Baker but always praise for her superior abilities and scholarship, her depth and independence of thought, and not least, [her] spiritual mindedness. . . ." A. S. B. G. Corser, reminiscence, August 4, 1902.

5. A. Gilbert Carpenter, reminiscence, p. 23.

6. A. *Ibid.*

7. *Historic Towns of the Southern States* by Powell, p. 259.

8. *Ibid.,* by Powell, p. 275.

9. Lindley Murray's *Introduction to the English Reader,* p. 151.

10. A. Clara Shannon, reminiscence, pp. 11, 12.

11. A. Letter from Robert Grant to Alfred Farlow, January 21, 1907.

12. [Ed. Note: Powell's discussion about George Glover's slaves (here and in the next few pages) and their disposition after Glover's passing cannot be documented as well as one would wish. For other information on this subject, see Peel, *Mary Baker Eddy: The Years of Discovery*, p. 75; and footnotes numbered 126, 1 and 2 on pp. 322–323. Glover almost certainly had had slaves and very probably had had at least a manservant at the time of his passing. In her later years Mrs. Eddy said she had declined to sell them, and the presumption must be that she let them go free informally.]

13. A. Clara Shannon, reminiscence, p. 11. William R. Rathvon, in his reminiscences (also in Archives), provides the following diary entry: "May 29, 1909: Mrs. Eddy was in a reminiscent mood and speaking to me of her earlier experiences in Charleston, said, 'We found the people of the South generally kind and hospitable, so long as the question of slavery was not raised. My husband had the courage of his convictions and may not always have been discreet in voicing them. As a result he was once challenged to a duel by one who believed the Northerner would not fight. Being the challenged party Major Glover had the privilege of naming the weapons and conditions. He chose pistols "toe to toe, and muzzle in the mouth." These austere conditions settled the question of his courage for all time, and the challenger withdrew his challenge [as] quickly as he could and my husband was not again disturbed.' Such performances sound strange to us now, but this was in the days when dueling was the 'gentleman's test of honor and courage' and was approved by such eminent Southerners as Clay, Jackson, Calhoun, and Benton, all of whom, she said, fought notable duels."

14. Alfred Farlow, unpublished manuscript entitled "Historical Facts Concerning Mary Baker Eddy," p. 115.

15. See *Ret.*, p. 19:19–22.

16. The following is taken from a photographic copy of a Card, which appeared in the *Wilmington Chronicle,* August 21, 1844:

Through the columns of your paper, will you permit me, in behalf of the relatives and friends of the late Maj. George W. Glover, of Wilmington, and his bereaved lady, to return our thanks and express the feelings of gratitude we owe and cherish toward those friends of the deceased, who so kindly attended him during his last sickness, and who still extended their care and sympathy to the *lone,* feeble, and bereaved widow, after his decease. Much has often been said of the high feeling of honor, and noble generosity of heart which characterize the people of the South, yet when we listen to Mrs. Glover, (my sister,) whilst recounting the kind attentions paid to the deceased during his last illness, the sympathy extended to her after his death, and the assistance volunteered to restore her to her friends, at a distance of more than a thousand miles, the power of language would be but beggared by an attempt at expressing the feelings of the swelling bosom. The silent gush of grateful tears alone can tell the emotions of the thankful heart. Words are indeed but a meagre tribute for so noble an effort in behalf of the unfortunate, yet it is all we can award; will our friends at Wilmington accept it as the tribute of grateful hearts.

Many thanks are due Mr. Cooke, who engaged to accompany her only to New York but did not desert her, or remit his kind attentions until he saw her in the fond embrace of her friends.

Your friend and obedient servant,

GEORGE S. BAKER.

Sandbornton [sic] *Bridge, N. H., Aug. 12, 1844.*

The above text is reproduced in *My.,* pp. 331, 332.

17. Last stanza of poem "The Widow's Prayer." A. Mrs. Eddy's scrapbook, vol. 1, p. 37B.

18. Wilbur, p. 40.

19. Wilbur, p. 41. Mrs. Eddy's memory of this period is somewhat different. See her "Reply to *McClure's* Magazine," reprinted

in *My.,* p. 313.

20. "When a widow & I sat rocking to sleep my baby boy as I gazed into his sweet face a big tear fell upon his soft cheek & wakened him. Reaching up his little hand to my face & half asleep he murmured 'mama not 'onesome Georgie is comp'ny. Georgie not s'eep.'. . . his little hand fell & he slept on. Those tender words comforted me." Dictated to her secretary at Pleasant View. (A. A11024.)

21. Peel, *Mary Baker Eddy: The Years of Discovery,* p. 93.

22. *The Ladies' Home Journal,* June, 1911; reproduced here through the courtesy of the editor.

23. Wilbur, p. 51.

24. Reminiscence (written in 1911) of Elmira Smith Wilson, the blind girl, who was Mrs. Patterson's maid in North Groton and Rumney, p. 1.

25. Letter to Martha D. Rand, *Munsey's Magazine,* April, 1911, p. 12. Mary Baker's autograph album, given her March 21, 1846, indicates many admirers, all writing in the stilted verse of that day.

26. A. James Smith's letter to Mrs. Glover, December 8, 1849. Mrs. Eddy pasted the following verse, apparently written by James Smith, into her first scrapbook (p. 13A):

LINES

Written in a young lady's album.
Air — "The Bride."

I'd offer thee this heart of mine,
If I could love thee less;
But hearts as warm, as soft as thine,
Should never know distress.
My fortune is too hard for thee,
'Twould chill thy dearest joy;
I'd rather weep to see thee free,
Than win thee to destroy.

I leave thee in thy happiness,
As one too dear to love!
As one I'll think of but to bless,
Whilst wretchedly I rove.
But oh! when sorrow's cup I drink,
All bitter though it be,
How sweet to me 'twill be to think
It holds no drop for thee.

Then fare thee well; an exile now,
Without a friend or home,
With anguish written on my brow,
About the world I'll roam.
For all my dreams are sadly o'er —
Fate bade them all depart, —
And I will leave my native shore,
In brokenness of heart.

S.

27. See Ch. 2, p. 74. Also autograph album (in Archives).

28. *Munsey's Magazine* April, 1911.

29. Perhaps it was this failure of the homeopathic doses, given by her husband to help his wife, that led at last to the sentence in her textbook (p. 152): "Her experiments in homeopathy had made her skeptical as to material curative methods." See also *My.,* 345:15. The following extract from the recollections of "the blind girl" who lived with Mrs. Patterson at North Groton and Rumney affirms that Mrs. Patterson "read a great deal and studied a large Doctors book on Homeopathy, and there were some of the neighbors that would come occasionally for medicine which she would give them. She always kept under her pillow a little bottle of pellets and one day in making up the bed the bottle fell upon the floor and I stepped on it breaking it. While trying to find and pick up the little pills Mrs. Patterson noticed what I had done, but she did not scold me, but told me not to mind as they were no good any way." A. Wilson, reminiscence, pp. 3, 4.

30. Until the end, Mrs. Tilton's character presents a curious combination of generosity and stiffness. In her will dated May 6, 1886, she bequeathed the Tilton Episcopal Church five thousand dollars on condition that a former rector whom she disliked should not be recalled. Liberal provision was made for her many relatives including her nephew, George W. Glover, but Mrs. Eddy was omitted. Her business associate and his little daughter were directed to occupy the first carriage in her funeral procession; "then my direct family according to their years." Of her sister's attitude Mrs. Eddy wrote, "My oldest sister dearly loved me, but I wounded her pride when I adopted Christian Science, and to a Baker that was a sorry offence." *CSS*. 9:312, (January 5, 1907).

31. *Ret.,* p. 20.

32. A. Wilson, reminiscence. Additional information on Mrs. Eddy in North Groton can be found in the reminiscence of Sarah Turner, niece of the Cheneys (in Archives).

33. Her sister, Martha Pilsbury, loaned the thousand dollars to buy the sawmill and some land. A. Wilson, reminiscence, p. 1.

34. A. Wilson, reminiscence, p. 6.

35. A. *Ibid.,* p. 3.

36. A. Mrs. Sylvester Swett, reminiscence. See *S&H,* pp. 170 and 221 for evidence that Mrs. Eddy early became acquainted with the Graham and Cutter cures for dyspepsia.

37. The "blind girl," Elmira or "Myra" Smith Wilson, wrote in 1911 when she was 75 or 76: "Mrs. Tilton, her sister, and myself rode in the carriage with Mrs. Patterson. It was in the spring and the roads were very bad — in spots deep snow — other places mud. As we were leaving, the bell in the church was rung. It was said Joseph Wheat had his son Charles toll the bell. I walked the greater part of the way to Rumney and was very tired & Mrs. Tilton walking with me so that she would not hear the moans and grief of Mrs. [Patterson]." (A. L08898.)

38. A. Letter is dated April 2, 1862.

39. The author's book of 1907, pp. 43–45, 51; Haggard's *Devils, Drugs, and Doctors,* p. 306.

Grimes was a hypnotist and left behind him some crude observations in *Electro-Biology.*

John Bovee Dods, more businessman than philosopher, explained his clairvoyant methods in *The Philosophy of Electrical Psychology,* published in 1850.

Andrew Jackson Davis, born in 1826, had extraordinary vogue before the Civil War as a mesmerist. Elaborate pictures of his method are given in *The Magic Staff* (1857). His favorite thesis was there is no mind, only matter; and his cult faded out before he passed on. He is best remembered as the foremost leader of the spiritualist movement in America.

Warren F. Evans, too, was enamored of magnetism and in his *Mental Medicine* (1872) declared it to be "the torch by the light of which mankind will explore their way to an all-satisfying faith." He was more than a mesmerist. Having been both a Methodist and a Swedenborgian, the philosophy he brought to Quimby, to whom he came for treatment in 1863, was a "blend." Quimby's chief service to Evans, in addition to the improvement in his health, was to show Evans how definitely to heal. He described Quimby's method as "an exhibition of the force of suggestion," laying much stress in the last two chapters of *Mental Medicine* on both the value of "psychic force" and on the specific ways of using finger pressure at various points of the body. He began to practice mental healing after his return to his New Hampshire home, later conducted a mind-cure sanitarium at Salisbury, Massachusetts, and between 1869 and 1886 published several books more lucid than *The Quimby Manuscripts* on mental healing, which had a large place in the genesis and development of New Thought. No propagandist, Evans tried simply to give mental healing a place among the curative agencies in life, and in his last book, *Esoteric Christianity* (published in 1886) he described his teaching as largely "occult" and "phrenopathic."

40. A. L07796, dated February 15, 1866.

41. A. L10106, in Calvin A. Frye's handwriting.

42. *Ret.,* p. 6.

43. Ibid., p.. 13.

44. A. Gilbert C. Carpenter states in his reminiscence, p. 9: "To illustrate how easily she wrote poetry, Mrs. Eddy said to me one day, 'I think in poetry,' and without a moment's hesitation, she dictated a poem to me . . . :

> *Guide as gently, God,*
> *Through the cloud or on the sod;*
> *Be our everlasting stay*
> *Night or day.*

45. A. Mrs. Eddy's scrapbook, vol. 1, p. 37.

46. Mrs. Eddy wrote this letter to her future sister-in-law, Martha D. Rand, probably in 1848 (original in LY). It was published in *Munsey's Magazine,* April, 1911, p. 12.

47. A. Letter from Mary B. Glover to Daniel Patterson, probably early 1853.

48. A. Sarah Turner, reminiscence.

49. H. A. L. Fisher, *Our New Religion,* p. 44.

50. Georgine Milmine, *The Life of Mary Baker G. Eddy and the History of Christian Science,* p. 56.

51. Even at the age of sixty-four, Mrs. Eddy looked about forty, as Mr. Farlow testifies. A. Alfred Farlow, reminiscence, p. 2.

52. A. V03340. Original is in Library of Congress, Quimby papers.

53. A. V03341. Original is in Library of Congress, Quimby papers.

54. A. A10225.

55. She perhaps meant "excited."

56. A. V03342. Original is in Library of Congress, Quimby papers.

57. Milmine, p. 44.

58. Wilbur, pp. 86–87.

59. Reports another patient: "His mode of treating the sick was to immerse his hands in water and manipulate their heads." Emma A. Thompson, *CSJ,* 4:184 (November, 1886).

60. Wilbur, p. 87. Also Matt. 9:21; and *Emmanuel Movement,* by Powell, p. 176.

61. *Portland Courier,* 1862.

62. See (in Archives) V03344, V03345, V03346, V03352, and V03351. Originals are in Library of Congress, Quimby papers. Mrs. Eddy wrote in later years: "At first, my case improved wonderfully under his treatment, but it relapsed." (*My.,* p. 307.)

63. A. V03351. Original is in Library of Congress, Quimby papers.

64. In Archives.

65. *Portland Courier,* November 7, 1862.

66. Milmine, p. 58.

67. A. Abigail Dyer Thompson, reminiscence, October 1928. Also Miss Thompson writes on January 20, 1930, "With regard to the statement made by Dr. Quimby in introducing Mrs. Eddy to my mother, I have heard her tell the entire experience, including that statement, repeatedly since my childhood; and also know that when mother recalled it to our Leader's mind, Mrs. Eddy replied that Dr. Quimby had paid her the same tribute many times during her stay in Portland."

68. A. V03344. Original is in Library of Congress, Quimby papers.

69. John 1:9.

70. From a poem published in the *Lynn Reporter,* February 14, 1866, entitled "Lines on the Death of Dr. P. P. Quimby . . . ."

71. Matt. 17:20. *Ret.,* p. 24. Also Milmine, p. 61.

72. Till the end George A. Quimby was both jealous for his father's reputation and adverse to Christian Science, but on November 11, 1901, he wrote of Mrs. Eddy: "The *religion* which she teaches certainly *is hers,* for which I cannot be too thankful; for I should be loath to go down to my grave feeling that my

father was in any way connected with 'Christian Science.' " He
went on to state his belief that Mrs. Eddy had gotten her "inspiration and idea" from his father. A. Collection of George
Quimby letters.

73. This letter is reproduced by the permission of Mrs. Julius
A. Dresser. Additional information (in Archives) indicates that
Julius Dresser was somewhat sensitive, and would not willingly
become a target of criticism for ministers and doctors. He spent
his time for a while in newspaper work, first in Portland, Maine,
and then in Webster, Massachusetts. As his health failed again,
he went to California to remain till 1882. Mrs. Eddy then had
attracted a following in Boston, and established Christian Science.
The reason Mr. and Mrs. Julius Dresser gave in explanation of
their return in 1882 to take up "the Quimby work" was that
they "had heard what was going on in Boston" and "they
believed the time was now ripe for action."

74. *My.*, pp. 306, 307. In *S&H*, vol. I, 6th edition, (pp. 4, 5),
Mrs. Eddy wrote: "The only manuscript that we ever held of his,
longer than to correct it, was one of perhaps a dozen pages,
most of which we had composed.... Not one of our printed
works was ever copied or abstracted from the published or from
the unpublished writings of any one."

75. A. L07796. Mrs. Patterson's poem entitled "Lines on the
Death of P. P. Quimby..." published in the *Lynn Reporter,*
February 14, 1866. In later years she spoke of "his rare humanity
and sympathy" (*Mis.*, p. 379:18), and also described him as "a
remarkable man." (*My.*, p. 307:22.)

76. The earliest names Mrs. Eddy called her teachings were
*Moral Science, Christian Healing, Mental Healing, Christian Science
Mind-Healing.* But we read in *S&H*, p. 107, that "In the year
1866, I discovered the Christ Science or divine laws of Life,
Truth, and Love, and named my discovery Christian Science."

77. For discussion of its authorship the reader is referred to
CSM, February 25, 1927.

78. Apparently, Quimby did not use the phrase "Science and Health."

79. *'02,* p. 16.

80. Love — II Cor. 13:11, I John 4:7, 8, 16.

Spirit — Gen. 1:2; Job 33:4; John 4:24; Rom. 8:16; Eph. 4:30; I John 4:13.

Truth — Deut. 32:4; Psalms 31:5; Isa. 65:16; Jer. 10:10.

Life — John 1:4; 3:26; Rom. 8:2, 10; Eph. 4:18; Col. 3:4; I John 1:2; 5:12, 20; Rev. 11:11.

81. *Mansions of Philosophy,* by Durant, 55ff; Powell's *Christian Science,* 1907, p. 108.

82. Durant, p. 58.

83. *Memoirs of Jonathan Edwards,* p. 51; and *Heavenly Heretics,* by Powell, p. 22ff.

84. She actually paid visits to Quimby in July 1863, in late 1863 through early 1864, in May 1864, and finally in April and September 1865.

85. A. A11050, recorded by Calvin Frye.

86. Milmine, p. 62, quoting Mrs. Crosby. Also *A Message to the Well,* by Dresser, p. 88.

87. A. S. B. G. Corser, reminiscence, August 4, 1902.

88. Browning's *Paracelsus.*

89. A. Letter of December 11, 1909. The author has a letter which Mrs. Crosby wrote to him, dated May 16, 1907, again summing up her indebtedness: "I am sure my experience with Mrs. Eddy gave me a clearer understanding of my own capabilities as well as a better knowledge of the world."

90. *S&H,* p. 107.

Chapter 4

1. *Human Life,* July, 1907.

2. A. L08660. Asa Eddy states, "Please secure a Charter for the College having the same officers. . . . Mrs. Eddy is the rightful head and we have never yet succeeded unless she filled that

place and we abided by her direction."

3. *Human Life,* July, 1907.

4. A. Julia Bartlett, reminiscence, pp. 9, 10. Although Bartlett's description of Mrs. Eddy is in character, it is actually describing her in 1880.

5. *McClure's,* April, 1907, p. 613.

6. Memorandum April 11, 1930, from executive offices of The Mother Church.

7. [Ed. Note: *Questions and Answers* was also the title of a Quimby manuscript which Mrs. Eddy carried with her for several years after 1866, and which she allowed Mrs. Wentworth to copy. Mrs. Eddy's own manuscript entitled *Questions and Answers* was the basis of her class teaching, which commenced in 1870. This was a substantially different set of questions and answers, and evolved into the chapter "Recapitulation" in the Christian Science textbook after first being published as *The Science of Man.* Over the years, the unfortunate initial use of the title *Questions and Answers* has been a source of confusion regarding the time when Mrs. Eddy left behind any traces of Quimbyism in her own teachings. For more comment on this subject, see Peel, *Mary Baker Eddy: The Years of Discovery,* pp. 230–235.]

8. One of her hearers — not a follower — left this record: "She is a woman of one idea almost to wearisomeness." — Van Ness, *The Religion of New England,* p. 168.

9. Italics the author's.

10. A. L07801.

11. *McClure's,* May, 1907, p. 113.

12. Dakin, p. 96.

13. A. Farlow, "Historical Facts . . . ," pp. 88–89.

14. *My.,* p. 237. Also *CSS,* July 4, 1908.

15. A. Dr. Cushing to Powell, letter, dated June 17, 1907. Cushing states, "The *Reporter* is wrong, as she went home in the morning not afternoon." *S&H,* 3rd edition, pp. 155–157, confirms Dr. Cushing's statement.

16. Dr. Cushing's affidavit in *McClure's,* March, 1907, p. 512.

17. *McClure's,* March, 1907, p. 512.

18. Dr. Cushing's letter, June 17, 1907.

19. Powell's *Human Touch,* pp. 15–16. Sir William Osler (1849–1919) was a Canadian physician who taught for a while at the University of Pennsylvania and at Johns Hopkins. It was at the latter school where Powell, in the summer of 1891, helped edit Osler's *The Principles and Practice of Medicine,* an experience which early in life piqued Powell's interest in the healing arts. Osler, at Oxford after 1905, was knighted in 1911; he was considered the most brilliant professor of medicine of his time.

20. A. L07796. See *Mis.,* p. 24:7 for Mrs. Eddy's account.

21. *Lynn Reporter,* June 30, 1866. However, six months later, she withdrew her claim. See also V03291 in Archives.

22. *CSJ,* (June, 1887). Years later Mrs. Eddy describes as follows the deeper meaning of the fall: "For three years after my discovery, I sought the solution of this problem of Mind-healing, searched the Scriptures and read little else, kept aloof from society, and devoted time and energies to discovering a positive rule. The search was sweet, calm, and buoyant with hope, not selfish nor depressing. I knew the Principle of all harmonious Mind-action to be God, and that cures were produced in primitive Christian healing by holy, uplifting faith; but I must know the Science of this healing, and I won my way to absolute conclusions through divine revelation, reason, and demonstration. The revelation of Truth in the understanding came to me gradually and apparently through divine power." (*S&H,* p. 109.)

"In following these leadings of scientific revelation, the Bible was my only textbook. The Scriptures were illumined; reason and revelation were reconciled, and afterwards the truth of Christian Science was demonstrated. No human pen nor tongue taught me the Science contained in this book, SCIENCE AND HEALTH; and neither tongue nor pen can overthrow it. This book may be distorted by shallow criticism or by careless or malicious students, and its ideas may be temporarily abused and misrepresented; but the Science and truth therein will forever remain to be discerned and demonstrated." (P. 110.)

"After a lengthy examination of my discovery and its demonstration in healing the sick, this fact became evident to me, — that Mind governs the body, not partially but wholly. I submitted my metaphysical system of treating disease to the broadest practical tests. Since then this system has gradually gained ground, and has proved itself, whenever scientifically employed, to be the most effective curative agent in medical practice." *(S&H,* p. 111.)

23. Fisher's *Our New Religion,* p. 45.

24. Farlow, "Historical Facts . . . ," p. 88.

25. In *Ret.,* pp. 24, 28, she calls her experience "The Great Discovery" that "Mind reconstructed the body, and that nothing else could. . . . It was a mystery to me then, but I have since understood it. All Science is a revelation. Its Principle is divine, not human, reaching higher than the stars of heaven."

26. Gen. 32:30.

27. This she paid back with interest, amounting to ninety-six dollars, thirty-eight years later, in 1900 in reply to an appeal from John Patterson, then eighty years old and destitute. (A. John Patterson, letter to Mrs. Eddy.)

28. Dr. Cushing wrote the author in 1907 that Dr. Patterson was not even at home when his wife had her fall in Lynn, and had to be brought down from New Hampshire by telegram the next day. He was rarely where he should have been when needed.

29. Report in Archives.

30. A. Affidavit of R. D. Rounsevel, proprietor of the White Mountain House, Fabyans, N.H., February 3, 1900.

31. Wilbur, pp. 166, 167.

32. A. Clara Shannon, reminiscence, pp. 26, 27.

33. A. L07811, December 30, 1876.

34. A. Clara E. Choate, reminiscence, dated October 12, 1914.

35. A. L08737, to Mrs. Anna Kingsbury.

36. A. Julia Bartlett, reminiscence, p. 9.

37. A. L07691.

38. *Po.,* p. 4.

39. A. He wrote Mrs. Eddy February 24, 1902, that he had had one sheet of the first manuscript typewritten for her that she had written while with him.

40. But, as Mrs. Eddy's little notebook before the author indicates, neither the Crafts nor the Wentworths ever paid her any cash, though it is evident that what they received from her came to far more than her "keep," liberally estimated. H. S. Crafts was lifted out of the manual labor class by her, into at least a semi-professional status with income to match.

41. A. Fred Ellis letters to Mrs. Eddy. She to him, L05663–L05670.

42. Hiram S. Crafts, in a letter written December 14, 1901 (in Archives), states that though a spiritualist when he began to study under Mrs. Eddy, her teachings changed his views and led him altogether away from spiritualism. The author had the privilege in his youth of spending two days in the home of the daughter of Judge Edmunds, a leader of the spiritualistic movement in New York in Mrs. Eddy's earlier womanhood, and of observing that the daughter, once his medium, at the time the author in her old age met her was convinced that under emotional strain the Edmunds family had misinterpreted their experiences. Scarcely anyone of intelligence in the middle of the nineteenth century but had at least a passing interest in spiritualism. In fact, with C. C. Helberg's *A Book of Spirit Writings* and Mrs. M. E. Williams's article in the latest issue of *Psychic Research* available, there is as reliable evidence that Abraham Lincoln was a spiritualist as that Mrs. Eddy, with no more than gossip gathered up a generation later to go by, ever had a profound interest in spiritualism.

43. Not merely did many of these students receive — as the little notebook shows — instruction without charge but also in some cases, where there was actual want, she loaned them money to live on while they studied with her, — that, too, at a time when to make both ends meet she often added to the ordinary cares of a homekeeper scrubbing the floors and living on a meagre diet. She could never, perhaps, have gotten on at all had she not budgeted her time and strength and means. Among the many evidences in the little notebook that she counted her every penny is the following memorandum:

Sept. 26, 1874 Postage 18 cts.
Sept. 26, 1874 Expressage 15 cts.

See also recollections of Miss Emma C. Shipman in Archives.

44. A. L07799.

45. A. Farlow, "Historical Facts . . . ," pp. 94–97.

46. Mrs. Eddy's little notebook, (in A.), in which she kept a careful record of her receipts and expenditures in those days, is a touching revelation of her serious situation. She counted every penny of outlay, as well as of income. Early training may have been a contributory force in this respect, for at Pleasant View she once related to a friend: "When they [Mary and her siblings] were children, in the winter evenings they used to shell corn for food for the chickens, etc. On one occasion little Mary was sitting by the fire, and as she shelled, a grain of corn fell off her lap. She pushed it with her little foot towards the burning log. Her Mother said, 'Mary, get down and pick up that corn.' She answered, 'Oh! Mother, it is only one grain.' 'Never mind,' said her Mother, 'It will help to make a meal for a little chick.' " A. Clara Shannon, reminiscence, p. 8.

47. *Man.,* p. 46.

48. Bancroft's *Mrs. Eddy as I knew her in 1870,* p. 2.

49. In addition, without charge, she opened her little home in Lynn to him and his family, setting aside five of her seven available rooms, and unconsciously revealing the wealth of her tenderness in the words: "Now you have a home offered you and

no rent to pay for it So do not be cast down I thank God more for this than anything that I have a shelter if it is humble to go to in an hour of want and to welcome those who need a little time to meet the hour." A. L08659, written in 1880.

50. A. L02469.

51. *Ret.,* p. 50.

52. Matt. 6:33.

53. *S&H,* p. 60.

54. *S&H,* p. 89.

55. A. Sarah A. Farlow, reminiscence, p. 6.

56. A. From Elizabeth Patterson Baker, April 6, 1875.

57. Wilbur, p. 178. Kennedy also told the author substantially this in 1907.

58. A. Emma Shipman, reminiscence, p. 16.

59. Richard Kennedy, as quoted by Wilbur, p. 278.

60. A. L08304 to Sarah Bagley.

61. Wilbur, p. 139.

62. He called her Mrs. Patterson. Wilbur, p. 140.

63. A. Hiram Crafts' letter to Mrs. Eddy.

64. A. Charles O. Wentworth, reminiscence.

65. Wilbur, p. 179. Of the Wentworths Mrs. Eddy wrote: "they are very kind[.] Don't you think they wont take a cent for board and want me to remain so long as I live." (A. L08307, letter to Sarah Bagley.)

66. *Lynn Transcript,* Wright's letter.

67. Her little notebook contains the full record of her percentage month by month from Kennedy's healing, for a year:

June, 1870	$225
July, 1870	200
August, 1870	137
September, 1870	167
October, 1870	90
November, 1870	200
December, 1870	130
January, 1871	147

February, 1871	100
March, 1871	136
April, 1871	110
May, 1871	100
Total	$1742

68. A. Mrs. Eddy's notebook.

69. But when personalities faded far into the past, Daniel Spofford, near his threescore years and ten, once in his quiet way indicated to a friend of the author that what Mrs. Eddy did for him was beyond all estimation.

70. How Mrs. Eddy dealt with the shock of the defection is such a revelation of her character that Miss Bartlett's personal recollection of the extraordinary experience is given at length: "In October, 1881, eight students who had allowed error to enter their thought, united in writing a disloyal letter of false accusations to their Leader and signed their names to the same. This cruel letter was read by one of their number at a meeting of the Christian Scientists Association in the presence of Mrs. Eddy. She made no reply, and when the meeting, which was held in her house, was closed, she went to her room and all the students went to their homes with the exception of two. These two remained with their beloved teacher to comfort her in her sorrow and anguish. . . . On hearing what had transpired I took the first train for Lynn, desiring to be with my dear teacher and to be of some service in her hour of trial. Dr. Eddy admitted me to the house. I found Mrs. Eddy seated by the table and the two students who had spent the night with her sitting near. I quietly took a seat near them as did Dr. Eddy also, and listened to Mrs. Eddy who was talking with a power such as I had never heard before. They were wonderful words she was speaking while we young students were receiving of the great spiritual illumination which had come through her glorious triumph over evil.

"Just before I had entered the room she was sitting with the others and the burden was still heavy upon her, when all at once she rose from her chair, stepped out in the room, her face radiant and with a far-away look as if she was beholding things the eye could not see. She began to talk and to prophesy of the blessings which would reward the faithful while the transgressor cannot escape the punishment which evil brings on itself. Her language was somewhat in the style of the Scriptures. When she began, the three with her, seeing how it was, caught up their pencils and paper and took down what she said. When she was through speaking, she put down her hand and said, 'Why, I haven't any body,' and as she came back to the thought of those about her, they were so moved by what they had seen and heard their eyes were filled with tears and one was kneeling by the couch sobbing. . . . Those three days were wonderful. It was as if God was talking to her and she would come to us and tell us the wonderful revelations that came. We were on the Mount. We felt that we must take the shoes from off our feet, that we were standing on holy ground. What came to me at that time will never leave me." Julia Bartlett, reminiscence, pp. 16–18. See also Wilbur, p. 259ff.

71. George Walter Fiske's *The Changing Family,* p. 222.

72. Wilbur, pp. 205, 206.

73. A. Irving C. Tomlinson, reminiscence.

74. *The Religion of New England,* by Thomas Van Ness, p. 166.

75. *Christian Science Hymnal* (1932 Edition), pp. 96, 142, 170, 217, 229, 230, 238, 372.

76. A. A10063, undated recollections, dictated by Mrs. Eddy to Calvin Frye. [Ed. Note: Powell evidently substituted "thee" and "thy," which do not appear in the original document.]

77. *Pul.,* p. 5. Bronson Alcott (1799–1888) was an American educational and social reformer. His experiment in group living in Harvard, Mass., lasted for only one year (1843). Alcott was the father of the author Louisa May Alcott. His Concord School of Philosophy, begun in 1879, held annual symposia, and it was in

this capacity that he became acquainted briefly with Mrs. Eddy.

78. A. Bronson Alcott's letter to Mrs. Eddy, January 17, 1876. [Ed. Note: There was very little public comment, pro or con, with respect to the first edition. However, Mrs. Eddy's correspondence at the time indicates that she immediately felt the mental reaction from some of those reading the book.]

79. A. Bronson Alcott's letter to Mrs. Eddy, March 5, 1876.

80. *Christian Scientist Association* records, vol. 1, p. 17.

81. A. Bronson Alcott's letter to Mrs. Eddy, February 6, 1876.

82. A. See Hiram S. Crafts' letter of December 14, 1901, stating that she was not a spiritualist.

83. Mrs. Emilie B. Hulin, often with Mrs. Eddy in her Concord days, told the author in April, 1930, that Mrs. Eddy in speaking of this period said that sometimes, as she wrote, her hands would grow so cold she would go down to the kitchen to warm them over the stove.

84. A. L08866.

85. "When," writes Mrs. Eddy in *Science of Man,* 1876 edition, p. 12, "we commenced teaching this science, we permitted students to manipulate the head, ignorant that it could do harm, or hinder the power of mind acting in an opposite direction, viz.: spiritually, while the hands were at work and the mind directing material action. We regret to say it was the sins of a young student, that called our attention to this question for the first time, and placed it in a new moral and physical aspect. By thorough examination and tests, we learned manipulation hinders instead of helps mental healing."

In further confirmation of the fact that Mrs. Eddy had completely done with Quimbyism, the author, in 1907, was informed by George A. Quimby that he believed that Mrs. Eddy had finally landed in prayer-cure pure and simple.

86. *Cambridge History of American Literature,* Vol. III, p. 526.

87. The weather report, in and about Boston in 1875, indicates an average temperature of 72 for July, and 71 for August, with

a rainfall of 3.93 and 3.50 respectively.

88. A. Clara Shannon, reminiscence, p. 5.

89. George Clark's boys' story of sea life was accepted, and all the way home Mrs. Eddy rejoiced with him, as though she, herself, had not suffered a grievous disappointment. Wilbur, pp. 202–203.

90. The bill itself is in Archives.

91. A. L07808.

92. In her personal notebook Mrs. Eddy records: "490 typographical errors in words besides paragraphs and pages wrong and punctuation."

93. *S&H,* 1st edition, p. 300.

94. *S&H,* p. 43.

95. *S&H,* 1st edition, p. 386.

96. Since Mrs. Eddy passed away in 1910, no changes have appeared in *Science and Health,* other than those already indicated by her.

97. *S&H,* 1907 edition, p. 390. This quotation appears on the same page in the present edition.

98. Flyleaf of *Science and Health,* 1907 edition.

99. For account of "Next Friends" see Chapter VI. See full account in Peel, *Mary Baker Eddy: The Years of Authority,* chapter VIII.

100. A. John Wilson, letter to Mrs. Eddy, December 18, 1896.

101. A. William Nixon served as Mrs. Eddy's agent, October 1889 to December 1892. Also see Mrs. Eddy, letters to Nixon; some of these concern *Science and Health.*

102. A. L09002.

103. A. A facsimile of this letter appears on p. 147.

104. A. William B. Reid, reminiscence, January 16, 1930, pp. 16–18.

105. *In Quest of the Perfect Book,* by William Dana Orcutt, pp. 52–54.

106. My., p. 319.

107. A. L02159, L02179, L02181, and L02219.

108. *My.*, p. 318.

Chapter 5

1. The reader who cares for the information is referred to the following descriptions of Boston:

Drake's *Old Landmarks of Boston;* Ticknor's *Doctor Holmes's Boston;* E. M. Bacon's *Rambles Round Old Boston;* Shackleton's *The Book of Boston;* Powell's *Historic Towns of New England.* Also certain letters written to the author, beginning in 1893, by Oliver Wendell Holmes, T. W. Higginson, Edward Everett Hale, George P. Morris, Charles Carlton Coffin, Frank B. Sanborn, Hezekiah Butterworth, William E. Barton, W. W. Goodwin, Edwin D. Mead, James Schouler, James F. Rhodes, and President Charles W. Eliot.

2. Brook Farm in West Roxbury, Mass., was an experiment in group living from 1841 until 1847. Founded by two Transcendentalists, it became known for its high thinking and its good school. The farming part of the venture was less successful.

3. Francis Marion Crawford (1854–1909) was an American novelist and historian, and the nephew of Julia Ward Howe. Born in Italy, he returned there after his American education. Beginning in 1882, he wrote some 40 novels in the next 25 years, sometimes turning out three books in a single year.

4. Powell's *Heavenly Heretics,* p. 126.

5. "A beautiful spot by the sea where sometimes she loved to go by herself." (A. Julia Bartlett, reminiscence, p. 10.)

6. After going the limit in free will service for affection's sake, Barry in a temper foolishly turned to the law to secure him repayment in cash.

Spofford had the distinction of being the only American of his day to have a legal action brought against him for witchcraft; then of disappearing under circumstances so mysterious that a charge was laid against two of his former friends that they had murdered him, which was not dropped until Spofford reappeared in two weeks. He lived to become a kindly old man, who left on record a final opinion that Mrs. Eddy was "the sole author of her famous book."

Richard Kennedy became a respected Vestryman of St. Paul's Episcopal Church in Boston and lived on into the twentieth century. In a conversation with the author in his old age he deplored the pettiness of the men and women around Mrs. Eddy those days in Lynn and observed that it all seemed unworthy of men and women in this work-a-day world of ours.

In jauntily passing off Mrs. Eddy's writings as his own Edward J. Arens seemed to forget what he perhaps had never learned, that they were copyrighted, and that infringement of copyright — a subject on which Asa Gilbert Eddy subsequently made himself an authority — is a serious matter in the eyes of the law; but when the court so ruled, Arens had at last to quit, and dropped into the background.

7. A. Julia Bartlett, reminiscence, p. 9. See also *We Knew Mary Baker Eddy,* p. 31.

8. A. L01138.

9. A. L02059.

10. A. L05212.

11. *Genealogy and Life of Asa Gilbert Eddy,* by Mary Beecher Longyear.

12. A. L08660, Asa Eddy, letter to James C. Howard (August 5, 1880).

13. A. Asa Eddy, letter to Mr. and Mrs. Choate, June 23, 1878.

14. "My last marriage was with Asa Gilbert Eddy, and was a blessed and spiritual union, solemnized at Lynn, Massachusetts, by the Rev. Samuel Barrett Stewart, in the year 1877. Dr. Eddy was the first student publicly to announce himself a Christian Scientist, and place these symbolic words on his office sign. He

forsook all to follow in this line of light. He was the first organizer of a Christian Science Sunday School, which he superintended. He also taught a special Bible-class; and he lectured so ably on Scriptural topics that clergymen of other denominations listened to him with deep interest. He was remarkably successful in Mind-healing, and untiring in his chosen work. In 1882 he passed away, with a smile of peace and love resting on his serene countenance. 'Mark the perfect *man,* and behold the upright: for the end of *that* man *is* peace.' (Psalms xxxvii. 37.)" *Ret.,* p. 42.

15. Professor Traquair's plea in *The Atlantic,* March, 1929, for "equal rights for men" in these days when women have without the asking the position which Mrs. Eddy won long years ago by worth and work, finds no illustration in the career of Asa Gilbert Eddy.

16. The original is in Archives. See also Peel, *Mary Baker Eddy: The Years of Discovery,* pp. 286–287.

17. "After our dinner was over we assembled in the parlor for a sing in which Mrs. Eddy joined us usually. My son, Warren, was about 5 yrs. old, & every one petted him more or less for he sang nicely and both Dr. and Mrs. Eddy delighted to hear him. This eve Mrs. Eddy grew silent as she often did when impressed by unusual thought arising for her consideration. The singing ceased, & one after another left the room for various reasons. There seemed such good feeling, we spoke of the progress we were making in the cause & felt this was a demonstration of the love she was trying to establish. The boy had climbed into her lap & gave her some caresses. She began to talk to him in something of this fashion, 'Now Warren dear you behaved splendidly today.' 'Well,' he replied, 'I know I did for you didn't look at me any all the time you talked, & now you love me, don't you?' To this Mrs. Eddy tenderly assented, and she told him she had a plan for him to speak on the platform with her. This greatly interested myself of course, as well as the boy. Mrs. Eddy

still embraced with loving hugs now & then as their two heads leaned together as if in concurring confidence. Mrs. Eddy continued, 'well, we *must* have a Sunday School, Warren. You shall be the first scholar.' He fell in with the plans but immediately said, 'how can we have a Sunday School with only *me*.' Mrs. Eddy smilingly told him that was only to begin with, & soon other little boys & girls would come & he would have them to listen to & to play with, but he could not comprehend how so much was to follow, tho if Mrs. Eddy said so & they must come if she told them to. I, the one onlooker, thought it all prattle to amuse the child, & gave no serious thought to either of them nor to what they were saying. I gave special attention tho to Mrs. Eddy's loving tenderness with the child & it found a like response in my own heart's love for her, & at the time she was so beset and distracted by worldly trials & evils on every hand. The boy grew sleepy & was soon abed, while Mrs. Eddy retired to her apartments, to no doubt formulate plans so suddenly started then & there. The following morning Mrs. Eddy asked Warren if he would come upstairs to her parlor awhile to which he readily consented. We never questioned Mrs. Eddy why nor wherefore in those days. So after Warren had an extra touch to his hair & a general looking over of face, hands & clothes, that he might not offend in any way, we kissed & he went to keep his important appointment — to explain the extra care Warren continually reminded us that 'Mrs. Eddy *is fussy* & won't like it so & so.' After quite a stay the boy reappeared full of enthusiasm & fun. We asked him what it meant & he mysteriously replied 'Mrs. Eddy has been rehearsing me.' Further questioning was for a time useless except that some important affair was afoot & the child was alive with its importance. Every little while he would recite in a most dramatic way a line from a song later another line and with each subsequent visit with Mrs. Eddy during the next few days, new words and new lines, were recited in all sorts of ways over & over. Then a message came from Mrs. Eddy, thro him, she would like him to look his best for the coming Sunday, for she was going to open her Sabbath School & he was to speak from the platform at the Hawthorne rooms on Park St., one verse before she began the regular services of the church. We all gladly consented and the boy's best frock a white pique kilt with wide collar & cuffs, a wide blue sash was all carefully attended to for Warren continued to assert 'Mrs. Eddy was terrible fussy,' and she told *him* he was just as important on the platform as she was & must look nice & behave nice & he thought her handsome if she *'was fussy.'* So each day of this very important & busy week was varied with plans & talk over the idea of a Sabbath School. Some praised & others discouraged the project, in the meantime Mrs. Eddy with all her manifold duties of church work, lectures forthcoming & manuscript to be revised, found time to *'rehearse'* the child in the verse he was to recite on Sunday at 3 P.M., Mrs. Eddy was as we all know quite particular in manners. She objected to our saying *thanks* & felt it better manners to say 'thank you' if occasion required.

"So she taught the boy how to walk to the front of the platform, how to bow to the audience, how to scrape his foot or draw it backward and the general fine gestures before his recitation. I don't know which enjoyed most these times, he or Mrs. Eddy. In giving these details his attention & which he practised daily, he caused us endless amusement & many a laugh & scream in which Dr. and Mrs. Eddy joined heartily. But the boy did finely in them all and with watchful coaching of such a woman as Mrs. Eddy, is it any wonder he should meet the excellence she expected. The wonder to me is she could ever find time to attend to these details. It all enforces the fact, however, of her thoroughness in laying foundations. In her mind the idea of the church with a Sabbath School was a truly engrossing affair, so she frequently said, & to this end we must help her. The starting was not easy and numbers, or material to work with were not then plentiful. Most of those interested or attracted to

the cause were above the age desirable for such a movement.
The younger element being Miss Lilly, Miss Potter, Mr. Orne,
Mr. Bancroft, my young sister & myself. I know of only one
other *child* besides Warren, the son of Mrs. Rice, about my boy's
age, but he was living in Lynn & quite a care, so he did not
come to the services regularly with either his mother or his aunt,
Miss Rawson, who usually attended. I do not now remember so
much of the services on this particular Sunday only we assembled at 3 P.M. as usual, for Mrs. Eddy was very prompt. She had
taken greatest pains to look nice as an example to us, who were
not as the boy termed '*so fussy.*' She even placed a rose in her
hair to the delight of the boy whose beaming face betrayed not
the least anxiety, but a consequential air pervaded him which
pleased Mrs. Eddy, who so wisely said to us, 'We don't know
where this will all end do we,' but we as ever unthinkingly
replied 'Well, it won't amount to much anyway,' at least not
impressively for the church or for the cause. But Mrs. Eddy
made no reply & with undaunted quiet refrained from argument.
With her reticule containing some leaves for her sermon she
entered the hall from the dressing room in the rear, hand in
hand with the boy. They ascended the few steps at the side of
the platform. With a graceful bow to an ever respectful audience,
she stepped to the front of the platform at the side of the pulpit, and spoke of the Sabbath School in a few words, & as *if it
already existed.* She then introduced this little boy, Warren, as one
of the representatives of the school, who would recite a short
verse. He had followed in her wake & stood deferentially quiet
beside her and as she retired, with a face full of smiles he bowed
profoundly. In the most assured tones he then recited the following verse Mrs. Eddy had taught him to say & had so often
'*rehearsed*' him, that full credit might be done to her & to the
school he represented —

> 'And right is right — since God is God;
> And right the day must win;

> To doubt would be disloyalty,
> To falter would be sin!'

Then another graceful bow and he came down to sit with Dr. Eddy, who seldom was on the platform with Mrs. Eddy, & who enjoyed the company of the boy, relieving me of care, while I sang a solo part, or led the congregational hymns with the quartette.

"The sermon was beautiful, full of the glory of Truth, the healing Truth of Christ. She seemed inspired & it uplifted us all by her positive & explanatory revelations. She referred to 'A little child shall lead them.' The Dr. looked with admiration from her to the boy, who had done so well, for 'a sensitive little chap,' as the Dr. said & by her directing. The singing was fine & the contribution generous. We all felt a new era of the cause was coming. As the audience of less than one hundred parted, more harmony was manifest and a mutual resolution to loyally abide by Mrs. Eddy's leadership. Upon our return at the dinner table the Dr. remarked with so much love, Mary, you have done a great work today, a grand work, & she turning to the boy with a smile said 'It is because I let this little child lead me.' Of course we all looked the adoring love of her we could not speak, and retired to the parlor for our singing with a *God praise* few companies can ever know." (A. Clara E. Choate, reminiscence.)

Mrs. Choate's many affectionate references, during 1914, to Mrs. Eddy are the more informing because in the eighties Mrs. Eddy more than once lovingly — as was her lifelong habit — reproved her young friend and student in accordance with St. Paul's counsel (II Timothy 4:2) to his young friend Timothy to "reprove, rebuke, exhort, with all longsuffering"; and also in illustration of her own words in the *Man.,* (Art. VIII, Sec. 1): "a Christian Scientist reflects the sweet amenities of Love, in rebuking sin, in true brotherliness, charitableness, and forgiveness."

18. A. Mary Harris Curtis, reminiscence.

19. Before undertaking to give an impression of Mrs. Eddy's appearance in her Boston pulpit, the author in years past talked with many who then heard her — including the late Miss Frances J. Dyer, then of *The Congregationalist.* He has also read the unpublished recollections now in the possession of The Mother Church of Mrs. Clara E. Choate, Miss Julia S. Bartlett, Miss Mary Alice Dayton, Miss Elsie Lincoln, Miss Mary A. Daggett, Miss Sarah A. Farlow, Mrs. Mary E. Foye, Mrs. Annie R. Hessler, Mr. William B. Reid, and Mr. William Lyman Johnson.

On all, Mrs. Eddy, near threescore years and ten, made the impression of eternal youth, and often imparted the impression to others. Miss Lilian Whiting wrote in the Ohio *Leader,* July 2, 1885, when Mrs. Eddy was sixty-four, that she came away from her first interview with "an utterly unprecedented buoyancy and energy which lasted days."

Mrs. Emma Easton Newman reports in her recollections that when Mrs. Eddy was sixty-seven, Mrs. Newman's father guessed she was about fifty-five. (A. Emma E. Newman, reminiscence.)

Mr. Farlow first met Mrs. Eddy when she was sixty-four and observed "she might easily be taken for a lady of forty." (A. Alfred Farlow, reminiscence, p. 2.)

At fifty-six Mrs. Eddy looked so young that Asa Gilbert Eddy, never once having thought to ask her age, assumed that it was forty when he applied for the marriage license, and it was not till many years after his passing that Mrs. Eddy ever heard of the occurrence. (A. Farlow, "Historical Facts...," p. 123.) See also Peel, *Mary Baker Eddy: The Years of Trial,* p. 20.

Mrs. Eddy writes in *Science and Health:* "Comeliness and grace are independent of matter. Being possesses its qualities before they are perceived humanly. Beauty is a thing of life, which dwells forever in the eternal Mind and reflects the charms of His goodness in expression, form, outline, and color. It is Love which paints the petal with myriad hues, glances in the warm sunbeam, arches the cloud with the bow of beauty, blazons the night with starry gems, and covers earth with loveliness." *(S&H,* p. 247.)

20. Mrs. Eddy wrote an early student: "a Baptist clergyman in Boston (now more of an Adventist) sent for me to supply his pulpit and I did, that gave me the opportunity for six months to keep the 'good tidings' circulating. I healed a large number by my sermons and they owned it at the close of them." (A.   L02050.)

21. *Man.,* p. 48.

22. A.   C. Lulu Blackman, reminiscence.

23. A.   *Ibid.*

24. A.   Sarah A. Farlow, reminiscence, p. 2.

25. A.   Mary Alice Dayton, reminiscence, October 10, 1917.

26. *S&H,* p. 465.

27. William Leroy Stidger (1885–1949) was a Methodist clergyman who pioneered religious broadcasting. For a while he was head of the department of preaching in Boston University's School of Theology, where he gave the first course (1938) on radio preaching.

28. A.   Sarah A. Farlow, reminiscence, pp. 4–5.

29. A.   Mary E. Foye, reminiscence, p. 5.

30. *Ira Oscar Knapp and Flavia Stickney Knapp,* by Bliss Knapp, p. 15.

31. *Mis.,* p. 99.

32. A.   L14502.

33. A.   L13271.

34. *Faith Work, Christian Science, and Other Cures,* p. 46.

35. John 9:25.

36. A.   Julia Bartlett, reminiscence, pp. 7–8.

37. *Ira Oscar Knapp and Flavia Stickney Knapp,* by Bliss Knapp, p. 6.

38. *Ibid.,* pp. 8–9.

39. *CSJ,* 10:68, 71 (May, 1892).

40. A.   Joseph G. Mann, reminiscence, p. 69.

41. Frances Burnett (1849–1924), was an American author, known for her children's books, among which were *Little Lord Fauntleroy* and *The Secret Garden.* Louisa May Alcott (1832–1888)

was the daughter of Bronson Alcott. She is remembered mainly
for her book *Little Women,* which appeared in the late 1860s, as
well as for other children's novels which she wrote throughout
the 1870s. Rose Cleveland was the sister of Grover Cleveland.
When Cleveland became president in 1885, he was still a bachelor, and Rose went to live at The White House.

42. At first it was called the *Journal of Christian Science.* Her
great happiness in editing the *Journal* is indicated in a letter
written January 31, 1884, to Colonel E. J. Smith, to whom she
also says "Never was a time when the Cause was in better condition." (A. L02065.)

43. *CSJ,* (September, 1886).

44. *The Genealogy and Life of Asa Gilbert Eddy,* by Mary
Beecher Longyear.

45. The following is an excerpt from one of George W. Glover's letters to his mother, dated January 31, 1895:

"I have a very valuable mining property which lies next to and
adjoining the property of a company that is shipping ore. The
company is anxious to get it and have offered seven thousand
five hundred dollars, but that is only a pittance.

"If I had two thousand dollars to open it I would realize a
good figure as it is now I haven't the money and can't open it
out so as to receive what it is worth.

"I do not wish you to feel as if I was asking any thing of you
for nothing but if you can assist me at present it would be of
great help and I would secure you." (In Archives.)

46. Mrs. Eddy's Petition.

47. It is difficult to square this assertion with the fact that he
joined on March 11, 1907, in bringing the "Next Friends' Suit,"
a suit that troubled Mrs. Eddy gravely.

48. A. Petition filed in Probate Court of Suffolk County.

49. A. E. J. Foster-Eddy, letter to William Lyman Johnson,
February 23, 1920. Foster-Eddy passed away November 13, 1930.

50. Of this visit she wrote Colonel E. J. Smith June 25, 1884:
"I went in May to Chicago at the imperative call of people there

and my own sense of the need. This great work had been started but my students needed me to give it a right foundation and impulse in that city of ceaseless enterprise. So I went, and in three weeks taught a class of 25 pupils, lectured ... to a *full* house, got 20 subscriptions for my Journal, sold about thirty copies of Science and Health, etc. In the class were three M.D.'s and two clergymen — one Methodist, the other Universalist both · good thinkers and scholarly." A. L02069.

51. Powell's *Historic Towns of the Western States,* p. 228.

52. *Mis.,* p. 134.

53. Mark Sullivan (*Our Times,* I, pp. 123–131) says that Bryan's historic speech was extemporaneous only in its arrangement. In paragraphs he had made the speech scores of times the two years before up and down the Missouri Valley. Once at least on the floor of Congress he had closed a speech with the phrase: "You shall not press down upon the brow of labor this crown of thorns, you shall not crucify mankind upon a cross of gold."

54. *Mis.,* pp. 98–106.

55. *CSJ,* 6:209 (July, 1888).

56. Mrs. Annie Macmillan Knott, who was present in Central Music Hall and later attended the reception in the Palmer House, tells the author that Mrs. Eddy remained at the hotel reception only a few minutes. "She shrank from personal adulation and everything of that sort."

57. Wilbur, p. 311.

58. New Thought, too, is a revolt against materialism, and is altogether idealistic. Both in theory and in practice it differs from Christian Science.

59. [Ed. Note: The steps which Mrs. Eddy took in changing the organizational form of her Church between 1889, when she dissolved most of the then existing organization, and 1892, when she established the church under The Christian Science Board of Directors, do not appear to have been directly the result of the growth of Christian Science into a nationwide movement. However, the organization which eventually unfolded in her thought

was indeed one whose structure would accommodate both a nationwide and eventually a global membership. She had come by bitter experience to recognize that a movement under the direct control of all its members would be unable to withstand the passions of the moment and therefore would not be a stable enough institution to fulfill its purpose.]

60. *Mis.*, p. 359. The following personal letter, November 28, 1889, addressed to the Church takes us back across the years:

"The Church of Christ (Scientist) in Boston was my patient seven years. When I would think she was well nigh healed a relapse came and a large portion of her flock would forsake the better portion, and betake themselves to the world's various hospitals for the cure of moral maladies. These straying sheep would either set up claims of improvements on Christian Science and oppose the Mother Church, or sink out of sight in religious history. This state of the Church has lasted ten years. It even grew rapidly worse when about three years ago I for lack of time to adjust her continual difficulties and a conscientious purpose to labor in higher fields and broader ways for the advancement of the glorious hope of Christian Science put students in my pulpit.

"As one who is treating patients without success remembers that they are depending on material hygiene, consulting their own organizations and thus leaning on matter instead of Spirit, saith to these relapsing patients, 'now quit your material props and leave all for Christ, spiritual power, and you will recover.' So I admonish this Church after ten years of sad experience in material bonds to cast them off and cast her net on the spiritual side of Christianity. To drop all material rules whereby to regulate Christ, Christianity, and adopt alone the golden rule for unification, progress, and a better example as the Mother Church." (A. L00008.)

On December 2, 1889, the church members at 9:30 p.m. unanimously adopted the following resolutions:

"(1.) That the time has come when this Church should free itself from the thraldom of man-made laws, and rise into spiritual latitudes where the law of love is the only bond of union.

(2.) That the Regulations and By-Laws of this Church be and are hereby declared to be, in all their articles and clauses except that part of Article 1 which fixes its name, null and void.

(3.) That the Corporation be and is declared dissolved and that the present Clerk of the Church be hereby requested to take the steps necessary to give legal effect to this resolution.

(4.) The members of this Church hereby declare that this action is taken in order to realize more perfectly the purposes of its institution as an organization viz. growth in spiritual life and the spread of the 'glad tidings' — and that they will continue as a Voluntary Association of Christians knowing no law but the law of Love, and no Master but Christ in the exercise of all the ministrations and activities heretofore performed by them as a Church of Christ (Scientist).

(5.) That the members of this Church hereby make loving recognition of the services and guidance of the founder and late pastor of the church, and also the expression of their grateful thanks to those who in the capacities of assistant pastor or otherwise have fostered its growth." A. Minutes of The Church of Christ (Scientist).

61. *CSJ,* 8:249 (September, 1890). Also Mrs. Eddy, letter to Miss Julia Bartlett, July 21, 1889 (A. L07695):

"Now I repeat that whatever questions in any of the C.S. organizations come up — no reference be made to me, for I hereby state that I *will not* entertain the question nor consider it, and why?

"Because under the counteracting mental influences, if I do this, my counsel is liable to be either carried out too late, or misunderstood, or carried out only in part, and because of all these things the wisdom and necessity of it is not seen nor the good it might do accomplished, and many will say she is a 'hard master.' I have borne this many years and think at this period of my retirement it should be seen that this is why I left the field. Again my students must learn sooner or later to *guard themselves,* to *watch* and not be misled.

"I appreciate your tasks far more than you can mine and have rewar[d]ed you by incessant care for you many years. It is a *grave mistake* not to do *quickly* all that is worth doing, *delay* gives all away, under our circumstances."

62. Wilbur, p. 203.

Chapter 6

1. A. L05227B. To another she wrote: "I cannot and do not recieve [sic] visits any more from any one but from those who come at my request to help me or who are my students.

"This dear one is the reason, viz. I have so much writing and care as a leader in a cause to which I devote my entire life that I have not time to visit or to be visited.

"Now this is not because I would not enjoy seeing you but because I *cannot* give more than one hour to any one unless it be to work with me in my field of labor." A. L02124.

2. When Mrs. Eddy first settled, June, 1889, in Concord, she lived at 62 North State Street. In the spring of 1891, she moved to Roslindale, Massachusetts; but within a few weeks she returned to 62 North State Street. In December, 1891, she bought a farm of about seventy acres beyond the city limits, and remodeled the farmhouse which she found there into the comfortable home to which, because of its broad and attractive outlook, she gave the name of Pleasant View.

3. Joseph G. Mann, reminiscence, p. 33.

4. A. M. Adelaide Still, reminiscence.

5. *S&H,* p. 254.

6. A. Margaret Macdonald, letter to The Christian Science Board of Directors, April 12, 1926.

7. See Abigail Dyer Thompson, reminiscence (in A.), p. 2: "One day when she asked the gardener to bring a basket of vegetables, carefully packed, to send on the train to one of her students who lived in an adjoining town ... she sent the gardener to the basement for a generous piece of salt pork. This she had carefully wrapped in paper and tied to the side of the handle so it would be held securely in the basket; she then slipped in a note expressing her pleasure at sending the vegetables from her own garden, and added: 'With the salt pork I think you have all the ingredients necessary for a good meal.' "

8. A member of the Chestnut Hill household tells the author that this practice was continued at Chestnut Hill.

9. *The Meaning of Culture,* p. 237.

10. "The fact is I am allowed no earthly peace and it is this that keeps me from visiting my church oftener, from not one week for vacation, and nothing save servitude. At my age this is all wrong." (A. L02429.)

11. A. Charles Welch, citing Clara Shannon, in letter to Board of Directors, March 26, 1928.

12. "The dissolution of the visible organization of the Church is the sequence and complement of that of the College Corporation and Association. The College disappeared, 'that the spirit of Christ might have freer course among its students and all who come into the understanding of Divine Science'; the bonds of organization of the Church were thrown away, so that its members might assemble themselves together and 'provoke one another to good works' in the bond only of Love." *CSJ,* 16:566 (February, 1899).

Later, however, with characteristic timeliness, Mrs. Eddy wrote a student: "You recall his [Jesus']... turning water into wine for the marriage feast, and even being baptized to meet the necessity of 'suffer it to be so now for thus it becometh us to fulfil all righteousness.' His age or the age in which he lived required what he did and his wisdom caused his concession to its requirements in some instances. Just as this age requires organization to maintain Christian Science." (A. L04756.)

13. A. L05213.

14. Leigh Mitchell Hodges to the author.

15. A. Joseph G. Mann, reminiscence, pp. 48, 49.

16. A. L00021. [Ed. Note: The author often compresses several years of history into brief paragraphs. The quotation here is from a letter Mrs. Eddy wrote in 1892, just before reorganizing her Church; however, in placing the substance of church over form, the letter expresses a sentiment that was enduring with her.]

17. Mrs. Eddy tells her own story of her relationship with the building of that earlier church (*'02,* pp. 13–14).

"During the last seven years I have transferred to The Mother Church, of my personal property and funds, to the value of about one hundred and twenty thousand dollars; and the net profits from the business of The Christian Science Publishing Society (which was a part of this transfer) yield this church a liberal income. I receive no personal benefit therefrom except the privilege of publishing my books in their publishing house, and desire none other.

"The land on which to build The First Church of Christ, Scientist, in Boston, had been negotiated for, and about one half the price paid, when a loss of funds occurred, and I came to the rescue, purchased the mortgage on the lot corner of Falmouth and Caledonia (now Norway) Streets; paying for it the sum of $4,963.50 and interest, through my legal counsel. After the mortgage had expired and the note therewith became due, legal proceedings were instituted by my counsel advertising the property in the Boston newspapers, and giving opportunity for those who had previously negotiated for the property to redeem the land by paying the amount due on the mortgage. But no one offering the price I had paid for it, nor to take the property off my hands, the mortgage was foreclosed, and the land legally conveyed to me, by my counsel. This land, now valued at twenty thousand dollars, I afterwards gave to my church through trustees, who were to be known as 'The Christian Science Board of Directors.' A copy of this deed is published in our Church Manual. About five thousand dollars had been paid on the land when I redeemed it. The only interest I retain in this property is to save it for my church. I can neither rent, mortgage, nor sell this church edifice nor the land whereon it stands."

18. Concord citizens of responsibility never lost an opportunity to express their great regard for Mrs. Eddy; and the author has before him letters of that time from the Mayor, the Concord editors, a United States Senator, and others agreeing with Mr. Josiah E. Fernald's appreciation which is the more impressive because he has never been a Christian Scientist.

19. The *Christian Science Sentinel* first had the title of *The Christian Science Weekly,* but received its present name January 26, 1899.

20. John Oxenham.

21. A. L03278.

22. '02, pp. 12–13.

23. Wilbur, pp. 342–343.

24.   *The Class of 1898*

Adams, George Wendell	McBean, Mrs. Catherine
Andrews, Mrs. Effie	McDonald, Miss Margaret S.
Baker, Mrs. Anna B. White	McKee, David N.
Baker, Dr. Alfred E.	McKenzie, Rev. Wm. P.
Betts, Edgar K.	Mann, Mrs. Frances Mack
Betts, Mrs. Harriet L.	Mann, Joseph G.
Blain, Julian	Meehan, Albert
Bond, Mrs. Lulu H.	Metcalf, Albert
Brown, Miss Alice Seward	Metcalf, Mrs. Mary C.
Buswell, Ezra M.	Miller, Mrs. Frederica L.
Chamberlain, Miss Jessie C.	Miller, William N.
Chanfrau, Mrs. Henrietta E.	Mims, Mrs. Sue Harper

Clark, Joseph B.
Clarkson, Judge Joseph R.
Coates, Lewis B.
Cochrane, Mrs. E. Rose
Colles, Mrs. Marjorie
Davis, Mrs. Emma S.
Dole, Rev. Walter
Easton, Miss Emma Gould
Eaton, Miss Mary E.
Fiske, Rev. Henry S.
Foster, Mrs. Adeline
Frame, Mrs. Caroline W.
Hanna, Mrs. Camilla
Hanna, Judge Septimus J.
Higman, Mrs. Elizabeth W.
Higman, Ormond
Kent, Mrs. Rose E.
Kimball, Edward A.
Kimball, Mrs. Kate Davidson
King, Mrs. Frances I.
Knapp, Miss Daphne S.
Lathrop, John Carroll

Moore, George H.
Neal, James A.
Norton, Carol
Norwood, Edward Everett
Pearson, Charles W.
Robertson, Mrs. Annie Louise
Robertson, Miss Nemi
Shipman, Miss Emma C.
Smith, J. Edward
Smith, Richard
Speakman, Miss Rachel T.
Stewart, John H.
Stewart, Miss Mary
Stocking, Miss Daisette D.
Stone, Mrs. Lida Stocking
Sulcer, Dr. Abraham A.
Thompson, Miss Abigail Dyer
Thompson, Mrs. Emma A.
Tomlinson, Rev. Irving C.
Members of the press:
    George H. Moses
    Allan H. Robinson
Also present:
Calvin A. Frye

25. Hanna's *Christian Science History,* p. 11.

26. There are many accounts (in Archives) left by members of the class of 1898, including George Wendell Adams, Judge Septimus J. Hanna, Joseph G. Mann, Mary Stewart, Mary E. Eaton, Emma C. Shipman, Lida S. Stone, Sue Harper Mims; and U.S. Senator George H. Moses.

27. Willis J. Abbot's interview with Senator Moses reported in *The Christian Science Monitor* for June 19, 1929.

28. A. Lida S. Stone, reminiscence, p. 4.

29. A. Mary Stewart, reminiscence, p. 1.

30. A. Abigail Dyer Thompson, notes written at the close of the 1898 class, pp. 2–3.

31. A. Mary Stewart, reminiscence, p. 6.

32. A. *Ibid., p. 4.*

33. A. Mary E. Eaton, reminiscence.

34. A. George Wendell Adams, reminiscence. Mr. Adams was sometime clerk of The Mother Church, and later a member of The Christian Science Board of Directors.

35. *Conversations with Eckermann.* Bohn's Library Translation, pp. 258–259.

36. Rom. 7:21.

37. Luke 10:17–20.

38. II Cor. 12:7.

39. Powell's *Heavenly Heretics,* p. 7.

40. A. Clara Shannon, reminiscence, pp. 50, 51.

41. *A Ballad of Trees and the Master,* by Sidney Lanier.

42. A. Mary E. Eaton, reminiscence, p. 3.

43. Hanna's *Christian Science History,* p. 11: Mrs. Eddy to Judge Hanna: "I did not refer to mental malpractice, — its members generally had taken the primary course, and this instruction properly comes before that class."

44. A. Joseph G. Mann, reminiscence, p. 11; also *S&H,* p. 406.

45. A. L02615.

46. A. Statement of Charles R. Corning.

47. A. Michael Meehan, reminiscence, p. 5.

48. A. Frank S. Streeter's statement dated October 28, 1906.

49. A. Grace A. Greene, reminiscence, pp. 3–4.

50. Matt. 5:44.

51. A. Joseph G. Mann, reminiscence, p. 89.

52. *Ret.,* p. 81.

53. A. L04996.

54. A. L05140.

55. A. L00090.

56. A. L00019.

57. A. L00053.

58. This is the Christian Science equivalent for "carnal mind," found in the Epistles of St. Paul. Tagore is still here, and thus he personalizes "mortal mind":

"Who is this that follows me into the silent dark? I move aside to avoid his presence, but I escape him not. He makes the dust rise from the earth with his swagger; he adds his loud voice to every word that I utter. He is my own little self, my lord, he knows no shame; but I am ashamed to come to thy door in his company."

59. *S&H,* p. 226.

60. A. L04777.

61. A. Clara Shannon, reminiscence, pp. 53–54.

62. A. L00325.

63. *Man.,* pp. 15, 16.

64. *Ibid.,* p. 97.

65. *CSS,* December 21, 1929.

66. *My.,* p. 130.

67. *Ret.,* p. 79.

68. *CSM,* January 8, 1930.

69. Owen Wister (1860–1938) was an American author of both short stories and novels. His most successful novel, *The Virginian,* was written in 1902.

70. *What Mrs. Eddy Said to Arthur Brisbane,* p. 41. Arthur Brisbane (1864–1936) was editor of the *New York Evening Journal,* as well as of other Hearst newspapers. He also conducted a famous interview with Mrs. Eddy at the time of the Next Friends' Suit in 1906. William E. Curtis (1850–1911) was a wide-ranging American journalist and author of many books on various parts of the world. He was the first director of what became the Pan-American Union. For many years he had a daily column (then a novel idea) in the *Chicago Record.* Isaac Marcosson (1877–1961) was a journalist and author. He was financial

editor of *The Saturday Evening Post* from 1907 to 1910, and then
a staff contributor to that magazine from 1913 to 1936.

71. A. Michael Meehan, reminiscence, pp. 8–10.

72. Michael Meehan's *Mrs. Eddy and the Late Suit in Equity,*
p. 25. Copyrighted and used by permission. In studying the testimony, the author has used Mrs. Eddy's own marked copy. For
various reasons the court hearing did not occur till August 13,
1907. On March 6, 1907, Mrs. Eddy had placed her property in
trust to Archibald McLellan, Henry M. Baker, and Josiah E. Fernald, — the last two not being Christian Scientists at all.

Among the many outside of Christian Science to whom the
author is under greater obligation than can be described for counsel and cooperation are distinctively Mr. Talcott Powell of the
New York Telegram, and Mr. Josiah E. Fernald of Concord, New
Hampshire, who has added to substantial assistance in procuring
material for the author, the following authentic personal recollection of Mrs. Eddy:

"After Mrs. Mary Baker Eddy came to Concord to live, she did
her banking with the National State Capital Bank, and started
her account with the bank on May 16, 1890. Mr. Fernald being
Cashier at that time, Mrs. Eddy asked him to look after some
business matters for her, and in that way he came to know her.
She in turn sent for him to come to her home to consult with
him and give such directions as she wished about the business in
hand.

"It was a great pleasure to Mr. Fernald to be called upon by
Mrs. Eddy to attend to any of her business matters. He always
found her a person who knew exactly what she wanted him to do
and how it should be carried out. Mrs. Eddy signed her own
checks, and ordered such securities as she chose to purchase, having a good knowledge of her business.

"Mr. Fernald remembers Mrs. Eddy in her office or study,
which was on the second floor of the house, and was a very
bright and sunny southeast corner room facing to the North, with

her visitor in a chair at her left in an easy speaking distance. She was always prompt, alert and courteous.

"It was a great pleasure to Mr. Fernald to be chosen one of the three trustees March 6, 1907. He assisted Gen. Henry M. Baker in the settlement of her estate up to the time of Mr. Baker's death, and was then appointed to complete the administration of her estate. After that, with the five members of the Board of Directors of The Mother Church, he was appointed the sixth Trustee under the Will, and has served in that capacity up to the present time. He is very glad to do all in his power to help carry out the terms of the Trust as set forth in the Will.

"Mr. Fernald states that in his relations with his co-trustees, and with the many Christian Science Workers, he has found some of the finest Christian people in the world; and that it is a great joy to be associated with such people, and to be of some assistance in carrying on a work that extends all over the world."

Another valued helper has been Miss Ida Belle Little.

73. *Mrs. Eddy and the Late Suit in Equity,* by Michael Meehan, p. 27.

74. *Ibid.,* p. 153.

75. *Ibid.,* pp. 157–159.

76. A. Adelaide Still, reminiscence, pp. 15–16.

77. A. L09772. April 20, 1908, to Hayne Davis.

78. Professor Hermann S. Hering's talk with the author.

79. A. Adelaide Still, reminiscence, p. 6.

80. A. L02632.

81. A. Joseph G. Mann, reminiscence, p. 93.

82. A. Michael Meehan, reminiscence, pp. 13–14, as well as *Mrs. Eddy and the Late Suit in Equity.*

83. *Mrs. Eddy and the Late Suit in Equity,* by Michael Meehan, p. 12.

Chapter 7

1. *Farmington* (N. H.) *News,* January 31, 1908. In preparation for the writing of this chapter, the author has read many recollections in the Archives. He has also talked with many of the

men and women — still living — who were then associated with Mrs. Eddy. Mr. William R. Rathvon has been of special service; but the author has also profited by the words of Mrs. Annie Macmillan Knott, Reverend Irving C. Tomlinson, Professor Hermann S. Hering, William P. McKenzie, Judge Clifford P. Smith, John C. Lathrop, John G. Salchow, Joseph G. Mann, Miss M. Adelaide Still, Mrs. Emilie B. Hulin, Miss Minnie B. Weygandt, Miss Emma H. McLauthlin, Mrs. Emma Easton Newman, Mrs. Ella W. Hoag, Miss Sarah A. Farlow, Mrs. Lauretta W. Blish, Mrs. Martha W. Wilcox, and Mrs. Minnie A. Scott.

2. John G. Salchow served a longer term of unbroken service to Mrs. Eddy than anyone else, except Calvin A. Frye.

3. *Mrs. Eddy and the Late Suit in Equity,* by Michael Meehan, p. 156.

4. In fact Mrs. Eddy once wrote a student: "I have had no vacation for over 30 years." (A. L05250.)

5. I Cor. 15:54.

6. *The Portsmouth Chronicle* for January 28, 1908, states: "Mrs. Eddy was instrumental in many improvements and charity, and the latter was very little known about for she gave quietly and her gifts were always with the understanding that the name of the giver should not be known."

7. *CSS,* February 15, 1908. Also, *My.,* pp. 365–366.

8. Letter on this point see p. 224.

9. Arthur Brisbane thus indicated at the time.

10. *Boston Globe,* January 27, 1908.

11. John G. Salchow's account of this memorable occasion as told to the author.

12. "OPPORTUNITY FOR SERVING THE LEADER. SECT. 11. At the written request of the Pastor Emeritus, Mrs. Eddy, the Board of Directors shall immediately notify a person who has been a member of this Church at least three years to go in ten days to her, and it shall be the duty of the member thus notified to

remain with Mrs. Eddy three years consecutively. A member who leaves her in less time without the Directors' consent or who declines to obey this call to duty, upon Mrs. Eddy's complaint thereof shall be excommunicated from The Mother Church. Members thus serving the Leader shall be paid semi-annually at the rate of one thousand dollars yearly in addition to rent and board. Those members whom she teaches the course in Divinity, and who remain with her three consecutive years, receive the degree of the Massachusetts Metaphysical College." *(Man.,* p. 67.)

13. Matt. 19:29.
14. Mark 13:33.
15. Joseph G. Mann's letter to the author.
16. *S&H,* p. 471.
17. *American Magazine,* June, 1930, p. 51.
18.

"For Rain

"O God, heavenly Father, who by thy Son Jesus Christ hast promised to all those who seek thy kingdom, and the righteousness thereof, all things necessary to their bodily sustenance; Send us, we beseech thee, in this our necessity, such moderate rain and showers, that we may receive the fruits of the earth to our comfort, and to thy honour; through Jesus Christ our Lord. *Amen.*"

"For Fair Weather

"Almighty and most merciful Father, we humbly beseech thee, of thy great goodness to restrain those immoderate rains, wherewith, for our sins, thou hast afflicted us. And we pray thee to send us such seasonable weather, that the earth may, in due time, yield her increase for our use and benefit. And give us grace, that we may learn by thy punishments to amend our lives, and for thy clemency to give thee thanks and praise; through Jesus Christ our Lord. *Amen.*"

Other Christians besides Episcopalians still pray for rain. During the summer drought of 1930 all Christians — totalling

625,000 — in Arkansas were called to pray for rain, and notice was sent to all the daily papers.

19. A. Adam H. Dickey, reminiscence, pp. 51–52. Dickey was a member of Mrs. Eddy's household at Chestnut Hill and served on The Christian Science Board of Directors from 1910 to 1925.

20. Through the courtesy of Mr. Rathvon, the author has examined the song book from which Mrs. Ella S. Rathvon many times sang to Mrs. Eddy the songs and hymns which Mrs. Eddy loved.

21. John C. Lathrop served for two short periods in Mrs. Eddy's household and later served on The Christian Science Board of Lectureship.

22. A. William R. Rathvon, reminiscence, June 11, 1930. Rathvon states that the wording of this quotation is accurate "as nearly as I can remember" it.

23. A. William R. Rathvon, reminiscence, June 11, 1930.

24. A. William R. Rathvon records that Mrs. Eddy spoke these words on November 27, 1909. In a talk he gave on February 14, 1931, Rathvon recounted Mrs. Eddy's quoting of Milton on his birthday.

25. Author's interview with John Salchow, June 11, 1930. Partial transcription is in Archives.

26. See John Lathrop, reminiscence, p. 6 (in Archives), or *We Knew Mary Baker Eddy,* p. 113, for a firsthand account of this exchange.

27. A. L07344.

28. A. John Lathrop, reminiscence.

29. A. William R. Rathvon, reminiscence, p. 33. Rathvon has "Mr. Dickey" for "one of us."

30. A. L05820.

31. Sam Shoemaker (1893–1963) was an Episcopalian priest and writer. When rector of Calvary Episcopal Church in New York, Shoemaker became involved in the Oxford Group Movement. This may have been what first brought him to Powell's attention.

32. *Pul.,* p. 75.

33. *'02,* p. 4.

34. Phil. 3:13, 14. Also Mrs. Eddy's *'00,* p. 6.

35. A. L04667.

36. These excerpts, which go to the heart of Mrs. Eddy's concept of Christmas, are from a longer article originally written for *The Ladies' Home Journal,* December 1907, p. 15. (See also *My.,* p. 262.)

37. *Po.,* p. 30.

38. A. L08757.

39. *My.,* p. 191.

40. A. Joseph G. Mann, reminiscence, p. 99. Mann prefaces this quotation with the following: "One Easter Sunday morning Mrs. Eddy called her household to her and gave us an Easter lesson to which I cannot hope to do justice from memory; but I want to hint the spirit of it and to share a few of the quickening points which I noted at the time."

41. *Mis.,* p. 7.

42. Mrs. Eddy's secretary wrote November 24, 1908, to Mr. Archibald McLellan: "Our Leader prefers the heavy style of type shown in the title of the paper which I enclose herewith, but insists that the article 'The' properly belongs in the title and wishes it placed there. This will necessitate making another design that can be as easily read as the one enclosed." (A. L07178.) This is another indication of Mrs. Eddy's constant overseeing of details in the establishment of her Cause.

43. A. L07268.

44. Mr. McLellan, a resident of Chicago, had been attorney with R. G. Dun & Co. for eighteen years, when he was called in 1902 by Mrs. Eddy to assume the Editorship of the Christian Science periodicals. When *The Christian Science Monitor* was established, Mr. McLellan became its Editor-in-Chief. Up to the time when Mrs. Eddy desired to make Mr. McLellan a Director, there were but four members of the Board. She caused the By-Law, Article I, Section 5, of the *Church Manual* to be amended

to provide that the Board "shall consist of five members." Then Mr. McLellan was elected the fifth member of the Board.

45. A. L03191.

46. *CSS.*, 13:524 (March 11, 1911).

47. Translated from the German.

48. A. Minnie A. Scott, reminiscence, p. 12.

49. Such an instance of reproof which Mrs. Eddy gave one of her beloved students had to do with the student's failure to observe the counsel of Matthew 18:15–17: "Moreover if thy brother shall trespass against thee, go and tell him his fault between thee, and him alone: if he shall hear thee, thou hast gained thy brother. But if he will not hear thee, then take with thee one or two more, that in the mouth of two or three witnesses every word may be established. And if he shall neglect to hear them, tell it unto the church: but if he neglect to hear the church, let him be unto thee as a heathen man and a publican." This Scripture has been a preliminary requirement of discipline since the early history of the Church. Mrs. Eddy wrote: "You are committing an unpardonable sin by talking as you do about the —s. What you say against them to others you should say *to them.* The Mother Church By-Laws forbid doing otherwise.... Unpardonable sin means one that we are never pardoned of — but taught through suffering that it is a sin."

50. *S&H*, p. 113.

51. A. L05066. [Ed. Note: The times to which the author refers were most probably a decade or so earlier, when Mrs. Eddy had first established the subjects for the Lesson-Sermons. The letter from which he quotes was written in 1898. During the last few years of her life she had largely withdrawn from active involvement in the various activities she had established.]

52. Powell's manuscript indicates that this quotation is from George Herbert Palmer (1842–1933), who was professor of natural religion, moral philosophy, and civil polity at Harvard. Palmer held various academic positions at Harvard from 1872 to 1913.

53. A. Mrs. Eddy's notebook.

54. A. Michael Meehan, reminiscence, p. 5.

55. John Hay (1838–1905) was an American author and diplomat. He wrote a ten-volume biography of Abraham Lincoln, whom he had served as private secretary in The White House. For the last seven years of his life, from 1898 until 1905, he was the U.S. Secretary of State.

56. A. L02345.

57. A. L00258.

58. A. L04755.

59. A. L01721.

60. A. L01832.

61. A. L04095.

62. A. L02372.

63. Wilbur, p. 6 note.

64. A. L07682.

65. A. Lydia B. Hall, reminiscence, p. 3.

66. A. Sarah A. Farlow, reminiscence, p. 2.

67. *My.,* p. 138. Perhaps nowhere has Mrs. Eddy indicated more vividly her love and loyalty to Christ Jesus than in her poem:

CHRIST MY REFUGE

O'er waiting harpstrings of the mind
   There sweeps a strain,
Low, sad, and sweet, whose measures bind
   The power of pain,

And wake a white-winged angel throng
   Of thoughts, illumed
By faith, and breathed in raptured song,
   With love perfumed.

Then His unveiled, sweet mercies show
   Life's burdens light.
I kiss the cross, and wake to know
   A world more bright.

And o'er earth's troubled, angry sea
    I see Christ walk,
And come to me, and tenderly,
    Divinely talk.

Thus Truth engrounds me on the rock,
    Upon Life's shore,
'Gainst which the winds and waves can shock,
    Oh, nevermore!

From tired joy and grief afar,
    And nearer Thee, —
Father, where Thine own children are,
    I love to be.

My prayer, some daily good to do
    To Thine, for Thee;
An offering pure of Love, whereto
    God leadeth me.

Po., p. 12.

68. [Although she might have made a similar statement in the final weeks, this actual quote is from a comment she made to Ella Rathvon in April of the same year.] An earlier New England village word for a little, restless fusser.

69. A. L00636A.

70. The following statement (in Archives) was made by the undertakers in attendance:

To Whom it may Concern:

We were called to the residence of Mrs. Mary Baker Eddy in Chestnut Hill, Mass., at 8-15 A.M., Sunday December 4, 1910, to care for her body. We found it in an excellent state of preservation when first called, and also fifty eight hours after death. No preserving compounds were used until that time. The tissues were remarkably normal; the skin was well preserved, soft, pliable, smooth and healthy. I do not remember having found the body of a person of such advanced age in so good a physical condition. The walls of the arteries were unusually firm and in as healthy a state as might be expected in the body of a young person. The usual accompaniments of age were lacking, and no outward appearance of any disease, no lesion or other conditions common to one having died at such an advanced age were noticeable.

In the process of embalming we found the body at sixty hours after death, in as good condition of preservation as we always find at twelve to twenty-four hours after death.

This is our voluntary statement made without solicitation or influence of any kind.

71. During his career Judge Smith served as First Reader of The Mother Church, a member of The Christian Science Board of Lectureship, manager of Committees on Publication, Editor of the Christian Science periodicals, and Editor of the Bureau of History and Records. (The Bureau later became the Archives and Library of The Mother Church.)

72.

O gentle presence, peace and joy and power;
    O Life divine, that owns each waiting hour,
Thou Love that guards the nestling's faltering flight!
    Keep Thou my child on upward wing tonight.

Love is our refuge; only with mine eye
    Can I behold the snare, the pit, the fall:
His habitation high is here, and nigh,
    His arm encircles me, and mine, and all,

O make me glad for every scalding tear,
    For hope deferred, ingratitude, disdain!
Wait, and love more for every hate, and fear
    No ill, since God is good, and loss is gain.

Beneath the shadow of His mighty wing;
    In that sweet secret of the narrow way,
Seeking and finding, with the angels sing:
    "Lo, I am with you alway," — watch and pray.

No snare, no fowler, pestilence or pain;
    No night drops down upon the troubled breast,

When heaven's aftersmile earth's teardrops gain,
And mother finds her home and heav'nly rest.
                                              Po., p. 40.

Chapter 8

1. Once in her old age asked by the author how she kept her youthfulness, Ellen Terry answered:

I pray devoutly,
I hammer stoutly,
And always get my way.
                        POWELL'S *The Human Touch,* p. 136.

2. *America Set Free,* p. 572.

3. Reported in *Christian World,* London, England, March 8, 1928.

4. *Time,* June 16, 1930, p. 21.

Compare the following editorial from *CSM.,* June 18, 1930:

One of the most noteworthy features of many of the recent theories of the physical scientists is the fact that their authors have recognized the necessity of looking right through the fluctuating testimony of the senses in an endeavor to reach basically correct ideas of fundamentals. Of none can this be said more truly than of Prof. Albert Einstein, who just the other day, before the delegates of the World Power Conference in Berlin, discussed, for the first time in more or less popular fashion, his ideas of space, time and relativity.

His opening sentence was startling in its metaphysical significance. "Conceptions and conceptional systems," he declared, "logically regarded, never originate from sense experiences." It is clear, therefore, that thought must lie behind those things that seem real to human testimony. From this point of view, Professor Einstein proceeded to show how, through the centuries of past investigation, gradually what he designated as "space" has obtained a foundational sense of reality.

One by one the earlier theories had been disproved or corrected until, in his words, "space ... has swallowed up ether and time and is about to swallow up the field theory and the corpuscular theory as well, so that it will remain as the only theory representing reality."

"Space," however, is not used in an entirely popular sense. It refers more to a structural framework of the universe. This, prior to the theory of relativity, was represented as absolute in itself, "as something the inner substance of which was not capable of being influenced and was in no wise changeable." Later, however, as "the last bit of substance" was removed from ether, "a structure of greater richness of form" for space had to be sought. This was necessary to reconcile the idea with further theories which were found to clash with the primary space hypothesis.

Of course, it is not possible to describe the Einstein theories in a short article. That they constitute a decided advance in the direction of a broadening concept of the unity of power and a clearer realization of the metaphysical nature of the universe is undeniable. It cannot be said that they represent absolute statements of Truth, because at best they aim simply at the explanation of the phenomena of the physical world. Still they are, without any question, aspects of that increase of knowledge welcomed as productive of the human invention that will be succeeded by even more important phases of experience.

There is little doubt that the development of these theories will be far-reaching and will greatly help in relieving mankind of its shackles of limitation. It is important, however, that the theories be seen in their right light, while being recognized as included among the most important contributions to twentieth century material progress.

5. *American Magazine,* June 1930, p. 138. M. K. Wisehart was a reporter for the *Evening Sun* (New York), (1911–1918), and a staff contributor on the *American Magazine* from 1920 until 1931.

6. The famous class of 1898 — the last — with its sixty-seven members, was an exception.

7. No preacher in Protestantism is more courageous or more understanding of American conditions than Dr. Burris Jenkins of

Kansas City. His church is always filled; and yet in his book, *The World's Debt to Protestantism,* p. 248, he writes: "Dean Inge has recently said that the golden age of preaching is past. He speaks for England, to be sure; but what happens in England sooner or later is likely to happen in America. The golden age of preaching no doubt recedes into the past in this country as well as in the motherland. The names of commanding preachers in America may be counted on the fingers of one hand. Country people who would listen eagerly for an hour or two hours to a preacher have given place to city people who will not listen with patience for twenty to thirty minutes. It is impossible in the cities to gather evening audiences even for the most powerful men. The 'foolishness' of preaching no longer gathers a gaping crowd on Sunday nights."

8. *The New Case,* p. 220. Rufus Jones (1863–1948) was a minister of the Society of Friends (Quakers). He was a founder of the American Friends Service Committee in 1917 and its chairman until 1928. He was a prolific writer on the history and outlook of the Quakers.

9. *Mary Baker Eddy, Her Purpose and Accomplishment,* by Frederick Dixon (1915) — reprint from *Cosmopolitan* (February 1911).

10. *S&H,* p. 411.

11. *S&H,* p. 125.

12. Powell's *Emmanuel Movement,* p. 154.

13. *S&H,* p. 325.

14. Bunting's *The Radiant Life,* p. 174.

15. In Mrs. Eddy's earlier days in Boston, Mr. Neal was a bank cashier in a Kansas town. His attention was brought to Christian Science by a friend. He bought a copy of *Science and Health,* and was soon launched on a notable career of Christian Science healing. In 1889 he was under Mrs. Eddy's class instruction in Boston, and from 1892 until he passed on in 1930 he practised healing in Boston and served as a member of the Board

of Directors from July 1912 to October 1929, when he resigned. It was to Mr. Neal that Mrs. Eddy, January 28, 1897, wrote with her own pen the following letter, which is unsurpassed in its revelation of her affection for the faithful and of the high value she set on healing.

My beloved Student,

Your letter is my best New Year's gift. I had felt for sometime the fitness you possess for healing I knew it when you were a member of my College class. It looked a waste of your talents to have you in a counting room. Now, thank God, I have at least one student in Boston that promises to be a Healer such I have long waited and hoped to see. Oh may the Love that looks on you and all guide your every thought and act up to the impersonal, spiritual model that is the only ideal — and constitutes the only scientific Healer.

To this glorious end I ask you to still press on and have no other ambition or aim. A real scientific *Healer* is the highest position attainable in this sphere of being. Its altitude is far above a Teacher or preacher; it includes all that is divinely high and holy. Darling James, leave behind all else and strive for this great achievement. Mother sighs to see how much her students need this attainment and longs to live to see one Christian Scientist attain it. Your aid to reach this goal is *spiritualization.* To achieve this you must have *one God,* one affection, one way, one Mind. Society, flattery, popularity are temptations in your pursuit of growth spiritual. Avoid them as much as in you lies. Pray daily, never miss praying, no matter how often: "Lead me not into temptation" — scientifically rendered, — lead me not to lose sight of strict purity, clean pure thoughts; let all my thoughts and aims be high, unselfish, charitable, meek, — *spiritually minded.* With this altitude of thought your mind is losing materiality and gaining spirituality and this is the state of mind that *heals* the *sick.* My new book will do you much good. Do not purchase one,

Mother wants to give you one. I welcome you into the *sanctum* of my fold. God bless you.

Your loving Teacher

M B Eddy (A. L03524.)

16. *S&H,* p. 292.

17. Bicknell Young of Chicago, for many years a member of The Christian Science Board of Lectureship.

18. Bliss Knapp, member of The Christian Science Board of Lectureship for many years.

19. A. Michael Meehan, reminiscence, p. 20.

20. *S&H,* p. 468.

21. *Mis.,* p. 287.

22. *Ibid.,* p. 287.

23. This letter is in the collection the author has presented to the Board of Directors. The word "friendship" in the last phrase Mrs. Eddy used, like Henry Clay Trumbull in his standard book on *Friendship — The Master Passion,* was thus hyphenated "friendship-love."

24. *My.,* p. 210.

25. Miss Mary Burt Messer was an authority on the family before she wrote "The Family in the Making" (1928). At one time connected in New York with the Association for Improving the Condition of the Poor and the Charity Organization Society, for seven years engaged in research for Wisconsin, teacher at Stout Institute, and finally lecturer on the family for the University of California Extension Division, she says (p. 351): "Breaking through the entire scheme of accepted values, and carrying its methods into all quarters of the world, the movement of Christian Science stands forth as a conception of the Christian religion drawn from woman's insight, quietly advancing women to a position of equality with man in the Christian church, and, conceiving the spiritual or creative principle in feminine as well as in masculine terms. The maternal attribute of the divine is thus

advanced in connection with the paternal attribute — not as in the poetic overtones of Virgin worship, but with the living potencies of an operative truth, a conception intimately associated with the restoration to Christianity of its lost power of healing."

26. Matt. 7:20.

Twenty Years After

1. *My.,* p. 357.
2. *S&H,* p. 126.
3. Matt. 28:20.
4. *S&H,* xi. In the *Christian Science Sentinel,* March 28, 1931, Judge Clifford P. Smith writes that Mrs. Eddy "has made Christianity more comprehensible to modern thought, less miraculous or mysterious, and more spiritually sensible than original Christianity was known to be before she discovered its Science."
5. *My.,* p. 4.
6. *S&H,* p. 146.
7. *Mis.,* p. 184.
8. A. L00325. This letter is quoted in full on p. 207.
9. Mark Twain quoted in Powell's *Christian Science,* 1917, XV.
10. Page 211 in "Sonny's Father."
11. Torrance Parker in the *CSS.,* June 7, 1924.
12. Matt. 6:34.

Index

T

Tilton, New Hampshire, 69, 78, 80, 86, 87, 88, 90, 92, 105, 121, 139, 178, 217

Tomlinson, Rev. Irving C., 78, 218, 231

Trustees of The Christian Science Publishing Society, 48, 247, 248

Trustees Under the Will of Mary Baker Eddy, 48

Twain, Mark, 41, 146, 213

U

Unity of Good, 175

W

Whittier, John Greenleaf, 134, 135, 151

Wiggin, Rev. James Henry, 146, 147, 148, 149

Wilson, John, 145, 146, 147, 148, 149